Putting Nigeria to Work

Putting Nigeria to Work

A Strategy for Employment and Growth

Volker Treichel
Editor

THE WORLD BANK
Washington, D.C.

ISBN: 978-0-8213-8072-7
eISBN: 978-0-8213-8073-4
DOI: 10.1596/978-0-8213-8072-7

Cover photo: Curt Carnemark/World Bank; © iStockphoto.com/hronos7 (flag).

Cataloging-in-Publication data is available from the Library of Congress.

Contents

Boxes

Figures

Tables

Foreword

Since 2001, macroeconomic stability and a range of structural reforms have laid the foundation for sustained growth in Nigeria. This represents the longest period of sustained high non-oil growth since independence. However, while growth has been broad-based, it has not led to a decline in unemployment. Youth unemployment has, in fact, exploded in all sectors but one. Only subsistence agriculture on small family plantations has seen a substantial increase in employment and in incomes. Growth without creation of formal sector jobs has left the economy largely trapped in the pre-2001 trajectory, dominated by agriculture and the wholesale and retail sectors.

These are some of the main findings of *Putting Nigeria to Work: A Strategy for Employment and Growth*. Based on the analytical work of a team of World Bank economists led by Volker Treichel, this book develops a growth strategy tailored specifically to Nigerian circumstances that should further strengthen job creation and sustain high growth. At the center of this strategy are interventions aimed at removing binding constraints to more rapid growth in sectors that are already growing fast, but could grow even faster, and hold substantial employment potential. These interventions would target specific physical infrastructure constraints, shortcomings in the investment environment and in access to finance, skills gaps, and distortionary trade policies.

How can the recommendations of the book, which is enriched by a review of successful growth-promoting policies in other countries, be implemented in Nigeria? First, it will be critical that there is further detailed analysis of binding constraints to growth in specific value chains in geographical areas that have the potential to become regional growth hubs. The book already identifies some of these constraints. They include a skills gap in the construction sector, the lack of modern technologies in the information and communications technology sector, and the absence of an integrated logistics program for the food processing industry.

Second, this analysis could be used to build consensus between the public and the private sector on the sharing of responsibilities in addressing these constraints. For example, mitigating shortcomings in physical infrastructure will require interventions led by the public sector, such as the development of industrial clusters. Training to bridge the skills gap will best be done in partnership between the public and the private sectors, as already successfully demonstrated in the recent establishment of Innovation Enterprise Institutions (IEIs). Access to finance can be improved through innovations led by the private sector, such as the development of special mortgage facilities.

Third, implementation of any agreed measures will need to be regularly monitored by the relevant stakeholders. Nigeria already has a number of fora where representatives from the public and the private sectors meet regularly, and where the status of agreed upon actions aimed at improving the competitiveness of certain sectors could be discussed. Such reviews should be open to the public.

Experience in many countries has shown the potential of interventions targeted at sectors with the highest growth and employment potential. While sector-wide reforms remain necessary, measures aimed at specific value chains can help bring about desired results over the short term. However, a fundamental condition for the successful implementation of this growth strategy will be continued sound macroeconomic policies. The adoption of an oil-price-based fiscal rule since 2003 was central to bringing an end to the boom-bust cycles of the past that were characterized by excessive government spending. The benefits of its implementation were apparent during the global financial crisis when Nigeria was able to draw on the Excess Crude Account to compensate for shortfalls in oil revenue and maintain fiscal spending at appropriate levels. Prudent monetary and fiscal policies and sound debt management will be the basis for continued macroeconomic stability, without which any growth strategy aimed at harnessing Nigeria's full economic potential cannot become effective.

I hope that the recommendations of this book and the way forward for sustained job-generating growth in Nigeria will be debated widely inside and outside the country. I also hope that the outcome of such a debate will contribute to the development and implementation of a cost-effective, high-quality, and uniquely Nigerian growth strategy that will meet the expectations of the people, particularly the aspirations of vulnerable groups, such as women, youth, and the rural and urban poor.

Obiageli Katryn Ezekwesili
Vice President, Africa Region
The World Bank

Preface

Since 1999, Nigeria has made significant progress in economic reform. Sound macroeconomic policies, combined with structural reforms aimed at increasing the supply responsiveness of the economy, ushered in sustained high growth, driven by the non-oil economy. The October 2005 debt relief by the Paris Club recognized Nigeria's success in economic reform and allowed the country to largely eliminate its external debt.

Yet, the impact of the recent period of economic reform and high growth on the living standards of the population has not been evident. The public discourse in Nigeria is dominated by a perception that unemployment and poverty have not been declining in recent years; and, in fact, youth unemployment has been on the rise.

The purpose of this book is to review Nigeria's recent growth performance and its impact on the labor market, and to develop a growth strategy aimed at increasing the employment intensity of growth, while ensuring its sustainability.

The response to the report by the Nigerian government, both at the federal and the state levels, was positive. The report was discussed at a Townhall Meeting organized by the Nigerian newspaper *This Day*. The meeting, held in Abuja on December 7, 2009, was attended by several government ministers. Key recommendations of the report are reflected in the draft Vision 2020 document, which aims at laying out the official growth and development strategy of the federal government of Nigeria. The report was also discussed at a meeting of Nigeria's Ministry of Finance; chapters 5 and 6 were discussed at specific stakeholder discussions.

At the Townhall Meeting, the minister of agriculture noted that the expanded use of arable land since 1999 was partly attributable to a range of government interventions. He also stated that Nigeria had considerable short-term potential as an exporter of agricultural commodities, including cassava and yam, especially in the region; and that the government was in the process of undertaking specific steps to fully realize this potential over the short term, including the construction of new warehouses and better enforcement of quality standards. By doing so, the minister suggested that the report's recommendation to adopt an export-driven growth strategy over the medium term may already be a viable approach in the agricultural sector in the short run.

Acknowledgments

This report was prepared by a World Bank team led by Volker Treichel, who is the overall editor of the study. The principal authors are Volker Treichel (chapter 1), Luke Haywood and Francis Teal (chapter 2), Markus Eberhardt and Francis Teal (chapter 3), Peter Mousley (chapter 4), Jorgen Billetoft (chapter 5), and Gaël Raballand and Edmond Mjekiqi (chapter 6).

The team benefited from contributions and comments by Ismail Radwan and Sunil Sinha (value chain analysis); Simeon Ehui, Lucas Akapa, and Abimbola Adubi (agriculture); Louise Fox (labor market analysis); John Ngwafon (labor market statistics) and Marcus Powell and Arvil van Adams (skills development). Gloria Joseph-Raji coordinated the analysis of labor market data in chapter 2 as well as the review of Nigeria's technical and vocational education system in chapter 5.

Peer reviewers were Paul Brenton, Andrew Dabalen, Sanjay Dhar, John Giles, and Brian Pinto.

The final version of the report benefited from comments by several Nigerian government ministers: Dr. Shamsudeen Usman, Minister of National Planning; Abbas Rumah, Minister of Agriculture; Adetokunbo Kayode, Minister of Labor and Productivity; and Akilanbi Olasunkanmi, Minister of Youth. The labor market and skills development analysis was conducted in close collaboration with Mrs. O. Ajayi of the Ministry of Labor and Productivity and with Mr. Ekezie of the National Bureau of Statistics and was discussed at a stakeholder workshop. The chapter on import bans benefited from comments by Mr. Sunday Oghayei of the Ministry of Commerce and Industry, and was discussed at a stakeholder workshop.

The report was edited by Deborah Davis.

Abbreviations and Measurements

AfDB	African Development Bank
AGOA	African Growth and Opportunities Act
BOI	Bank of Industry [Nigeria]
CAC	Corporate Affairs Commission
CAD	competitive advantage defying
CAF	comparative advantage following
CCI	clean certificate of inspection
CET	common external tariff
COMTRADE	United Nations Commodity Trade Statistics Database
CRI	clean report of inspection
DFID	Department for International Development
EBA	everything but arms
ECA	Excess Crude Account
ECOWAS	Economic Community of West African States
EEG	export expansion grant
EME	emerging market economy
EPA	Economic Partnership Agreement
EPZ	export processing zone
FCT	federal capital territory
FDI	foreign direct investment

FIAS	Foreign Investment Advisory Service (World Bank)
FIRS	Federal Inland Revenue Service
FMCIT	Federal Ministry of Commerce, Industry, and Trade
FMOF	Federal Ministry of Finance
FPSRP	Federal Public Service Program
FSS	financial sector strategy
FTZ	free trade zone
GDP	gross domestic product
GHS	General Household Survey
HND	higher national diploma
ICA	investment climate assessment
ICT	information and communications technology
IDG	Industrial Development Group
IDR	Industrial Development Report
IEI	innovation enterprise institution
IMF	International Monetary Fund
IRC	import requirement certificate
ISI	import substitution industrialization
ITF	industrial training fund
JICA	Japan International Cooperation Agency
LADOL	Lagos Deep Offshore Logistics Support Services
LIC	low income country
LWIL	Lekki Worldwide Investment Ltd.
MAN	Manufacturing Association of Nigeria
MDA	ministries, departments, and agencies
MFB	micro-finance bank
MFN	most favored nation
MIBS	manufacture-in-bond scheme
MSME	micro, small, and medium enterprises
NASSI	Nigerian Association of Small-Scale Industries
NACRDB	Nigeria Agricultural Cooperative and Rural Development Bank
NAFDAC	National Agency for Food and Drug Administration and Control
NBCI	National Bank for Commerce and Industry
NBS	National Bureau of Statistics
NBTE	National Board of Technical Education
NCC	Nigerian Communications Commission
NCS	Nigerian Customs Service

ND	national diploma
NDE	National Directorate of Employment
NEEDS	National Economic Empowerment and Development Strategy 2004–2009
NEPC	Nigerian Export Promotion Council
NEPZA	Nigerian Export Processing Zone Authority
NERFUND	National Economic Reconstruction Fund
NEXIM	Nigerian Export-Import Bank
NGO	nongovernmental organization
NID	national innovative diploma
NIDB	Nigerian Industrial Development Bank
NIPC	Nigerian Investment Promotion Commission
NISER	Nigerian Institute for Social and Economic Research
NLSS	Nigeria Living Standard Survey
NPA	Nigerian Ports Authority
NVC	national vocational certificate
NVQF	National Vocational Qualifications Framework
NYS	national youth service
OILSS	Oil Integrated Logistics Support Services
OLFTZ	Oshogbo Living Spring Free Trade Zone
PPP	public–private partnership
R&D	research and development
RAR	risk assessment report
SABI	state accelerated broadband initiative
SEZ	special economic zone
SGD	single good declaration
SITC	standard international trade classification
SIWES	student industrial work experience scheme
SME	small and medium-sized enterprise
SMEDAN	Small and Medium Enterprises Development Agency of Nigeria
SMIEIS	Small and Medium Enterprises Equity Investment Scheme
SON	standards organization of nigeria
SSI	small-scale industry
TFP	total factor productivity
TEU	twenty-foot equivalent unit
TVE	technical and vocational education
UK	United Kingdom

UNDP	United Nations Development Programme
UNESCO	United Nations Educational, Scientific, and Cultural Organization
UNIDO	United Nations Industrial Development Organization
VAT	value-added tax
VEI	vocational enterprise institution
WARDA	West African Rice Development Association
WDI	World Development Indicators
WEC	weighted eligibility criteria
WTO	World Trade Organization

Currency and Measurements

Unit of currency is the Nigerian naira.

Exchange rate effective November 3, 2009: US$1 = naira 151

Weights and measures: Metric system

Fiscal year of budget: January 1st–December 31st

Overview

Public debate in Nigeria on the country's progress has been dominated by two seemingly opposite themes. The first is the strong growth performance of the non-oil economy since the return to democracy in 1999, and especially since 2003, which ushered in a period during which the Federal Government of Nigeria undertook debt restructuring and fiscal, financial, infrastructure, and institutional reforms. Strong growth during this period has been manifested by sharp increases in agriculture production, wholesale and retail trade, and construction, and by the emergence of new industries, particularly in the financial, telecommunications, and entertainment sectors. The second, opposing theme is that Nigeria's much improved economic performance seems to have done little to reduce unemployment, especially among the young. The consensus in society is that youth unemployment is on the rise, with an associated negative impact on public order and an increase in militancy.

The goal of this book is to shed light on the extent to which Nigeria's much improved economic performance has impacted the labor market, and to develop a growth strategy that can enhance the employment intensity of growth. The report consists of six chapters. Chapter 1 provides an overview of the book's main findings, reviews Nigeria's growth performance from 2001 to 2007, and addresses the question of the sustainability of that growth performance. Chapter 2 analyzes the evolution of the labor market since 1999. The analysis focuses on the share of the formal and informal sectors in employment, the trend in incomes in the formal and the informal sectors, and the unemployment rate. Chapter 3 addresses the question of what Nigeria can do to increase the availability of quality jobs and reduce rising youth unemployment. Chapter 4 discusses Nigeria's industrial policy and investment environment. Chapter 5 proposes strategies for skills development; and Chapter 6 analyzes the effects of restrictive trade policies.

The book's main findings and conclusions are summarized below.

Nigeria's Growth Performance

Since 2001, Nigeria has enjoyed a long period of sustained expansion of the non-oil economy, with growth occurring across all sectors of the economy and accelerating. While non-oil growth averaged about 3 to 4 percent in 1995–2000, it more than doubled, to about 7 percent, since 2003, and rose to 8 to 9 percent in recent years. Even in the wake of the global financial crisis, Nigeria's growth performance in 2009 remained above 7 percent. The development of the non-oil economy has been in contrast to that of the oil economy, whose contribution has been declining owing to unrest in the Niger Delta.

Nigeria's growth performance can be ascribed to a number of factors:

- Seventy percent of growth is attributable to the agriculture, wholesale, and retail sectors.
- Relatively new sectors, such as construction, the financial sector, and information and communications technology (ICT) recorded high growth and have initiated a structural transformation of the Nigerian economy towards the services sector.
- Macroeconomic and structural reforms instilled greater confidence among the business community and boosted foreign direct investment and remittances from Nigerians living abroad, thus raising aggregate demand and private investment.
- Growth was largely the result of factor accumulation, with only minor contributions of productivity increases. In the agriculture sector, in particular, productivity has stagnated and growth has been largely the result of increased land use.

Nigeria's growth path is distinct from that of other countries whose strong performance has relied extensively on the services and manufacturing sectors. In India, in particular, the contribution of the agriculture sector to GDP was on a rapidly declining path since 1950, and had fallen to 21 percent in 2004–05 from 57 percent in 1950–51. At the same time, the contribution of manufacturing in India doubled, from 9 to 17 percent, and that of services nearly doubled, from 28 to 52 percent. Over Nigeria's period of high growth since 2001, by contrast, the contribution of agriculture in Nigeria's GDP has declined only marginally, which is remarkable in that growth has been sustained and has even accelerated for some time.

Evolution of the Labor Market

How have employment and incomes responded to this strong growth performance? An analysis of the General Household Survey (GHS) since 1999 leads to the following conclusions:

- The number of jobs seems to have grown in line with the labor force; and unemployment (both voluntary and involuntary) has remained constant.
- Youth unemployment seems to be on the rise.
- Most jobs have been created in family agriculture.
- Incomes in family agriculture have almost doubled in real terms and are now on a par with those in the self-employed non-agriculture sector.
- Wage employment has declined, as retrenchment in the civil service and the impact of privatization on employment in state-owned enterprises has not been compensated by job creation in new industries.

The Need for a New Growth Strategy

Nigeria faces a growing employment crisis: The share of young people between the ages of 15 and 24 outside the labor force is increasing, despite the country's strong growth performance. Unless constraints to growth are systematically removed in those industries that are particularly employment intensive and stand a chance of being globally competitive, it is unlikely that these trends will be reversed, further exacerbating tensions and youth unrest.

Nigeria should follow a growth strategy based on the following pillars:

- Domestic led, with a focus on exports to regional and international markets at a later stage.
- Targeted interventions to remove constraints in both formal and informal sector (including self-employment sector) value chains with high employment and growth potential.

- Adoption of a national skills development framework.
- Liberalization of trade policy.

The growth strategy would follow three phases: phase 1 directed at capturing larger shares of the domestic market; phase 2 aimed at extending Nigeria's access to regional markets; and phase 3 at promoting access to the international market. These phases do not need to be sequential, although it is likely that phase 3 would occur later than phases 1 and 2. This phased approach would differ considerably from the approach of countries that grew through an initial focus on the manufacturing sector, and would be distinctly Nigerian.

The phased approach focuses on the domestic market at the outset because, in view of the severe cost disadvantage of Nigerian industry, resulting primarily from the lack of power and the high costs of transportation, it is unrealistic to expect Nigeria to be able to compete in the international marketplace *in the short term*. Instead, growth is likely to continue to be driven by sectors focused on domestic demand, especially in those service industries that have already contributed significantly to growth. Through development of appropriate infrastructure, phase 1 would create the platform for the growth of manufacturing industries, which would be oriented towards the regional and international markets in phases 2 and 3.

How to Implement the Growth Strategy—Sectoral Interventions and Geographic Focus

In devising implementation strategies for this phased growth, the choice of sectors and policies is central.

Which Sectors?

A recently completed competitiveness assessment of some 14 value chains[1] in the economic corridors of Lagos, Kano-Kaduna, and the South-Eastern region centered on Calabar, reached the following conclusions with regard to value chains as a source of sustainable growth and employment creation.

- Sectors with the highest employment potential include light manufacturing, construction, ICT, wholesale/retail, meat and poultry, oil palm, and cocoa. The growth strategy, with its focus on the services and manufacturing sectors, is consistent with this finding. The feasibility of accomplishing growth in these sectors varies widely by geographical area. In Lagos, for example, ICT, construction, wholesale/retail, and light manufacturing have high degrees of feasibility; while in Kano, the feasibility of light manufacturing is lower. This analysis confirms the need for geographically focused interventions.

- Only two value chains with high employment potential—oil palm and cocoa—are in the agriculture sector. Indeed, the employment potential of the agriculture sector is limited relative to other value chains, given that future growth in this sector will rely largely on improvements in productivity. As modern technologies and extension services are adopted, the ratio of output to labor will rise, thus limiting the potential for large-scale job creation, but also improving prospects for increased income. However, higher growth in meat and poultry and food processing, which have high employment potential, will stimulate growth and employment in agriculture. Rice and dairy, while having more limited growth and employment potential, are also of interest, given their high degree of feasibility.

- While the agriculture sector's potential for job creation is limited relative to the other value chains, it remains considerable in view of the size of the labor force employed in agriculture and the fact that, in spite of the need for productivity gains, there are still significant possibilities to expand the use of arable land. Key ways to improve agricultural performance include (1) reforming the policy environment, especially reformulating fertilizer policy; (2) improving rural infrastructure; (3) increasing agricultural expenditure; (4) reducing vulnerability and enhancing food security; (5) improving market access; and (6) strengthening the rural investment climate.

Which Interventions?

The common denominator of the proposed interventions is the need to increase productivity, as this is the key to reducing costs and prices so that demand can rise. Productivity growth is at the heart of any successful strategy for job creation. Improving productivity growth will, in turn, improve Nigeria's competitiveness in the global economy.

The root causes of Nigeria's pattern of jobless growth—the five binding constraints to growth—are:

- Inadequate physical infrastructure, in particular power and transport.
- Inadequate access to finance.

- A poor investment climate and slow bureaucratic procedures.
- A shortage of skilled staff.
- The high cost of inputs due to import bans and other restrictive trade policies.

Addressing the Five Binding Constraints to Growth

Over the short term, employment generation can be fast tracked if the binding constraints to growth in the most promising value chains are addressed in a selective manner. This is the central argument of this book.

Physical infrastructure constraints could be addressed through:

- The provision of well-functioning infrastructure (electricity, water, roads, telephones) to locally concentrated areas (e.g., export processing zones and free trade zones). This approach would be particularly suitable for three value chains: light manufacturing, especially in Lagos; food processing; and meat and poultry production.
- A review of how responsibility for infrastructure development is allocated among different levels of government. This would be particularly applicable to value chains such as construction, where the responsibility for improving infrastructure lies mainly with local governments, which suffer from limited capacity.
- For the food sector, delivery of an integrated logistics program from farmgate to the processing stage, using a cluster-based approach. This would be particularly suitable for the food processing industry in Kano.

Access to finance could be enhanced through:

- Regulatory interventions to develop all sectors of the credit market, from microfinance to larger corporations. Existing microfinance banks could be given incentives (e.g., lower capital requirements) to establish branches around the country.
- Acceleration of credit market reform measures already underway, including dispute resolution mechanisms, credit bureau regulations, and leasing laws.
- For the construction sector, development of a new and innovative means of providing access to finance, such as a public-private partnership

framework for housing, a mortgage liquidity facility, reform of the legal framework for rental markets, and development of a coordinated federal-state housing policy.

The investment climate could benefit from selective efforts such as:

- Simplification of the approval process for the development of new businesses, based on careful process mapping.
- Launch of targeted capacity-building programs to revive the functions of quality control agencies such as the Standards Organization of Nigeria.
- Harmonization of the roles of agencies in charge of quality inspection for seamless cooperation.

The skills gap could be reduced through targeted interventions such as:

- Reprioritizing government resource allocation to the technical and vocation education and training (TVET) stream of the educational system, and reconsidering the importance of the tertiary education system.
- Refocusing policies for skills development towards the identified employment-intensive value chains; and delivering training programs with a practical focus and content (e.g., meat sector programs leading to a Certificate of Hygiene or Master Butcher Certificate).
- Accelerating the process of establishing a National Vocational Qualifications Framework (NVQF).
- Empowering the National Board of Technical Education (NBTE) as the national authority for TVET, with responsibility for regulating and monitoring formal and informal TVET.
- Empowering informal sector trade associations to take part in skills upgrading and certification of their members; and establishing a facility to support trade associations in acting as advocates and service providers for their constituencies.
- Establishing tripartite governance frameworks involving training institutions, public sector agencies, and the private sector, with private sector institutions leading vocational training. The program of Vocational Enterprise Institutes (VEIs) and Innovation Enterprise Institutes (IEIs) initiated by NBTE is a step in the right direction. Government support to such institutions would be limited to standardization of curricula and accreditation of programs.

- Developing new and strengthening existing vocational institutes to increase access by the unskilled informal labor sector, including to programs that teach practical skills (e.g., the Vocational Training Center of Excellence in Lagos for the construction sector).
- Providing financial incentives to reward schools that produce graduates who find employment in the private sector.
- Equipping enterprise clusters and zones with training and counseling facilities for small-scale informal business operators.
- Creating a government-funded voucher system (possibly spearheaded by the Industrial Training Fund, ITF) to help fund skills programs for the informal system.

The high cost of inputs could be reduced by reconsidering import bans and high tariff barriers, which have been found to significantly increase costs in key value chains with high employment and growth potential. Import bans should be replaced by tariffs, with a view to creating incentives to formalize trade and promoting customs reform.

Note

1. The selection of the 14 value chains for competitive and growth assessments was based on extensive discussions with key public and private sector stakeholders at the federal and state levels. The selections included more established industries where there was a continued perception of long-term growth potential, and new industries where there was a more limited track record but a perception of high potential.

CHAPTER 1

Employment and Growth in Nigeria

Volker Treichel

Overview

Nigeria faces a growing employment crisis. Notwithstanding sustained, high, and broad-based growth in the non-oil economy, unemployment has not fallen materially since 1999. More importantly, youth unemployment has risen markedly over the same period. Nigeria's growth performance has not responded to the aspirations of its population as a whole, especially the young generation. While the number of jobs seems to have grown in line with the labor force, most of these jobs have been created in family agriculture. Wage employment, however, has declined. Job creation in family agriculture was accompanied by rapid income growth and falling rates of poverty in rural areas.

The main purpose of this study is to assess the impact of the recent strong growth performance on employment and to propose a strategy to sustain and further accelerate Nigeria's growth performance and enhance the growth elasticity and quality of employment.

This chapter provides a synoptic overview of the book. Chapter 2 analyzes the evolution of the labor market since 1999. The analysis focuses on the share of the formal and informal sectors in employment, the development of incomes, and the unemployment rate. Chapter 3 addresses the question of what Nigeria could do to increase the availability of quality jobs and reduce rising youth unemployment. Chapter 4 discusses Nigeria's industrial policy and investment environment and proposes an alternative approach to promote growth. Chapter 5 proposes strategies for skills development, and chapter 6 analyzes the effects of restrictive trade policies.

The book concludes that enhancing the growth elasticity of employment and restructuring the economy toward long-term sustainable growth will require a three-pronged strategy:

- **Targeted interventions to address binding constraints in value chains with high growth and employment potential.** These binding constraints include poor physical infrastructure (especially power and transportation), poor investment climate, lack of access to finance, pervasive skills gaps, and restrictive trade policies. Successful interventions in these value chains need to be designed on the basis of an assessment of what *is most relevant, feasible, and cost effective* and *provides the greatest near and medium-term benefits.* To be effective, these interventions should emanate from a dialogue with the private sector and be designed to allow swift correction and suitable governance arrangements.

- **Comprehensive reform of the technical and vocational education system.** While addressing the skills gap may, to some extent, be feasible through targeted interventions, a comprehensive reform of the technical and vocational education system is needed not only to create conditions for more rapid growth, but also to combat youth unemployment. Private sector–led approaches to improve vocational training, where government plays the role of standardizing curricula and accrediting programs, are the most promising route for education system reform.

- **Trade policy reform.** Import bans and high tariff barriers substantially increase the cost of doing business in value chains with high employment potential. Further trade liberalization will be essential to allow a restructuring of the economy toward sectors in which Nigeria is globally competitive.

According to this strategy, growth would be driven by those sectors of the economy that are already growing fast—such as services and manufacturing—but have the potential to grow even faster. Growth in the agriculture sector will continue to be a key element in poverty reduction and employment creation, and further efforts to deepen research and extension services, facilitate access to finance, and strengthen sector governance and the regulatory framework will be essential. However, in view of the need for productivity increases to sustain growth in agriculture, the potential for large-scale job creation will be limited. In the initial phase, growth would continue to be driven by domestic demand, with exports to the region and international markets at a later stage. The potential for domestic-led growth has been manifest in Nigeria's recent strong growth performance, which has mostly been driven by domestically oriented sectors. Non-oil exports have remained negligible.

In view of the importance of addressing unemployment, the study reviews Nigeria's technical and vocational education and training (TVET) and finds that it barely contributes to the formation of skilled professionals, as the number of graduates is small and programs are outdated and insufficiently responsive to the requirements of the labor market. The absence of adequate TVET is a major impediment to the effective integration of youth into the labor market. In addition, it is an obstacle to the development of several value chains for which shortages of adequately trained staff are a major constraint to growth. Development of a national skills framework targeted at sectors of the economy with the highest growth and employment potential will be critical to faster growth and to enhancing the growth elasticity of employment.

Nigeria's trade regime has been substantially liberalized in recent years, especially with the partial adoption of the Economic Community of West African States (ECOWAS) common external tariff (CET), which resulted in a lowering of tariff rates and some phasing out of nontariff barriers. Nonetheless, Nigeria's trade regime remains heavily protectionist, resulting in distortions to the domestic production structure and the perpetuation of uncompetitive cost structures. The analysis of value chains finds that import bans and high tariffs are major constraints to the faster development of a number of employment-intensive sectors of Nigeria's economy. In addition, import bans are a significant constraint to improving the efficiency of customs and reducing the time for clearing imports. Greater availability of cheaper imports and enhanced access to export markets will be critical to a restructuring of the Nigerian economy toward competitive and employment-intensive sectors.

This study implicitly focuses on small and medium-size enterprises (SMEs) and larger corporations. Additional work on household, micro-, and nano-enterprises will be needed to specifically assess constraints to higher income and employment in these segments of the informal sector, as well as mechanisms to improve training for such enterprises.

The study was largely prepared before the onset of the current global financial crisis. The global financial crisis is affecting Nigeria primarily through the decline in oil prices and the fall in foreign direct investment and remittances. The resulting fall in oil revenue will lead to a marked rise in the fiscal deficit, while the decline in aggregate demand will dampen growth prospects. The global financial crisis substantially heightens the urgency of economic diversification away from oil and strengthens the case for a growth strategy built on targeting binding constraints in selected value chains with high employment potential. The main conclusions and recommendations of the study, therefore, remain valid.

Nigeria's Growth Performance

Since 2001, Nigeria has had the longest period of sustained expansion of its non-oil economy since independence. Growth has occurred across all sectors of the economy and has been accelerating. While non-oil growth averaged about 3 to 4 percent from 1995 to 2000, it more than doubled to more than 7 percent since 2003, and it rose to 8 to 9 percent in recent years. In spite of the financial crisis, growth of the non-oil economy is estimated to have remained above 7 percent in 2009. The development of the non-oil economy is in contrast to that of the oil economy, whose contribution has been declining owing to unrest in the Niger Delta (table 1.1).

Over the past five years, the growth of Nigeria's non-oil economy has been superior to that of most oil-exporting and non-oil-exporting countries in Sub-Saharan Africa (table 1.2). Only Angola and Equatorial Guinea had significantly higher growth rates.

An analysis of the sources of that growth shows that it was largely driven by faster accumulation of capital and labor, and that productivity has not improved significantly. Figure 1.1 plots the development of total

Table 1.1   Macroeconomic Aggregates, 2001, 2003–07

(percent)

	2001	2002	2003	2004	2005	2006	2007
Real GDP	8.4	21.4	10.2	10.5	6.5	6.0	6.3
Oil GDP	5.6	–5.7	23.8	3.3	0.5	–4.4	–5.5
Non-oil GDP	9.8	33.9	5.8	13.2	8.6	9.4	9.5
Inflation rate	18.9	12.9	14.0	15.0	17.9	8.0	5.4

Source: Nigerian National Bureau of Statistics.
Note: Data for 2002 are affected by a statistical break in the series. GDP = gross domestic product.

Table 1.2   Real Non-Oil Gross Domestic Product Growth, 2003–07
(percent per annum)

	2003	2004	2005	2006	2007	2003–07
Nigeria	5.8	13.2	8.6	9.4	9.5	9.3
Oil producers						
Angola	10.3	9.0	14.1	27.5	25.1	17.2
Cameroon	4.9	4.9	3.2	2.9	4.1	4.0
Chad	6.0	–0.5	11.0	4.7	3.1	4.9
Congo, Rep. of	5.4	5.0	5.4	5.9	6.6	5.7
Equatorial Guinea	3.7	15.4	25.8	17.6	37.8	20.1
Gabon	0.8	2.3	4.3	4.9	6.2	3.7
Non-oil producers						
Ghana	5.2	5.6	5.9	6.4	6.3	5.9
Kenya	2.9	5.1	5.7	6.1	6.9	5.3
South Africa	3.1	4.8	5.1	5.0	4.8	4.6
Tanzania	5.7	6.7	7.4	6.7	7.1	6.7

Sources: World Development Indicators database; International Monetary Fund data.

Figure 1.1   Cumulative Total Factor Productivity for Alternative Initial Capital–Output Ratios, 1960–2004

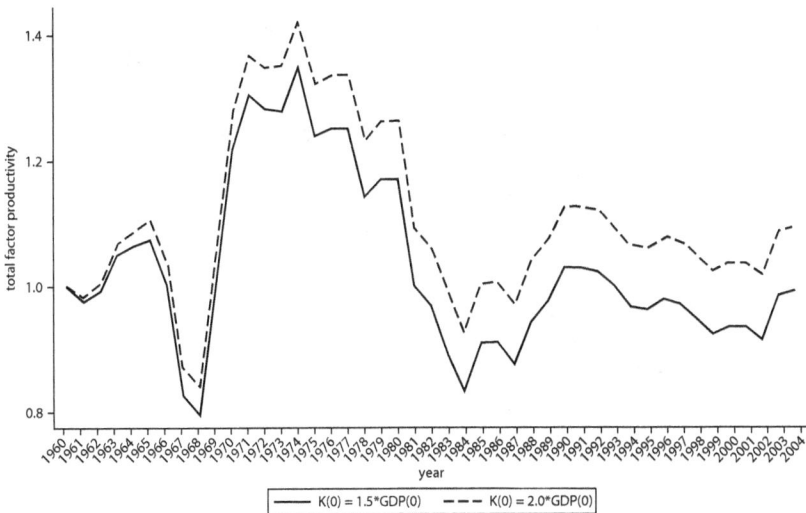

Source: World Bank 2007.

factor productivity (TFP) since 1960. From 1990 to 2002, the contribution of TFP to growth declined. In 2003 and 2004, some productivity improvements may have occurred, possibly related to the delayed impact on investment of the changed policy environment since 1999.[1]

Contribution to Growth by Sector

The growth of the non-oil economy was largely driven by the agriculture sector, which contributed, on average, more than 40 percent (table 1.3). The contribution of agriculture was followed by that of the wholesale and retail sector (about 30 percent), the telecommunications sector (7 to 8 percent), and the manufacturing and financial sectors.

Since 2001, changes in the services sector have led to a structural change in Nigeria's economy, manifested in substantial growth of the telecommunications, transportation, hotel and restaurant, construction and real estate, and financial sectors.

The fastest-growing sector has been telecommunications (at an average annual rate of more than 30 percent), followed by the wholesale and retail sectors (about 15 percent) and construction (about 13 percent). Also, solid minerals grew by more than 10 percent, on average, and manufacturing by about 8 to 9 percent. Agriculture grew by 6 to 7 percent, on average—the strongest sustained growth performance in more than a decade.

Explaining Nigeria's Growth Performance

In light of the recent oil boom, high oil prices would be the most obvious explanation for strong growth. However, the available evidence does not support the conclusion that non-oil growth was substantially driven by high oil prices. The adoption of an oil-price-based fiscal rule since 2003 essentially de-linked expenditure from oil prices. Nigeria's ratio of consolidated government expenditure to gross domestic product (GDP) has, in fact, largely *declined* since 2001 (table 1.4). By contrast, the ratio either remained flat or slightly increased for other producers.

Table 1.3   Contribution to Non-Oil Growth
(percent)

	2004	2005	2006	2007
Agriculture	46.7	45.3	42.8	40.6
Solid mineral	0.5	0.4	0.4	0.4
Manufacturing	6.3	5.5	5.0	4.5
Telecommunication and post	5.0	5.5	6.9	8.9
Finance and insurance	2.0	1.8	2.8	3.1
Wholesale and retail trade	21.3	27.3	29.4	29.4
Building and construction	2.5	2.7	2.8	3.0
Other	15.7	11.3	10.0	10.1

Sources: World Development Indicators database; International Monetary Fund data.

Table 1.4 Total Expenditure and Net Lending, 2001–07
(percentage of GDP)

	2001	2002	2003	2004	2005	2006	2007	2001–07 (average)
Nigeria	51.1	32.1	33.1	29.1	28.7	26.9	29.1	32.9
Other oil producers								
Angola	48.7	47.3	44.3	38.5	33.3	31.6	33.1	39.5
Cameroon	16.2	15.7	15.4	16.0	14.6	14.5	15.6	15.4
Chad	17.6	20.2	21.9	14.4	13.1	16.5	20.7	17.8
Congo, Rep. of	31.5	35.5	29.8	26.7	23.2	27.4	32.0	29.4
Equatorial Guinea	12.4	15.1	15.6	19.3	18.2	22.2	23.6	18.1
Gabon	30.8	28.0	22.8	22.6	22.8	22.5	21.5	24.4
Non-oil producers								
Ghana	30.9	24.5	28.8	33.3	30.7	34.3	34.3	31.0
Kenya	26.7	27.0	25.2	22.5	23.7	24.4	24.3	24.8
South Africa	25.9	25.9	26.7	26.9	27.3	27.4	27.7	26.8
Tanzania	14.4	14.6	16.4	18.1	20.3	21.8	22.1	18.3

Sources: World Economic Outlook database; International Monetary Fund 2008.
Note: Central government figures for Gabon and Ghana; general government figures for all other countries.

At the same time, excess oil revenue accumulated rapidly in the excess crude account and reached more than US$18 billion toward the end of 2008.[2] This suggests that there has not been a significant fiscal impulse driving the growth performance. However, it is conceivable that the quality of spending substantially improved since the return to democracy in 1999 and the adoption of more transparent expenditure policies. It is more likely, however, that the growth in aggregate domestic demand underlying the strong growth performance mostly reflected (a) higher foreign direct investment, notably in the oil and gas and telecommunications sectors; (b) increases in remittances from Nigerians living abroad; and (c) higher credit to the private sector (table 1.5).

Foreign direct investment and remittances responded directly to important changes in macroeconomic policies and to structural reforms. Notably, sound macroeconomic policies helped to stabilize the economic environment and lower inflation and real interest rates. Structural policies such as large-scale privatization, reforms to the regulatory environment, establishment of institutions combating corruption, and financial sector reforms (box 1.1) succeeded in improving the supply response.[3]

Generally, these macroeconomic and structural policies succeeded in instilling confidence in the business community that Nigeria had entered a new phase in its development and that the environment for private sector-led investment had fundamentally improved.

In the case of agriculture, growth was clearly driven by a sharp increase in the prices of agriculture commodities, which reflected (a) the rise in local demand due to the emergence of an urban middle class; (b) the increase in international prices; and (c) protectionist trade policies (notably import bans on food items such as cassava, vegetable oil, and poultry).[4] Table 1.6 shows the growth of different types of crops since 2001.

Table 1.5   Credit, Remittances, and Foreign Direct Investment

	2001	2002	2003	2004	2005	2006	2007	2008
Claims on private sector (% GDP)	16.7	13.1	13.6	12.8	13.2	13.5	22.8	28.9
Private remittances, net (US$ millions)	1,167	1,209	1,063	2,273	3,329	5,435	9,921	9,980
FDI, net (US$millions)	1,971	2,422	2,815	4,376	6,111	6,181	6,425	−3,109

Source: International Monetary Fund 2001–08.
Note: FDI = foreign direct investment.

Box 1.1

Financial Sector Reforms

The growth in the financial sector benefited from the banking consolidation exercise at the end of 2004, during which the minimum capital requirement was raised from about US$19 million to US$190 million. To meet new capital requirements, many of the existing 89 commercial banks merged with larger and financially more robust banks, resulting in the emergence of 25 commercial banks that were more solid. Another factor deepening the financial system was the reform of the pension fund, essentially the replacement of the pay-as-you-go system by a fully funded pension system. The new system allowed an end to the accumulation of arrears and had a catalytic effect on the capital markets. Since the banking consolidation, credit to the private sector has more than doubled as a percentage of GDP and is now above the average for Sub-Saharan Africa.

Table 1.6   Agriculture Production by Crop
(thousands of tons)

	2001	2003	2007
Cereals	20,090	22,736	30,850
Roots and tubers	65,282	73,905	92,718
Vegetables and melons	7,919	8,513	9,869

Source: Nigerian National Bureau of Statistics.

In conclusion, the key features of Nigeria's growth performance since 2001 include the following:

- Seventy percent of non-oil growth can be explained by the agriculture, wholesale, and retail sectors.
- Relatively new sectors, such as construction, the financial sector, telecommunications, and information and communications technology (ICT) have recorded high growth and have initiated a structural transformation of the Nigerian economy toward the services sector.
- Macroeconomic and structural reforms have instilled greater confidence among the business community and boosted foreign direct investment and remittances from Nigerians living abroad, thus raising aggregate demand and private investment.
- Growth has been largely the result of factor accumulation, with only minor contributions of productivity increases. In the agriculture sector,

in particular, productivity has stagnated and growth has been largely the result of increased land use. Also, as growth since 2003 was increasingly attributable to new, technology-driven sectors of the economy, such as the financial sector and ICT, it is likely that the importance of productivity improvements may have increased in recent years.

- Nigeria's growth path is distinct from that of other countries such as India, whose strong performance had relied extensively on the services and manufacturing sectors. In India, in particular, the contribution of the agriculture sector to GDP had been on a rapidly declining path since 1950 and had fallen to 21 percent in 2004–05 from 57 percent in 1950–51. At the same time, the contribution of manufacturing to India's GDP nearly doubled, from 9 to 17 percent, and that of services from 28 to 52 percent. In Nigeria, by contrast, over the period of high growth since 2001, the contribution of agriculture to GDP has declined only marginally, which is remarkable in that nonagricultural growth has been sustained and has even accelerated for some time.

How Sustainable is Nigeria's Growth Performance?

Nigeria's strong growth performance is all the more significant in that it occurred in spite of poor physical infrastructure and a business environment that has not been conducive to private investment. This performance can be largely attributed to the vibrant response of Nigeria's dynamic private sector to a more stable and predictable economic and political environment, as well as to some important structural reforms. Against this background, prospects for continued strong growth seem favorable, especially if the investment climate is reformed and physical infrastructure is improved in key areas. Such reforms will create the basis for productivity-enhancing investments in value chains that have the highest growth and employment potential. In this case and in view of the country's large unexploited potential, it is realistic to expect that growth will remain sustainable at high levels and possibly further accelerate to 11 or 12 percent. Recent estimates of the growth elasticity of poverty suggest that such growth rates would be consistent with a decline of poverty in line with the Millennium Development Goals.

Development of the Labor Market

How have employment and incomes responded to this strong growth performance? This question has been at the center of the public debate in Nigeria. A general perception in Nigeria is that the improvement in the country's economic environment has not translated into higher employment and poverty reduction. This section discusses the evolution of the labor force since 1999 and analyzes the development of employment and incomes. It also contrasts these findings with developments in other Sub-Saharan African countries.[5]

Structure of the Labor Force

The labor force is defined as people between the ages of 15 and 65 who are not in school. Table 1.7 presents the structure of Nigeria's labor force by gender and by rural and urban sectors in 2003–04.

A key feature of the working-age population is the high share (approximately one-fourth) of that population that is not in the labor force. The breakdown by gender shows that the share of females outside the labor force is at least three times that of males. As in other African countries, formal unemployment (measured as job seekers who cannot find a job) is extremely low. The vast majority of people outside the labor force consists of individuals who are either discouraged job seekers or who have not embarked upon a job search, as they do not consider prospects to be promising. The share of people outside the labor force is a more reliable indicator of unemployment than the official unemployment rate, which consists of individuals who are looking for but are unable to find employment.

Wage employment (about 8 to 10 percent of the labor force) is relatively small and dominated by the public sector. The share of informal sector employment (defined as self-employed workers outside the agriculture sector) is high compared to other Sub-Saharan African countries (table 1.8). Only Senegal has a more sizable informal sector.

Table 1.9 shows how the labor force has evolved since 1999.

Table 1.7   Composition of Labor Force, 2003–04
(percent)

| | By gender | | By sector | | |
	Female	Male	Rural	Urban	Total sample
In labor force	66.3	84.7	77.5	71.8	75.0
Not in labor force					
(voluntarily unemployed)	35.3	16.0	22.5	28.2	25.0
Memo items					
Unemployed	1.6	0.7	0.9	1.4	1.1
Employed	98.4	99.3	99.1	98.6	98.9

Source: Based on Nigeria Living Standards Survey 2003–04, population aged 15–65, not in school.
Note: Unemployed figures include only individuals who are actively looking for work. They do not include discouraged job seekers, who represent the largest share of people without jobs.

Table 1.8   Informal Sector Share of Labor Force
(percent)

Country	Year	Urban	Rural	Total
Burkina Faso	2003	42.7	3.7	9.6
Cameroon	2001	50.9	10.6	22.3
Mozambique	2002	28.1	3.5	11.1
Nigeria	2006	54.2	21.0	28.3
Senegal	2001	69.4	11.3	30.0
Uganda	2002	54.1	18.7	24.0

Sources: Fox and Gaël 2008; author's calculations.
Note: Informal sector defined as own account and unpaid family workers outside the agriculture sector.

Table 1.9   Sample Population Aged 15–65, Not in School
(percent, weighted)

	1999	2004	2006
Labor force status			
Not in the labor force	25.3	23.0	25.2
In the labor force	74.7	77.0	74.8
Unemployment status			
Employed	97.8	97.0	97.4
Unemployed	2.2	3.0	2.6

Source: Haywood and Teal 2008, based on Nigeria Living Standards Survey 2003–04 and General Household Survey 1999–2006.

The share of the population not in the labor force has remained broadly unchanged. This means that the number of jobs has risen broadly in line with the labor force, and that unemployment has remained basically unchanged.

Table 1.10 shows the evolution of employment broken down by family agriculture, nonagriculture self-employed (that is, mostly urban), and wage employment.

From 1999 to 2006, the most important structural changes that have occurred in Nigeria's labor force have been a shift *into* agricultural employment and *out of* wage employment: the proportion of the sample population aged 15 to 65 (excluding those in full-time education) with wage jobs *declined* over this period, from 15 percent in 1999 to 10 percent in 2006. The same is true for those classified as nonagriculture self-employed, whose share of the population fell from 24 percent to 22.9 percent. The category that saw a major increase in this share of the population was family agriculture, which rose from 30.8 percent to 37.8 percent.[6]

Table 1.10   Types of Employment as Percentage of Sample Population
(weighted)

	1999	2004	2006
Family agriculture	30.8	36.60	37.80
Nonagriculture self-employed	24.1	25.80	22.90
Nonagriculture unpaid family work	0	0.08	0.06
Wage employment	15.0	10.40	10.00
Apprenticeship	2.1	1.10	1.90
Unemployed	1.7	2.40	1.90
Not in the labor force	26.4	23.70	25.50

Source: Haywood and Teal 2008, based on Nigeria Living Standards Survey 2003–04 and General Household Survey 1999–2006.

This is an important finding. It essentially confirms the thrust of discussions of employment policy in Nigeria, which frequently asserts that the problem is the creation of an insufficient number of jobs. With the share of the population outside the labor force unchanged *in spite of sustained high non-oil growth,* Nigeria's pattern of growth has not responded to the aspirations of its population.

This pattern of change in the structure of the labor force is at variance with that observed in most of Sub-Saharan Africa in the 1990s. In Ghana, Tanzania, and Uganda, the proportion of the labor force working in family agriculture over the 1990s declined (figure 1.2)—in the case of Tanzania, dramatically so, from 80 percent to 70 percent of the labor force. This contrasts with a rise in Nigeria. Furthermore, these three countries saw an explosive growth in non-agriculture self-employment relative to wage employment.

Table 1.11 provides further insights into the development of wage employment since 1999. As would be expected, wage employment in parastatals, government agencies, and public companies has declined, while employment in the private sector and others (including nongovernmental organizations, international organizations, and associations) has risen.

The decline of wage employment reflects three developments:

- The retrenchment of civil servants and the privatization of many parastatals has led to a sharp decline in public service employment, which has long dominated employment in the formal sector and continues to represent the largest share of wage employment.
- Many private industries with large wage employment, notably the textile industry, have been in decline for a number of years and have shed a considerable part of their work force.

Figure 1.2   Trends in Nonagriculture Employment
(absolute number of workers, thousands)

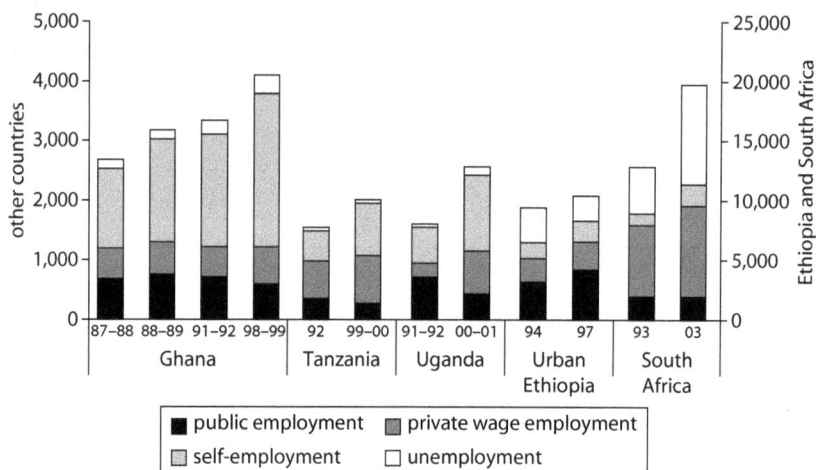

Source: Kingdon, Sandefur, and Teal 2006.

Table 1.11   Types of Wage Employment
(percent, weighted)

	1999	2004	2006
Parastatals and ministries	48.6	42.2	45.6
Private companies	17.0	20.5	18.0
Public companies	11.6	12.0	6.9
Other	22.8	25.2	29.6

Source: Haywood and Teal 2008, based on Nigeria Living Standards Survey 2003–04 and General Household Survey 1999–2006.
Note: Other includes NGOs, international organizations, and associations.

- Sectors of the economy that have grown quickly, such as wholesale and retail, construction, and agriculture, have been to a significant extent made up of informal workers, while industries in the formal sector, e.g., financial services and hospitality, are either not very employment intensive or have added labor from a very low base, failing to make a significant difference in the growth of wage employment.

This pattern of job creation is even more apparent in the youngest age bracket of the population. Table 1.12 shows the evolution of the types of

Table 1.12   Types of Employment of Population Aged 15–25
(percentage of sample population, weighted)

	1999	2004	2006
Urban			
Family agriculture	4.00	3.70	5.50
Nonagriculture self-employed	28.00	34.80	23.70
Nonagriculture unpaid family work	0.01	0.20	0.20
Wage employment	13.50	9.10	9.30
Apprenticeship	11.70	6.80	11.40
Unemployed	9.10	11.60	8.40
Not in the labor force	30.80	33.50	37.50
Rural			
Family agriculture	16.90	34.00	31.10
Nonagriculture self-employed	9.50	15.30	12.00
Nonagriculture unpaid family work	0.01	0.26	0.20
Wage employment	15.40	2.70	3.20
Apprenticeship	5.50	2.90	4.50
Unemployed	4.40	5.90	4.30
Not in the labor force	48.20	38.90	44.80

Source: Haywood and Teal 2008, based on Nigeria Living Standards Survey 2003–04 and General Household Survey 1999–2006.
Note: Excluding those in full-time education. The relatively high share of family agriculture in urban areas may reflect the fact that areas on the verge of urbanization may be counted as urban but have household members engaged in agriculture. It might also reflect household members living in urban areas who work in rural agriculture.

employment as a share of the sample population aged 15–24 (excluding those in full-time education). Two features stand out:

- Among the young in rural areas, the share of family agriculture almost doubled from 1999 to 2006.
- By 2006, the share of young people outside the labor force in urban areas had appreciably increased. A more detailed review of the share of the people outside the labor force suggests that most are women engaged in the household and men who have never had any employment experience.

This picture generally supports the conclusion that youth unemployment has been on the rise since 1999, an alarming trend in view of Nigeria's strong growth performance in recent years.

How Has Growth Affected Incomes?

The General Household Survey contains information on the development of incomes in the formal and informal rural and urban sectors since

1999 (table 1.13). These data strongly indicate that real incomes have substantially risen since 1999. Incomes in the formal wage sector and the informal urban sector have increased by about 50 percent in real terms. Most importantly, incomes in family agriculture have almost *doubled* in real terms and are now on par with those in the self-employed non-agriculture sector. At the beginning of the decade, incomes in the urban informal sector were about 30 to 40 percent higher in real terms than in family agriculture.

The evolution of incomes in Nigeria's agriculture sector compares favorably to that in other African countries (table 1.14). This shows the importance of the agricultural renaissance that Nigeria has experienced since 1999—not only for growth, but also for the development of incomes. At the same time, the development of incomes in the urban informal sector and in wage employment was closer to the average for comparator countries.

Table 1.13   Mean Earnings by Employment Type, 1999–2006
(weighted)

Earnings per month (constant naira)	1999	2004	2006
Family agriculture	4,573	8,219	8,851
Self-employed non-agriculture	6,065	9,174	9,049
Wage job	9,924	16,437	12,362
Total	5,785	9,739	9,427

Source: Haywood and Teal 2008, based on Nigeria Living Standards Survey 2003–04 and General Household Survey 1999–2006.

Table 1.14   Estimated Average Annual Growth in Earnings, by Sector of Employment
(percent)

Country	Years of survey	Agriculture	Wage and salary jobs	Informal sector
Burkina Faso	1998 and 2003	3.0	1.4	−1.5
Cameroon	1996 and 2001	0.8	2.8	6.8
Ghana	1991 and 1998	2.0	2.0	0.8
Mozambique	1996 and 2002	4.4	5.4	6.0
Nigeria	1999 and 2006	9.5	3.6	5.1
Senegal	1994 and 2001	0.4	−1.2	3.0
Uganda	1992 and 2002	3.7	4.4	1.8

Source: Author's calculations, based on General Household Survey 1999–2006.
Note: Earnings are measured as total household consumption per labor force participant.

Summary of findings. The pattern of growth in Nigeria and its relation to the evolution of Nigeria's labor market can be summarized as follows:

- Nigeria's strong growth in recent years has been dominated by the agriculture sector. In the labor market, this has been reflected in a shift of employment into family agriculture. The considerable growth of employment in the agriculture sector is consistent with the absence of improvements in agricultural productivity.
- Strong agriculture performance has reflected primarily the rise in the prices of agriculture commodities, owing to (a) the increase in international prices, (b) the increase in demand from the urban middle class, and (c) the impact of restrictive trade policies. This change in relative prices in favor of agricultural commodities is also an essential factor explaining the increase in incomes in family agriculture and is consistent with the marked decline of extreme rural poverty.
- The creation of contractual wage jobs in the rapidly growing sectors of the economy has been unable to compensate for the loss of wage jobs in the public sector, parastatals, and government agencies, leading to a decline in wage employment.

With the share of population outside the labor force unchanged for the population as a whole and rising for the lowest age bracket, Nigeria's growth performance has clearly not responded to the aspirations of its population.

What Have Been the Impediments to Faster Growth in the Formal Sector?

As discussed above, Nigeria's strong growth performance has reflected primarily two factors: (a) sound macroeconomic policies that created a more favorable environment for private investment and (b) sectoral policies, such as the banking consolidation exercise that directly boosted growth in specific sectors of the economy. Both macroeconomic and structural policies contributed to confidence in a new era in the Nigerian economy and thus promoted investment substantially fueled by foreign direct investment and remittances.

This investment, however, was more focused on capital-intensive industries than on employment-intensive industries. Investment occurred primarily in the oil and gas and the telecommunications industries, in which returns were particularly high. Few productivity improvements occurred in the employment-intensive sectors of the economy, such as manufacturing.

As a result, the infrastructure constraints became more binding in these sectors, limiting improvements in their productivity and competitiveness and, hence, their ability to generate employment. A forward-looking growth strategy needs to focus on improving productivity in the employment-intensive sectors of the economy.

This is particularly important because Nigeria's comparative advantage of relatively low labor costs is rapidly eroding, as the effect of low labor productivity is compounded by appreciation of the naira. In fact, the rise in U.S. dollar–denominated wages is larger than that in real naira by a factor of two. This much larger increase in incomes in U.S. dollar terms, rather than in domestic prices, implies that labor costs are becoming increasingly uncompetitive on the international market.

Nigeria's Growth Strategy Going Forward

Based on the analysis above, this section develops for Nigeria a growth strategy going forward that is specifically tailored to Nigeria's circumstances.

Why a Growth Strategy?

Many developing countries have followed *comparative-advantage-defying* strategies, which led to various distortions, poor growth performance, and more uneven income distribution (Lin 2008). A hallmark of such strategies was the development of the kinds of capital-intensive, technologically advanced heavy industries that prevailed in the developed countries as a symbol of modernization. However, with many developing countries being capital-scarce economies, capital-intensive industries have not been to their comparative advantage.

To promote such industries, governments opted to regulate entry to give firms in the priority sectors a monopoly position so that they could charge high prices. In addition, they used administrative measures, including distortions of interest and foreign exchange rates, to allocate capital, foreign exchange, and other inputs to lower their costs of investment and operations. These interventionist measures ultimately led to rent-seeking, crony capitalism, low efficiency, and poor development performance.

Many policies followed by Nigeria since independence have been in line with such a comparative-advantage-defying strategy. Key aspects of this strategy have been (a) the takeover of key sectors of the economy by the state, (b) a highly protectionist trade policy characterized by import bans and high tariff barriers, and (c) directed credit schemes. Although Nigeria adopted a private sector–led growth strategy in 2001, restrictive trade policy, direct support to industries of strategic interest, and state domination of all aspects of the oil and gas industry continue to characterize government policy.

Traditional growth theory argues that a stable macroeconomic framework and an environment free of distortions are sufficient to allow an economy to grow in line with its potential. However, many countries that have achieved high growth adopted strategies that actively supported employment and growth in specific sectors of the economy. Lin (2008) refers to these strategies as *comparative-advantage-following* strategies.

Rodrik (2004) conceptualized this new approach to growth-promoting policies. He stressed that the right way of thinking about industrial policy, such as the intervention in a firm's choice of location through the creation of industrial clusters, is a *discovery* process—one in which firms and governments learn about underlying costs and opportunities and engage in strategic coordination.

The importance of discovery, as opposed to innovation, rests on the finding that in many cases, differences in the production structure cannot be explained by differences in factor endowments. For instance, Bangladesh exports millions of dollars worth of hats, while Pakistan exports virtually none. Pakistan exports millions of dollars worth of footballs, which, in turn, Bangladesh hardly exports. These production patterns are less the outcome of a production structure determined by factor endowment than they are of random self-discovery attempts followed by imitative entry. In Nigeria, such imitative entry was the driving factor in the success of the Otigba computer cluster as well as the entertainment industry, which provides direct and indirect employment for one million people (box 1.2).

Experience around the world suggests that such discovery could be supported through proactive industrial policy. The question is in what way the experience of these countries could be adapted to Nigeria.

What Kind of Growth Strategy?

Nigeria faces a growing employment crisis: the share of young people between the ages of 15 and 24 outside the labor force is increasing despite strong growth performance. Unless constraints to growth are systematically removed in those industries that are particularly employment intensive and stand a chance of being competitive globally, it is unlikely that these trends will be reversed, further exacerbating tensions and youth unrest.

Nigeria should follow a growth strategy based on the following features:

- Domestic led initially, with a focus on exports to regional and international markets at a later stage.

Box 1.2

Nigeria's Entertainment Industry

The Nigerian film industry (known locally as Nollywood) is the most prolific in the world, producing no fewer than 40 new movies every week. It is the third largest movie industry in the world by value (US$250 million per year) after Hollywood and Bollywood (India's film industry). It employs an estimated 200,000 people directly and provides up to one million job opportunities indirectly. Most of those employed in the industry are young university graduates and school leavers.

Despite these achievements, the industry remains unstructured and loosely regulated. Production standards remain low, marketing and distribution links are ad hoc, and access to finance remains limited. There are few global links and a strong need to improve quality at all stages of the value chain, from production to post-production and retail distribution.

Copyright and piracy protection are priorities needed to grow the industry, since they would enable filmmakers and promoters to capture a greater part of the revenue stream generated by their movies. Other priorities for industry to improve performance include strengthening the distribution and marketing mechanisms and establishing a Nigerian film institute. Such an institute would help improve standards through training and capacity building for industry stakeholders, provision of a hub for key industry skills, and facilitation of equipment leasing.

- Targeted interventions to remove constraints in value chains with high employment and growth potential in both formal and informal sectors, including the self-employed sector.
- Adoption of a national skills development framework.
- Liberalization of trade policy.

Growth would follow three phases. The first phase would be dominated by capturing larger shares of the domestic market; phase 2 would focus on extending Nigeria's access to regional markets; and phase 3 would promote access to the international market. These phases do not need to be sequential. In particular, while Nigeria's growth over the short- to medium-term is likely to continue to be driven by higher domestic demand, phase 1 would likely also witness the increased export orientation of parts of the economy. In fact, encouragement by the Nigerian government to export would be a continuous feature of the growth strategy. This phased approach would differ considerably from that of other countries that have grown through an initial focus on the manufacturing sector and would be distinctly Nigerian.

The phased approach focuses on the domestic market at the outset because, in view of the severe cost disadvantage of Nigerian industry resulting primarily from the lack of power and high costs of transportation, it is unrealistic to expect Nigeria to be able to compete in the international marketplace *in the short term*. Instead, growth is likely to continue to be driven by sectors focused on domestic demand, especially in the service industries that have already significantly contributed to growth. Through the development of appropriate infrastructure, phase 1 would create the platform for growth of manufacturing industries, which would then be oriented towards the regional and international markets in phases 2 and 3.

Can incomes continue to rise without a growth in formal employment? Most of the rise in income during the recent period of strong growth occurred in the context of rising employment in the informal sector. However, the small scale of many informal sector operators, and their low productivity, will limit the potential of any strategy focused on the informal sector to bring incomes toward the levels seen in middle-income countries. Substantial increases in income will require an expansion of wage jobs.

A focus on wage jobs will facilitate income increases in both the formal *and* the informal sectors. This is because a rise in wage employment will lead to a relative decrease in the supply of workers in the self-employment sector—whether urban or rural. This decrease in relative supply will act to raise incomes in that sector, thus reversing the recent trend in which the continued influx into the informal sector in the absence of wage jobs has exerted downward pressure on incomes in the informal urban sector. Furthermore, higher wage employment will also increase the availability of higher-quality informal sector jobs. Most formal sector enterprises have backward and forward links with the informal sector, so growth in these enterprises will also stimulate growth in informal sector companies.

How feasible and realistic is a strategy focused on wage employment in the Nigerian context? Currently, few sectors of the Nigerian economy have a high share of contractual wage employment. The largest formal sector employers include food processing, ICT, and the leather industry. While these sectors have considerable growth potential, it is unlikely that even substantially faster growth will allow job creation to accelerate to levels required to make a significant dent in unemployment. Against this background, an employment-oriented growth strategy will need also to address key constraints in promising value chains dominated by the informal sector, such as light manufacturing, construction, wholesale and retail, palm oil, and cocoa. Employment growth in these value chains has been characterized by casualization; that is, companies have preferred to add labor through casual employment rather than through formal, contractual wage employment.

This casualization reflects essentially two constraints: (a) the uncertain policy environment and (b) the low level of skills of a considerable share of labor.[7] The often unpredictable policy and business environment makes it difficult for companies to be certain of incomes in the future.[8] Combined with the high degree of substitutability of labor, reflecting the low level of technical skills, this creates a preference for companies to hire casual labor and refrain from long-term commitments. However, specific interventions outlined below, especially in the area of skills development and the development of a more favorable business environment, could help address this situation and increase the share of wage employment.

Hence, while a focus on wage jobs is appropriate to enhance the sustainability of growth and raise incomes, it needs to be complemented by measures aimed at key informal sector value chains, as well as by policies to stem the casualization of labor. In fact, given the relatively small size of the formal sector, informal sector value chains could be the focus of an employment-creation strategy in the short run.

How good are the prospects for faster growth in the manufacturing sector? Given the manufacturing sector's lack of competitiveness, it may seem difficult to anticipate substantial growth in that sector. However, figure 1.3 shows that countries similar to Nigeria have been able to break into low-tech, labor-intensive goods production, even if starting points are relatively low, thus considerably expanding the number of manufacturing jobs and directly affecting the poverty rate (see also figure 1.4).[9] Growth in these phases would largely be driven by the discovery process outlined above. In the medium- and high-tech sectors, Nigeria already has been able to establish a foothold in skills-intensive computer repair and clone production (for example, the Otigba cluster in Lagos). Also, the success of the petroleum downstream operator, Oando, following its privatization, is evidence of the ability of the Nigerian private sector to break into sectors of the economy traditionally dominated by foreign companies.

Figure 1.3   Evolution of Production Intensity for Countries Similar to Nigeria

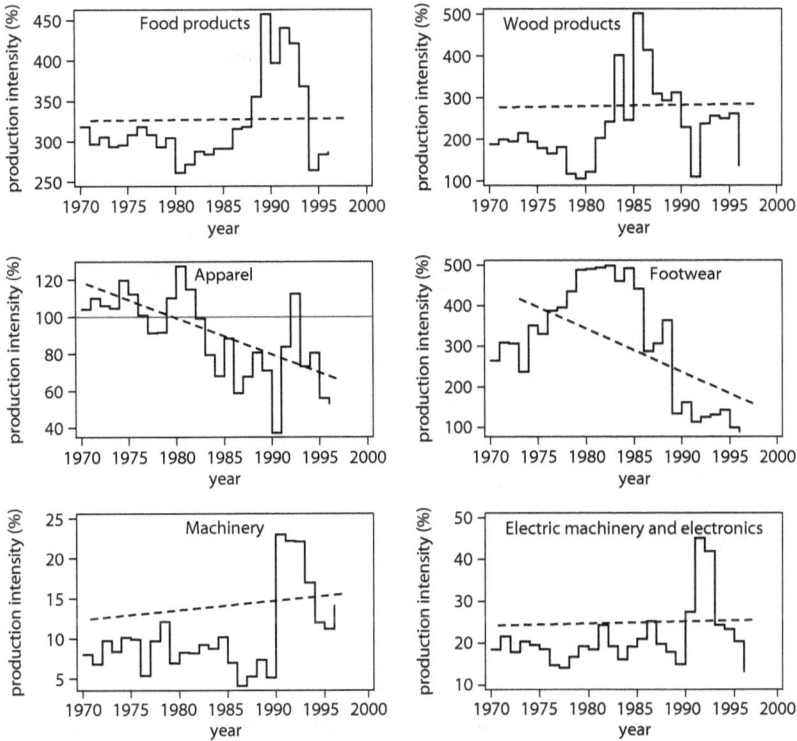

Source: Estimates by Eberhardt and Teal (authors of chapter 3 of this book).

How to Implement the Growth Strategy?

In devising implementation scenarios for this growth strategy, two questions are at the forefront. First, which sectors should be targeted and second, which policies would be best suited to promoting growth in these sectors?

Which sectors? A recently completed competitiveness assessment of some 14 value chains[10] in the economic corridors of Lagos, Kano, Kaduna, and the Southeastern region centered on Calabar (Emerging Market Economics 2008), analyzed the potential of value chains to provide a source of sustainable growth and employment creation. The findings are summarized in figure 1.5 and table 1.15.[11]

Sectors with the highest employment potential are light manufacturing, construction, ICT, wholesale and retail, meat and poultry, oil palm,

Figure 1.4   Evolution of Production Intensity for Some Successful Lower-Income Countries

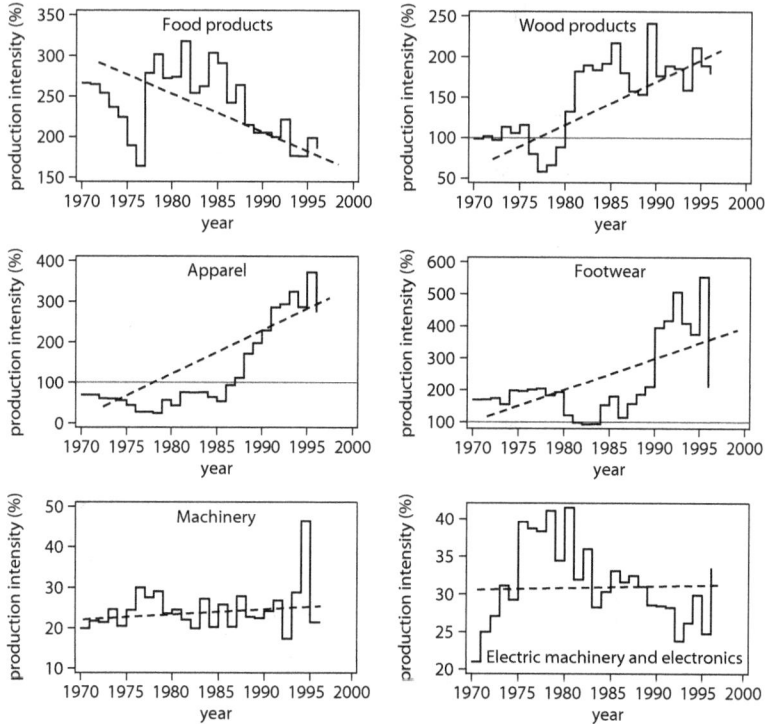

Source: Estimates by Eberhardt and Teal (authors of chapter 3 of this book).

and cocoa. Consistent with the thrust of the growth strategy, most sectors are in either services or the manufacturing industry. As illustrated in figure 1.5, the feasibility of accomplishing growth in these sectors varies widely by geographical area. For example, in Lagos, ICT, construction, wholesale and retail, and light manufacturing have high degrees of feasibility while in Kano, the feasibility of light manufacturing is lower. This analysis confirms the need for geographically focused interventions.

Only two value chains with high employment potential—oil palm and cocoa—are in the agriculture sector. Indeed, the employment potential of the agriculture sector is limited given that future growth in this sector will rely largely on improvements in productivity. As modern technologies and extension services are employed, the ratio of output to labor will rise, thereby limiting the potential for large-scale job creation but also improving prospects for income increases. However, higher growth in

Figure 1.5   Prioritization of Value Chains for Further Investigation

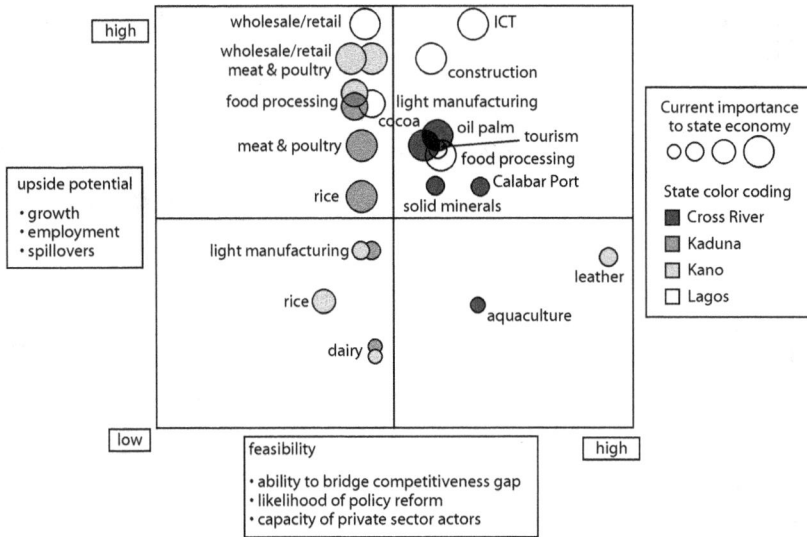

Source: Emerging Market Economics 2008.

meat and poultry and in food processing, which have high employment potential, will stimulate growth and employment in agriculture. Rice and dairy, while having more limited growth and employment potential, are also of interest given their high degree of feasibility.

While the agriculture sector's potential for job creation is limited relative to other value chains, it remains considerable in view of the size of the labor force employed in agriculture and the fact that, in spite of the need for productivity gains, there are still significant possibilities to expand the use of arable land. Box 1.3 summarizes key elements of the government's strategy for agriculture.

Which instruments? The development of *basic principles* for the implementation of a growth strategy needs to build on lessons learned in the promotion of sector-specific growth in the past. The main instruments of Nigeria's industrial policy are currently:

- *Tax and trade incentives,* including exporter grants, duty drawback and manufacturer-in-bond schemes, pioneer tax status, and other tax incentives provided to industry (excluding oil and gas exploration, development and production)

Table 1.15 Prioritization Criteria Scoring

	Growth	Employment	Spillovers	Upside total (y-axis)	Feasibility total (x-axis)	Competitiveness	Policy reform	Private sector capability
Lagos								
Light manufacturing	4	4	2	10	7	2	3	2
Construction	4	4	3	11	8	2	3	3
ICT	4	4	4	12	9	3	3	3
Wholesale and retail	4	4	4	12	7	2	3	2
Food processing	3	3	3	9	8	3	2	3
Kano								
Light manufacturing	2	2	3	7	7	3	2	2
Wholesale and retail	4	3	4	11	7	2	2	3
Food processing	3	3	4	10	7	2	2	3
Leather	3	2	2	7	11	4	3	4
Dairy	1	2	2	5	7	3	3	1
Rice	2	2	2	6	6	2	2	2
Meat and poultry	4	4	3	11	7	2	3	2
Kaduna								
Light manufacturing	2	2	3	7	7	3	2	2
Food processing	3	3	4	10	7	2	2	3
Dairy	1	2	2	5	7	3	3	1
Rice	3	3	2	8	6	3	2	2
Meat and poultry	3	3	3	9	7	3	2	2
Cross River								
Tourism	3	3	3	9	8	3	3	2
Solid minerals	4	2	2	8	8	3	1	4
Oil palm	3	4	2	9	8	3	2	3
Cocoa	3	4	2	9	8	3	2	3
Calabar port	2	2	4	8	9	3	2	4
Aquaculture	2	2	2	6	9	3	4	2

Source: Emerging Market Economics 2008.

Box 1.3

Improving Agricultural Productivity in Nigeria

Agriculture has contributed about 40 percent of the recent strong non-oil growth performance and employs about 50 percent of the labor force. It also provides 88 percent of non-oil foreign exchange earnings. It is a key strategic sector to address multiple challenges that keep the country from achieving broad-based economic growth, increasing household incomes and employment, and reducing food and nutrition insecurity and poverty. Sustaining and further accelerating growth in the agriculture sector is, therefore, important for Nigeria's growth and poverty reduction strategy, which sets an annual growth target of 10 percent for the sector.

To achieve this growth target, policymakers will need to address the following keys issues: (a) the policy environment, (b) rural infrastructure, (c) agricultural finance and expenditure, (d) reducing vulnerability and enhancing food security, (e) access to markets, and (f) the rural investment climate. Addressing these issues will require identifying the constraining factors and the appropriate institutions and agencies to foster the needed changes. In particular:

- **The policy environment** will need to be made more consistent, possibly through new legislation. There is need to reformulate fertilizer policy to reduce rent seeking and to leakages and to increase access by the intended beneficiaries. Pricing and marketing policies need to be designed to provide the incentives for farmers to expand investment in agriculture. Agricultural research policy should be designed to emphasize systemic innovation in the formulation of research and the implementation and engagement of local government councils as primary actors in a pluralistic extension delivery arrangement.
- **Rural infrastructure**, such as farm machinery, roads, electricity, water, storage facilities, transport, communications, and processing facilities, requires immediate attention. The Federal Ministry of Agriculture and Water Resources should be encouraged to work with other relevant arms of government to improve rural infrastructure for farmers.
- **Agriculture expenditure** has traditionally been low relative to the overall budget. Over the 2001–05 period, the government spent less than 2 percent of its budget on agriculture. There is an urgent need to maintain a minimum of 10 percent of budgetary allocation to agriculture, in line with the Maputo Declaration. In the 2009 budget, the government allocated about 12 percent

(continued)

Box 1.3 *(continued)*

of the federal budget to the agriculture sector, which is a clear indication of a shift of priorities toward agriculture. The government is also taking steps to restructure the Nigeria Agricultural Cooperative and Rural Development Bank (NACRDB) to help provide adequate funding to the sector.

- **Reducing vulnerability and enhancing food security** is an important growth driver in Nigeria because of the high level of poverty among the farming population. Key challenges include making weather forecasts available and useful to farmers; expansion of facilities for safety net and recovery mechanisms (such as strategic grains reserve); and improving women's participation in the agriculture sector through better access to land, credit, processing and marketing facilities, as well as reform of the land tenure system.
- **Improving the effectiveness of market access** as a growth driver needs to focus on the establishment of effective market institutions, associations, and unions; commodity exchanges; revenue collectors; regulators; market information systems; and the expansion of market space.
- **Improving the rural investment climate** is also a key driver of agricultural growth. Key areas where changes are needed include (a) removal of disincentives in relation to high costs of doing business and to multiple, high taxes and levies, (b) access to sufficient credit on a timely basis, (c) enhancement of security of lives and property, and (d) risk mitigation through the introduction of insurance schemes and early warning mechanisms to avert losses.

- *Free trade zone services*
- *The Bank of Industry,* which provides loans to SMEs.

Nigeria's current industrial policy is largely supply driven and suffers from the following shortcomings:

- *Lack of uptake by the private sector.* The outreach to firms from different policies and programs is, overall, quite limited. For example, only 94 firms have accessed the pioneer program over the past four years, and some 181 sought Bank of Industry loans in 2006. In the case of export zones, after some 15 years, very few outside the oil and gas sector are active.

- *Complex bureaucratic procedures and institutional capacity constraints limit the effectiveness of existing incentive arrangements.* In many cases, firms need to satisfy an extensive set of administrative requirements in order to access a program. A hierarchy of decision making, including interdepartmental committee reviews, adds complexity, time, and uncertainty to the process.
- *Overall, the various programs have had no significant economic outcome,* whether measured in terms of employment, revenue, foreign exchange, or technology transfer.

A new approach to industrial policy needs to be based on the following basic principles (table 1.16):

- *Performance agreements, monitoring, and accountability.* The impact of incentives on companies needs to be continuously monitored against agreed performance benchmarks, and incentives need to be withdrawn or modified if they do not show the intended results.
- *Governance and coordination.* The number of agencies in charge of industrial policy needs to be streamlined and the existing programs harmonized.
- *Interventions linked to feasibility, relevance, sustainability, and synergies.* The assessment of policy options needs to be based on relevance, feasibility, sustainability of costs, synergies, and impact. For instance, a value chain would be supported if it has the potential for high employment impact (relevance), if growth in that value chain is feasible based on political will and existing institutional capacity (feasibility), and if the costs of the interventions are sustainable (sustainability).

The new approach would target sectors with high growth potential in a framework that takes into account what is most relevant, feasible, and cost effective and provides the greatest near- and medium-term benefits. Critical to the effectiveness of these policies is not only the political commitment of the government, but also the dialogue with the private sector. *In fact, interventions in specific sectors need to emanate from in-depth discussions with the private sector, as opposed to being driven by the government.*

Table 1.17 shows how interventions could be designed to promote growth in the respective value chains. These interventions may be exclusively public- or private-sector driven, or jointly driven by both sectors. Actions that fall in the domain of government include changes in policy, the strengthening of institutions, and the targeted provision

Table 1.16   Assessing Policy Reform Options

Criteria	Variable	Description of variable
Relevance	Policy priority	Do the actions focus on improvements that can have a measurable impact in support of key policy or strategic objectives?
Feasibility	Political will and institutional capacity	• Does the political commitment for the policy exist? • Beyond the reform champions, is there sufficient institutional capability to implement certain measures?
	Sequencing	• Are there sequencing considerations? Do certain measures better suit shorter or longer-term timeframes?
Sustainability and cost	Budget and other resource implications	• Are there significant upfront or recurrent costs or revenue gain and loss considerations? • Is the reform financially sustainable? • Can gaps in institutional capacities essential for success be addressed in parallel with implementing the reform program?
Synergies and impact		Do the planned initiatives have the potential to catalyze a broader alliance for reform to follow through or scale up? Three elements by which to assess this potential are
	Demonstration	• Does the initiative offer quick wins and tangible impacts to lock in commitment and maintain momentum?
	Links	• Do the initiatives link to other stakeholders and have the capacity to *scale up reforms* or have positive *spillovers* to other areas (can an institution created for one reform apply knowledge gained and champion related or other reforms)? Are there *knock-on effects*, where a reform initiative raises awareness and interest in dealing with related reform areas?
	Measurement	• Can the policy impact be credibly measured? Do objective and broadly accepted benchmarks exist?

Source: Consilium International 2008.

Table 1.17 Value Chains—Reform and Instrument Interventions Matrix

	Value chains														
Interventions	Light manufacturing	Construction	ICT	Tourism	Solid minerals	Wholesale and retail	Food processing	Leather	Dairy	Rice	Cocoa	Oil palm	Meat and poultry	Aquaculture	Calabar Port and EPZ
Public															
Policy reform/ regulation	•	•	•	•	•	•	•	•		•	•	•	•		•
Institutions	•	•	•	•		•	•	•	•	•	•	•	•	•	•
Infrastructure	•	•	•	•	•	•	•	•	•	•	•	•	•	•	•
Other public goods[a]									•	•	•		•	•	•
Public/private															
Training	•	•	•	•			•	•	•	•	•	•	•	•	
Planning/coordination	•	•	•	•	•	•	•		•	•	•	•	•	•	
Business development/ support services	•	•	•	•	•	•	•		•	•	•	•	•	•	
Information systems	•	•	•	•		•	•		•	•	•	•	•	•	•
Technology transfer	•	•				•			•	•	•		•	•	
Private															
Supply chain logistics				•		•	•	•	•	•	•	•		•	
Market governance		•				•		•			•	•	•		
Access to finance	•		•	•	•	•	•	•	•	•	•	•	•	•	
Additionality[b]	3	3	2	4	1	3	4	1	4	3	3	3	3	3	2

Source: Emerging Market Economics 2008.

a. e.g., research. b. poor = 1, good = 4. EPZ = export processing zone.

of infrastructure. Areas for joint interventions by both the public and private sectors include training and technology transfer. Measures to improve supply logistics and strengthen access to finance would rely mostly on the private sector.

What share of the labor market? A key to the effectiveness of this strategy will be the *absolute* employment-generating potential within the proposed value chains. While each value chain has considerable growth and employment potential in relative terms (that is, measured as a percentage of the existing work force), the strategy will not achieve its objectives if the absolute employment number (as a percentage of total employment in both formal and informal sectors) is relatively small.

Based on data from the General Household Survey and the Manufacturing Association of Nigeria, total employment in the value chains discussed above was estimated at 14 million people, or about 15 percent of the labor force, of which 2 million were in wage employment and 12 million were self-employed. Included in the figures for self-employment are nearly 5 million agricultural households that keep livestock and grow cocoa, oil palm, and rice. Hence, the employment-generating potential of the targeted value chains is considerable.

Targeted Interventions

The common denominator of the proposed interventions is the need to increase productivity, as this is the key to reducing costs and prices so that demand can rise. Productivity growth is at the heart of any successful strategy for job creation. Nigeria's lack of competitiveness, which reflects inadequate improvements in productivity, is the root cause of the pattern of jobless growth.

Although specific to each value chain, binding constraints can be broadly categorized in the following five areas (annexes 1A and 1B):

- Inadequate physical infrastructure, in particular, power and transport
- Lack of access to finance
- Poor investment climate, leading to shortcomings in quality control and slow bureaucratic procedures
- Shortage of skilled staff and
- Effect of import bans and other restrictive trade policies on the cost of inputs

These binding constraints and their importance for growth have been extensively discussed in other documents (e.g., World Bank 2007; World Bank 2009; International Finance Corporation and World Bank 2008a). Clearly, if all of these constraints were addressed in a holistic way, Nigeria would be poised to quickly achieve middle-income status. However, this is an unlikely prospect given the complexity of the reforms involved. *Over the short term, employment generation can be fast-tracked if binding constraints to growth in the most promising value chains are addressed in a selective manner. This is the central argument of this study.*

Addressing these five types of binding constraints will require different responses.

Physical infrastructure. Both cluster-based approaches and shared public-private responsibility can be critical elements in the government's strategy for addressing infrastructure shortcomings in Nigeria. Clusters are advantageous when it is more efficient to geographically concentrate resources so that costs can be reduced in certain localities, rather than attempt a general countrywide increase in productivity. The government can also use clusters to selectively improve bureaucratic procedures (for example, customs clearance, licensing, land regulations, and governance) (box 1.4).

Box 1.4

The Use of Clusters to Improve Bureaucratic Procedures

The recent Industrial Development Report (UNIDO 2009) includes a case study of Malaysia's Penang export zone, which has evolved into a major industrial cluster. At the core of the government's intervention was the provision of excellent infrastructure in the zone, financed out of natural resource revenues. However, government policies went well beyond the provision of infrastructure. Attention was also paid to social infrastructure in the zone so that it would be an attractive place for high-skilled workers to live, thereby easing the recruitment problems facing firms that chose to set up in the zone. Finally, the government took care to put its own house in order by tackling corruption and delays in the regulatory and customs regime; in effect, the export zone became a good governance zone. In combination, these supportive policies succeeded in attracting very high inflows of foreign direct investment.

Geographical concentration has other benefits as well. Firms may be able to gain from clustering close to each other through agglomeration economies. The literature identifies potential knowledge externalities (related to information about marketing and technology), pecuniary externalities (access to suitably skilled "thick" labor markets), supply chain linkages (forward to customers, backward to suppliers of inputs), specialization (division of labor among firms), and competitive pressures to innovate and harness potential cross-sectoral synergies. A further benefit might be that firms organize themselves and carry out conscious joint action such as lobbying.

A cluster-based approach may be most suitable for the following industries, in view of the type of constraints affecting their growth: (a) light manufacturing, especially in Lagos, (b) food processing, and (c) meat and poultry production.

In food processing, for example, it is essential to deliver an integrated logistics program from farmgate to the processing stage, covering farm storage, drayage, wholesale markets, rural roads, and line haul transport to the processor using temperature control equipment. Given that it will be impossible to implement such an approach nationwide, a cluster-based approach would allow the targeting of public investment in those geographical areas that have natural advantages, such as proximity to markets or to the areas of production.

Not all employment-intensive sectors of the economy lend themselves to a cluster-based approach, however. The review of the construction and real estate value chain, for example, shows that one binding constraint to growth in this sector is the offloading of costly public access infrastructure to the developer. The responsibility for improving infrastructure lies with local governments, but their capacity is limited so that in practice, the developer tends to cover this task. To address this constraint, it may be preferable to review the allocation of responsibility among different levels of government with a view to assigning the task of building roads in critical real estate developments to state governments, possibly in the context of public-private partnerships.

Access to finance. Nigeria has made significant strides in the reform of its financial system, and credit to the private sector has been expanding rapidly. However, access to finance remains a problem in many sectors, since much of the growth of credit reflects an expansion of short-term trade credit. Important growth sectors of the economy, including SMEs, continue to have limited access to finance. This problem has been greatly exacerbated by the global financial crisis, which has led to a slowdown in credit to the private sector. Growth in the construction sector, for example, is constrained due to the high cost of commercial loans for real estate development and housing mortgages.

Interventions should aim at developing all sectors of the market, starting with microfinance and going up to larger corporations and international companies. At the lower end of the market, the Central Bank of Nigeria has already established a sensible microfinance policy that has resulted in the growth of formal, commercial microfinance banks. Further growth in the market and increased geographic coverage could be fostered by easing the capital requirements of microfinance banks that operate in more than one state. Nigeria is also experimenting with alternative dispute resolution mechanisms and credit bureau regulations and is introducing a new leasing law. Once implemented successfully, these measures will allow the expansion of credit to smaller businesses.

In many countries, businesses are often started by homeowners taking out a mortgage on their homes or borrowing against the value of their property. The mortgage industry in Nigeria remains at a nascent stage, with fewer than 50,000 formal sector mortgages. Mortgage finance represents a huge asset class and market potential that remains unleveraged. Nigeria could make progress in this area by developing a public-private partnership framework for effectively supervising housing finance and a mortgage liquidity facility that, with sound underwriting and strong regulation, would group together mortgages from various lenders and securitize them, allowing the lenders to effectively access the capital markets. Reform of the legal framework for rental markets and development of a coordinated federal-state housing policy could also assist in facilitating better access to finance for the construction sector. These interventions could also help in the design of similar reforms aimed at improving access to finance in other sectors where finance is a constraint.

At the top end of the market, Nigerian corporations are limited in their financing options for bank borrowing. The corporate bond market has been inactive for several years. However, the primary market in government bonds has grown rapidly in recent years. This, in turn, provides a yield curve against which to price corporate debt. The government is also considering installing a bond auction trading system that would include sovereign and non-sovereign debt. These measures, along with corporate credit ratings, will assist companies in accessing local and, in some cases, international capital markets.

Investment climate. There are two key obstacles to a better investment climate:

• First, key approvals needed for the development of new businesses, such as land registration, planning, and building permits, are subject to excessively complex bureaucratic procedures that raise costs and delay new start-ups. For example, transaction costs for land acquisition, including real estate appraisal fees, land registry search fees, and governor's consent fees, make up about 25 percent of total transaction costs; and the administrative procedures take approximately 6 months to complete. Similarly, the registration of property is time consuming and costly, leading to low levels of property registration. The impact of high real estate transaction costs extends to food wholesale and retail chains because of their dependence on the construction of commercial real estate. Dealing with these administrative barriers also places a high burden on management, which, as a consequence, has insufficient time for value-adding activities for the company. To address these shortcomings, it is essential to initiate a reform program aimed at speeding up the compliance and approval process. This will require a redesign of administrative procedures through process mapping as well as modernization of some parts of the legal framework.

• Second, many government agencies in charge of quality control are dysfunctional, leading to considerable quality problems. For example, domestic building materials—timber, wood products, rebar steel, and tiles—are of poor quality and non-standardized, as the Standards Organization of Nigeria does not have authority to enforce compliance. To strengthen the functions of these agencies, a strong capacity-building program needs to be launched. Also, where a series of inspections is involved, the inspection activities need to be harmonized to achieve seamless operations.

Skills gap. Labor constraints due to lack of vocational training and low productivity affect product quality and the growth of value chains. For instance, growth in the construction sector is constrained by the lack of skilled construction workers, while at the same time there is no vocational school to train tradesmen. Similarly, in the leather sector, a shortage of skilled labor inflates costs, leading to the use of less-skilled workers— which impacts the quality of the processed skins.

Targeted interventions to improve the technical and vocational education system in employment-intensive value chains will be crucial to address the growing skills gap. A promising avenue in this respect is the initiative by the Federal Ministry of Education to create Vocational Education Institutions (VEIs) and Innovation Enterprise Institutions (IEIs), discussed in more detail below. The major aim of this initiative is to widen access for secondary school leavers, both with and without degrees. In addition to school leavers, potential target groups include university graduates seeking employable skills and adults who need to re-skill themselves.

Another option would be for the Industrial Training Fund to open a window for targeted investments by enterprises, helping them to remove critical skill constraints in key value chains.

The lack of managerial capabilities is also an important skills gap. The recent Investment Climate Assessment (World Bank 2009) showed that better-managed firms are about 80 percent more productive than poorly managed firms. In fact, managerial capability almost eliminates the effect of a poor environment on firm productivity. Business development services may be a suitable means to support managerial capacity in critical value chains.

Trade regime. The pervasiveness of import bans and high tariffs significantly raises the price of factor inputs to consuming industries.

Building materials such as cement, rebar steel, and concrete blocks are an example of how trade policy can have an impact throughout the chain, as these materials are protected by high tariffs, while structural timber imports are banned. Combined with the ineffectiveness of quality controls by SON, this situation leads to an escalation of construction costs, limiting growth and employment creation in this sector. Similarly, the ban on oilseeds has impacted the retail price of domestic cooking oil through high factor input prices. The effectiveness of import bans and high tariff barriers should be reconsidered.

Summary. Targeted interventions along employment-intensive value chains with significant growth potential over the short to medium term will go a long way toward accelerating growth and increasing employment. Such interventions will create regionally concentrated zones of high growth intensity that are likely to have spillover effects in other regions of the country. They will also serve as pilots for reform in the five key areas identified as in need of reform—physical infrastructure, access to finance, investment climate, the skills gap, and trade policy.

Sustainable growth in Nigeria will need to go beyond targeted interventions, however, and aim at comprehensively reforming these five areas in the context of the work on value chains. Strategies exist for the development of modern physical infrastructure (especially in power, water, transportation, and rural roads), including through the promotion of public-private partnerships. Similarly, the Financial System Strategy 2020 (Central Bank of Nigeria 2007) develops a concrete plan for reform of the financial system to enable it to support more rapid growth. The Cost of Doing Business Survey and Investment Climate Enterprise Survey (World Bank 2008) also provide suitable roadmaps for the reform of government agencies and procedures (box 1.5). However, no reviews exist of the technical and vocational education system; and the impact of import

---

Box 1.5

Nigeria's Investment Climate

According to the 2008 Cost of Doing Business Survey, Nigeria's investment climate ranks 108th among 178 countries. However, widespread adoption of the best practice regulations that are already in place in some Nigerian states would bring the nation's ranking to 51st place—alongside such economies as Taiwan, China; Italy; Kuwait; and Botswana—and would go a long way toward substantially improving the investment climate.

These best practice regulations relate mainly to (a) starting a business, (b) permits and licenses, (c) registering property, and (d) enforcing contracts.

- The performance of all Nigerian states is weakest in the area of registering property. The main source of delays and the high cost of property transfers are associated with obtaining the requisite governor's consent. Currently, all Nigerian states would rank low in the global Doing Business ranking. Nigeria's top performer on this indicator, the Federal Capital Territory (FCT), would rank only 157th out of 178 economies worldwide.
- Registering a business has become significantly easier across Nigeria, thanks to computerization of the registry and establishment of zonal branches of the Corporate Affairs Commission (CAC) and Stamp Duty Offices. Company registration remains fastest in FCT, where CAC headquarters is located.

(continued)

Box 1.5 *(continued)*

- Compliance with building regulations is easier and cheaper in the northern states, while the cost of obtaining building permits varies widely across Nigeria. A permit to construct the same warehouse would cost just 25 percent of Nigeria's income per capita and take only 46 days in Sokoto (4th best in the world!), compared with 580 percent in Lagos. Dealing with licenses, on the other hand, is easier in Kaduna.
- There are also substantial differences in the time and cost of enforcing a commercial contract. Typically, court performance is better in states such as FCT, Lagos, and Kaduna that have already implemented the 2004 High Court rules, which stipulate mandatory processing deadlines and procedural steps aimed at fast-tracking court procedings. Across Nigeria, lack of enforcement is a significant factor in the delayed recovery of commercial debts.

bans on customs efficiency and the economy as a whole has not been comprehensively reviewed.

The following section reviews the technical and vocational education system with the aim of assessing its responsiveness to the demands of the labor market and developing a reform strategy. The subsequent section discusses the impact of import bans.

Skills Development in the Technical and Vocational Education System

The skills gap manifests itself in three ways: (a) the unavailability of highly qualified professionals in specialized areas such as engineering and business administration, which is partly addressed through recruitment of expatriate Nigerians; (b) the lack of entrepreneurial and management skills, which affects the ability of companies to cope with an often adverse business environment; and (c) the low quality of technical staff, which leads to productivity losses and poor competitiveness. Given the importance of TVET for the integration of youth into the labor market, as well as for the growth prospects of key value chains, this section reviews the structure of Nigeria's TVET and develops a set of proposals for its reform.

Formal Vocational Training

Formal vocational training is mainly provided through polytechnics, monotechnics, and technical colleges. In addition, many universities offer training similar to that of polytechnics. Also, the Industrial Training Fund facilitates the attachment of young graduates to enterprises for short periods to obtain practical experience.

Importantly, while the National Youth Service (NYS)—in which graduates of secondary and post-secondary training institutions carry out a specific practical assignment for one year—is designed to foster national unity by assigning individuals to regions of the country different from their home state, it has significant potential to be used as a tool for vocational training. This is particularly true given that for many young Nigerians, the NYS represents the first exposure to practical work, and that it is well organized and widely represented throughout the country.

While technical colleges emphasize practical skills, training at polytechnics has a substantially stronger academic thrust. The strong preference for academic education and the low esteem in which Nigerian youth hold blue collar occupations has led to very low enrollment at technical colleges. In fact, enrollment in technical colleges and science technical colleges accounts for less than 2.6 percent of senior secondary enrollment. While enrollment at polytechnics is substantially higher, it is still only about one-third the level of enrollment at universities.

Formal vocational training, therefore, produces only a small fraction of the available technical graduates. A substantial number of young people acquire work-related skills outside the formal education system, mostly through the open apprenticeship system; or they simply enter the labor market without any additional education and training.

Low demand for formal vocational training largely reflects the limited responsiveness of the available programs to the needs of the labor market and, consequently, the poor prospects of graduates finding employment. The gap between acquired competencies and available employment opportunities mainly reflects quality constraints and institutional deficiencies, especially in the technical colleges. Although the government has increased its allocation to the education sector, underqualified staff, shortages of equipment and materials, inadequate facilities for practical training, and outdated course programs are prevalent problems for most public institutions.

These problems are compounded by a shortage of data for monitoring and planning purposes at both the institutional and system levels. There is no systematic assessment of the labor market relevance of the education offered by the technical colleges and polytechnics. These shortcomings impede adequate assessment of performance and quality.

The corollary to the problems with formal training schemes is the high cost of training incurred by private companies and other agencies. In many cases, the quality of this private training compares favorably to that of government institutions. Two examples are the Nigerian Institute of Welding and the Shell Youth Development Scheme.[12]

Informal Sector Training

In the informal sector, skills are acquired in two principal ways: non-formal training and traditional apprenticeship.

The dominance of the traditional apprenticeship system was confirmed in a recent study by the Nigeria Institute for Social and Economic Research (NISER), which found that more than half the operators in the informal sector are trained by master craftsmen or master trainers. Only 20 percent receive their training through the National Directorate of Employment (NDE) or other specialized government training organizations or institutions (NISER 2007).

Non-formal training, by contrast, is conducted in a disjointed manner, with no uniform certification system and highly varying quality. Furthermore, much of the training seems to be conducted without proper assessment of the demand for the skills in question. As no government agency is responsible for coordinating or monitoring non-formal training, no systematic assessment of its relevance and quality takes place.

Summary

Linking growth sectors to skills development. The growth strategy outlined above clearly identifies sectors of the economy with high employment potential and pertinent skills gaps. Systematically linking these value chains with specific skills development programs in a strategic approach that takes account of geographical differences would be a critical step toward addressing pervasive skills gaps. A government agency such as the National Board of Technical Education (NBTE) could play an important role in coordinating the development and implementation of such a framework. The well-functioning trade associations that exist within major parts of the informal sector should be empowered to take part in the skills upgrading and certification of their members. These associations are also well positioned to participate in the design and management of the planned industrial zones and clusters. A facility to support trade associations in their capacity as advocates for and service providers to their constituencies should be established. In addition, Centers for Excellence, such as those already established recently in Lagos, might be encouraged to provide training for key value chains, including through the opening of a special window for targeted investment by enterprises in key value chains, to help them remove critical skills constraints.

Supporting private sector leadership in the context of PPP. Nigeria's private sector has been highly responsive to the improved policy environment and has successfully created pockets of excellence. Vocational training would ideally be led by training institutions run by the private sector, which would offer programs that respond to its specific needs and administer relevant exams. Government could support such institutions through standardization of curricula and accreditation of relevant programs.

The NBTE has taken the first steps to initiate this process through the VEI and IEI programs. VEIs and IEIs are private institutions offering vocational, technical, technological, or professional education and training at post-basic (VEI) and tertiary (IEI) levels, to equip secondary-school leavers (both with and without a degree) and working adults with vocational skills and knowledge to meet the increasing demand for technical manpower by various economic sectors.[13] VEIs and IEIs seek to address the shortcomings of existing vocational training programs, as they are driven and owned by the private sector, with the government limited to ensuring compliance with standards that have been established by the private sector. While the experience with VEIs, which have a somewhat lower standard than IEIs, is mixed, demand for IEIs has exceeded expectations.

An effective way to strengthen links between employers and training programs would be through tripartite governance frameworks involving training institutions, public sector agencies, and the private sector. These agencies could review and coordinate public expenditure on training and help to monitor quality control mechanisms.

Developing a National Vocational Qualifications Framework. Development of such tripartite frameworks could benefit from a more comprehensive National Vocational Qualifications Framework (NVQF). The existence of an NVQF would facilitate the development and certification of new short-term programs that address emerging and short-term needs, such as skills upgrading for the informal sector. An NVQF would, if appropriately managed, open the national certification procedures to private and community-based training institutions. Hence, establishment of an NVQF would provide opportunities for the large group of young people who have acquired their skills in the informal sector to obtain recognition for their competencies. An NVQF could also be an avenue for integrating the National Youth Service into the national strategy for skills development, including matching NYS postings to applicants with appropriate skills profiles.

Planning for labor demand. In order for government policies on skills development and employment to become more strategic, there is the need for a mechanism to monitor the labor market and show where employment absorption is highest, including what skills are required. The system should be able to produce information on broad employment trends and skills needs and specific skills in demand in different states.

Providing financial incentives for vocational training. Currently, the system offers few financial incentives for schools to produce graduates who find employment in the private sector. Providing financial rewards to such institutions requires effective monitoring and evaluation of their existing programs.

Reforming Trade: Import Bans and an Economic Partnership Agreement

Further liberalization of the trade regime is an integral component of any strategy aimed at promoting growth. Nigeria's trade regime, while somewhat liberalized in recent years with the adoption of the ECOWAS (Economic Community of West African States) Common External Tariff, remains highly restrictive and prevents a restructuring of the economy toward those sectors in which Nigeria is competitive. In fact, reforming trade is one of the key elements of moving toward a competitive-advantage-following strategy.

The section on targeted interventions in high-potential value chains already discussed the impact of import bans on production costs. A recent analysis of import bans shows not only that it is very difficult to enforce such bans, but that the pervasiveness of import bans has made it impossible to reform customs and reduce the time required for the clearance of imports. Moreover, import bans provide a strong incentive for smuggling.

Available data from Benin's trading partners indicate that Benin significantly underreports imports subject to import prohibition or high tariff rates in Nigeria—notably textiles, footwear, and manufactured products. However, Benin's trade statistics reveal little discrepancy for goods subject to low tariff rates in Nigeria. Moreover, the reintroduction of extensive import bans on textiles in 2004 was accompanied by a massive increase in unrecorded textile imports by Benin. Data further show that in 2005, per capita consumption of textile products in Benin was 18 times higher than in Nigeria.

Official data also indicate that 13 percent of Cotonou's port traffic originates from or is destined for Nigeria. However, port officials estimate

that 75 percent of the containers that land at Cotonou Port are headed
for Nigeria. Based on this estimate, the value of unofficial trade from
Benin to Nigeria would be around US$4 billion, or about 15 percent of
Nigeria's total imports. Textile smuggling alone amounts to an estimated
US$2.2 billion, against local production in Nigeria of US$40 million. This
figure is broadly in line with estimates by experts in the international textile industry on textile consumption in Nigeria.

The ineffectiveness of import bans is also supported by the seminal
decline of Nigeria's textile industry, where employment fell from 350,000
workers in the mid-1980s to 40,000 direct workers in 2004. Import bans
were an ineffective tool against the impact of inadequate infrastructure
and other factors driving up the cost of doing business in Nigeria.

Import bans have a significant adverse impact on the efficiency of
customs. The pervasiveness of cumbersome customs procedures and
the high number of physical checks reflect, to a significant extent, the
effect of import bans and significantly affect the cost of doing business.
The complexity and restrictive nature of trade policies has provided
ample opportunities and incentives for smuggling, leading to a substantial loss in revenue. Indeed, on a per-staff basis, Nigeria's customs
administration collects only about 15 percent of the amount collected
by Kenya's customs administration, and less than one-third that of
Cameroon's (table 1.18).

An important aspect of the Nigerian import regime is the pervasiveness of non-tariff barriers, including outright prohibitions (or import
bans) for reasons other than protecting health, safety, and the environment. Using a simple empirical model, it is estimated that replacing all
the bans with a 35 percent tariff would increase Nigeria's total imports by
US$2.4 billion (about 10 percent of official imports). Part of this increase
would actually be a formalization of existing informal trade or smuggling,
while the rest would be new imports driven by the more open trade
regime. The new imports would benefit consumers (through availability
and lower prices), and government tax revenue would expand since tariffs would now be collected on both formalized and new imports. The
welfare benefits from removing these import bans are likely to be substantial. At the sectoral level, the largest import response from replacing
the bans with tariffs would occur for used cars.

A more comprehensive reform of the trade regime could take place
in the context of an Economic Partnership Agreement (EPA) between
Nigeria and the European Union (EU), which has been under discussion
for a number of years. As most imports from the EU are already liberalized,
and 20 percent of imports can be exempted from liberalization under an

Table 1.18   Customs Revenue per Staff, Selected Countries

Country	Revenue collected per staff	Year
Kenya	954,181	2003
Romania	838,587	2003
Macedonia, FYR	646,282	2004
Russian Federation	644,134	2004
Armenia	603,925	2006
Tajikistan	520,545	2002
Bulgaria	497,917	2002
Thailand	474,051	2004
Bosnia-Herzegovina	466,306	2003
Albania	420,952	2003
Iran, Islamic Rep. of	407,122	2003
Indonesia	392,067	2003
Pakistan	378,169	2006
Cameroon	370,370	2006
Philippines	356,739	2003
Tunisia	342,216	2005
Vietnam	340,460	2004
Kazakhstan	321,695	2004
Yugoslavia, former	288,112	2004
Nigeria	153,846	2006
Georgia	153,530	2003
Moldova	145,257	2003

Sources: World Bank 2008c; various sources for African countries.

EPA, the impact of an EPA on imports would be limited. However, trade diversion may dominate in view of the EU's declining aggregate import market share and lower competitiveness relative to Asian suppliers.

The key conclusion of the analysis of the welfare impact of an EPA is that it would enhance Nigeria's welfare and that trade-creating effects would dominate the trade-diverting effects *provided* that the liberalization of trade with the EU is accompanied by simultaneous liberalization of trade with other partners. If that is not the case, trade diversion would exceed trade creation by a small margin.

Therefore, one way for Nigeria to limit these losses in welfare is to minimize the potential for trade diversion (and monopolistic pricing) through nonpreferential trade liberalization before (or at least at the same time as) implementing an EPA. Such liberalization would, in itself, be welfare improving. It would also reduce the welfare loss from a discriminatory EPA liberalization.

Annex 1A: Growth-Inhibiting Cross-Cutting Constraints, Interventions, and Expected Outcomes

Cross-cutting constraints	Real estate and construction	Food wholesale and retail	Leather	Intervention approach
Growth constraints				*Growth interventions*
Unreliable and high-cost infrastructure services				Establish public-private partnerships and sectoral reforms in the power sector and other key infra-structure areas (tariff and regulatory reform) supported by the World Bank.
Power	X	X	X	
Water	X	X	X	Construct independent power plants in geographical areas with high growth potential that already have a high concentration of promising value chains.
Transport	X	X	X	
Distortionary trade policy accompanied by poor border controls				Replacement of import bans with tariffs (preferentially a 15 percent tariff, which would maximize incentives for formalizing trade); reform of customs procedures, including through risk-based customs clearances.
Import bans affecting (a) factor inputs (construction materials, oilseeds, etc.) and (b) final products such as oil and other fast-moving consumer goods	X	X		
Tariffs and duties to protect domestic goods	X	X	X	
Porous borders that undermine trade policy	X	X	X	

Constraint			Recommended action
Onerous administrative procedures			Initiate an administrative reform program to simplify individual procedures in relevant agencies and speed up compliance and approval process.
Land registration	X		
Planning approvals and building permits	X		
Burdensome business regulations, including Export Expansion Grants		X	Redesign or re-engineer procedures through careful process mapping and streamline legal basis (amend administrative order and regulation) as necessary (ideally no law reform). Provide strong technical assistance in the preparation and design stage, followed by hands-on implementation with stakeholders.
Poor logistics and handling			Deliver an integrated logistics program for the food sector from farmgate to the processing stage covering farm storage, drayage, wholesale markets, rural roads, and line haul transport to the processor, complete with temperature control equipment as warranted.
Poor rural roads to dispersed small-scale farms	X	X	
Poor handling practices (e.g., no temperature control, improper bagging, storage.)	X	X	
Underdeveloped freight transport services system	X	X	X

Annex 1B: Quality-Inhibiting Cross-Cutting Constraints, Interventions, and Expected Outcomes

Cross-cutting constraints	Real estate and construction	Food wholesale and retail	Leather	Intervention approach
Quality constraints				*Quality interventions*
Low-quality and unproductive labor inputs				Explore possibility of using IEIs to deliver training programs.
Shortages of skilled labor	X	X	X	Sponsor technical advisory trips to international locations that incorporate religious and traditional practices of target groups (e.g., Islamic-run abattoirs and butchers in Dubai, Malaysia, South Africa).
Lack of vocational training	X	X	X	Develop new and strengthen existing vocational institutes to increase access by unskilled, informal labor sector, including through practical teaching programs (e.g., Vocational Training Center of Excellence in Lagos for the construction sector).
Unskilled labor exhibiting low productivity	X	X	X	

Lack of regulatory enforcement on product standards (inspections)			Deliver capacity-building program to strengthen inspection activities of relevant government authorities pertaining to quality and safety of products in the construction, agriculture, livestock, and food industries.
SON	X		
State departments of agriculture			
Veterinary services	X	X	
Livestock and poultry services	X	X	Harmonize roles of food inspection agencies—State Ministry of Agriculture, State Ministry of Health, NAFDAC—for seamless cooperation.
Agricultural services, pest control, produce inspection, and fisheries	X		
National Agency for Food and Drug Administration and Control (NAFDAC)	X		
Local town planning authority			
Poor environmental practices and enforcement			Provide technical assistance to the State Ministry of Environment to develop the appropriate level of resources and expertise, as well as the institutional authority to enforce environmental regulations under its statutory responsibility.
Inadequate procedures for disposal of construction materials	X		
Improper environmental control of animal waste at public abattoirs	X	X	
Improper chemical disposal practices by leather tanneries (3 out of 6 have no chemical treatment facilities)		X	

Notes

1. The two curves plot the development of TFP assuming different initial capital-output ratios (1.5 and 2.0).

2. The recent decision to share oil revenue from the excess crude account with the states does not change this conclusion, as they did not significantly increase the expenditure-to-GDP ratio. Allocations from the excess crude account prior to 2007 were largely for the power sector, but they remained mostly unspent due to difficulties in implementation.

3. Reforms to the regulatory environment particularly benefited growth in the telecommunications sector.

4. Although these import bans were only partly enforced, they somewhat increased the demand for locally produced goods.

5. Both the General Household Survey (GHS), which is conducted annually, and the Nigeria Living Standards Survey (NLSS), which was conducted in 2003, allow conclusions as to the evolution of the labor market. This chapter reports either the results of the GHS for inter-year comparisons (1999–2006), or for NLSS for 2003. Some variations in the data may be due to the quality of surveys and may not reflect actual changes on the ground.

6. This finding does not necessarily imply that people in wage employment moved into family agriculture. It could also mean that those who previously reported no activity (that is, were outside the labor force), but were at least temporarily involved in agriculture, became engaged in agriculture to an extent that they now reported employment in family agriculture. In other words, they moved from under-employment to employment.

7. The finding of low skill levels stands despite evidence that large segments of the labor force in the informal sector have high levels of education; it points to the low degree of responsiveness of the available education programs in the secondary and tertiary education systems to the requirements of the labor market.

8. The recent Country Economic Memorandum for Nigeria (World Bank 2007a) describes this problem as the "inappropriability of profits."

9. Production intensity is defined as the share of an economy's manufacturing value added, located within a specific sector compared to the world average. For example, 100 percent production intensity for a country group in, say, food products, indicates that it has the same industrial focus on food production as the average country in the world.

10. The list of sectors is not exhaustive but represents an attempt to capture those areas of the economy that hold potential. Similarly, the choice of value chains that is being reviewed is necessarily somewhat arbitrary and should not be seen as an exhaustive set of sectors with high potential.

11. To create this diagram, the sum of each value chain's score from 1 to 4 for growth, employment, and spillover determines their overall upside potential and hence their position on the vertical axis. The sum of the three scores for the feasibility criteria determines their position on the horizontal axis. The combination of upside and feasibility scores places the value chain on the diagram. The color of each circle indicates the state that is being considered, and the size of the circle represents the estimated current importance of that value chain to that state in terms of the proportion of state GDP. The smallest circle is <1 percent, then as the sizes move up, 1–2 percent, 2–3 percent, and >3 percent for the largest circle.

12. In collaboration with a South African partner and with support from the Niger Delta Development Authority, the Nigerian Institute of Welding, which was established by the Nigerian Welders' Association, offers accredited welding courses for young people with a science background. The training is modularized, with the basic courses lasting 6 weeks. The program is targeted to the oil and gas industry. The Shell Youth Development Scheme, established in the 1980s, follows an institutionalized training model, in conformity with the National Policy on Vocational Education.

13. Currently accredited programs include ICT, film industry, clothing, paralegal, welding, and building and construction.

CHAPTER 2

Employment, Unemployment, Joblessness, and Incomes in Nigeria, 1999–2006

Luke Haywood and Francis Teal

Overview

As argued in chapter 1, the question of how jobs can be created is critical to achieving sustained poverty reduction in Nigeria. Measuring jobs is a complex issue in an African economy, and how it can be done depends on the type of data that is available. This chapter draws on two complementary sources. One is the 2003–04 Nigeria Living Standards Survey (NLSS), the data from which are presented and analyzed in Haywood (2007). The second is the data from the Nigerian Bureau of Statistics General Household Survey (GHS). The existence of two sources for 2004 (one from the regular GHS and one from the NLSS, which was undertaken only in 2003–04) enabled a direct comparison of certain key measures for that year. Further, the GHS data enable us to investigate changes over time. This chapter documents the kinds of jobs that have been created, the level of incomes available from those jobs, and the way this picture has changed over the period 1999 to 2006.

The next section begins by showing how the data available from these two sources enable the measurement of employment, unemployment, and joblessness. First, a distinction is drawn between being in and out of the labor force, and—for Nigerians defined as being in the labor force—the rates of unemployment, using the standard definitions discussed below. Second, the section examines the three types of jobs that can be identified from the data—employment on farms, non-agricultural self-employment, and wage jobs. Employment is considered within the wage sector, which is by far the smallest employment category, but has the highest demand for relatively educated labor. Finally, the section examines the incomes available across these employment categories and assesses how incomes differ, how the returns to education have been changing, and the factors that determine access to wage employment. The final, section examines the characteristics of those not in the labor force.

Definitions in the Nigeria Living Standards Survey and the General Household Survey

The NLSS (2003–04) and the GHSs (1999, 2004, and 2006) use very different approaches to measure the labor force. The NLSS determines those who were available for work by asking the following four questions:

- During the past 12 months, have you done work for which you received a wage or any other payments?
- During the past 12 months, have you been paid money, including payment in kind through self-employment (for example, trading)?
- During the past 12 months, have you worked on a farm, in a field, or herding livestock?
- During the past 12 months, have you worked unpaid for an enterprise belonging to a member of your household?

Individuals who answered "yes" to at least one of these questions were counted as labor market participants. While these four questions identified only past activities in the labor market, a fifth question allowed the inclusion of people who were available for work even if they may not have worked in the past:

- Were you available for work in the last 7 days?

Individuals who were engaged in any of these activities plus those who were available for work during the last 7 days constitute the labor force. Attention is confined to those in the age group 15–65. People currently in educational institutions are excluded from the labor force. In a standard analysis of labor market data, it would be assumed that all of those not in the labor force, so defined, are economically inactive. Further, a standard analysis would divide those in the labor force between the employed and unemployed. The latter are people who were not active during the last 12 months but who were available for work during the last 7 days.

In contrast to the indirect approach used by the NLSS, the GHS adopts a direct approach by asking, "What was your main job in the last week?" The following possible options were listed in the 2006 version of the questionnaire.[1]

- Worked for pay
- Got job but did not work
- Worked for profit
- On attachment but did not work
- Apprenticeship
- Stayed home
- Went to school
- Did nothing

Using the GHS data, this study defines the labor force as those persons who are classified under any of the first five categories given above for "What was your main job in the last week?" The labor force also includes those who answered "did nothing" and gave as a reason for this inactivity one of the following:

- Looked for job
- Sick
- Believed no job available
- Laid off 30 days or less
- Waiting to begin work

Those who answered "stayed home" were classified as out of the labor force, as were those who answered "did nothing" and gave as a reason one of the following:

- Retired
- Invalid
- Other

The measure of unemployment was obtained by counting those who answered "did nothing" as their main job and who gave as a reason one of the following:

- Looked for job
- Believed no job available
- Laid off 30 days or less

Clearly, this manner of identifying those in the labor force and, conditional on being in the labor force, being unemployed, is very different from the procedure used in the NLSS. The differences in the overall structure of the labor force that emerge from the two data sources are discussed below. The advantage of the GHS is that it gives comparable data for three years: 1999, 2004, and 2006. For 2004, a direct comparison can be made between the NLSS and the GHS, so issues of comparability can be addressed directly.

There are several potential problems in comparing the NLSS approach with that of the GHS. The first is that for the GHS, the way of identifying whether the work is agricultural or non-agricultural self-employment is to use the industry classification. In contrast, the NLSS has a direct question: "During the past 12 months, have you worked on a farm, in a field, or herding livestock?" This study assumes that, for the GHS data, those who answered "worked for profit" and who are classified as working in agriculture, fishing, or forestry are working as self-employed in agricultural households. The study also assumes that all those who work in other industries and who reported their main job as "working for profit" are in non-farm self-employment. Thus, in seeking to establish the numbers in self-employment in and outside of agriculture, the NLSS and GHS data are not directly comparable. As will be shown below, the two surveys show different shares of workers between agricultural and urban self-employment. These differences may reflect the alternative methods of asking the questions.

A second problem, discussed in Haywood (2007), is that it is not possible to identify apprentices from the NLSS data. This is partly a matter of how the questionnaire was designed and partly due to how the questions were answered. As is clear from reviewing the questions, apprentices could possibly be classified as out of the labor force. Given the importance of this occupation for the young, this is a significant lacuna in the data. In contrast, in the GHS questionnaire, apprenticeship is one of the job choices, so this occupational choice can be explicitly identified.

Unemployment or Joblessness

A common problem across both questionnaires—indeed, with any labor market survey of African economies—is how the labor force is to be defined. There are several problems in an African context with the standard procedures used for both the NLSS and the GHS. The first is that all those who do not seek work because they know that there is no work available for them are likely to be classified as economically inactive. The second is that women who work in the household, but not on the farm or in an enterprise, may be classified as economically inactive, even though their activities are, in fact, part of the work of the farm or non-farm enterprise. Further, it is very likely that both men and women would take jobs if suitable ones were available.

For all these reasons, it is important not to confine attention to the labor force as conventionally measured. It may well be that some defined as out of the labor force (that is, economically inactive) are indeed that; but especially among the young, it seems far more likely that the definitions used are failing to capture those who seek jobs but for whom none exist.

This study will show that focusing on the unemployment numbers will be unhelpful in understanding the issues of how jobs are created and what impact the rate of job creation has on poverty. In the case of Nigeria, high rates of unemployment particularly among the young, are frequently cited (see, for example, NISER 2007). The data show that the problem in Nigeria is not unemployment, as measured in a conventional sense in labor market surveys; it is joblessness defined as the lack of economic opportunities that pay more than the reservation incomes (incomes where the opportunity cost of idleness is higher than that of working) of those out of the labor force.

It is sometimes argued that if reservation incomes or wages are above the level of income from a job, then the outcome—no job—is economically optimal. In one sense, it is. If the incomes generated by the available jobs are low, it is possible to be better off by not doing one. The other side of this issue, though, is why the available jobs generate such low incomes. The problem is not the lack of jobs but the lack of jobs that pay more than US$30 per month.

The Labor Force in Nigeria

Table 2.1 presents the breakdown of the population aged 15 to 65 who are not in school from the NLSS 2003–04 data and the GHS 2004 data (table 2.4), using the definitions set out above and, for those in the labor force, the rates of unemployment. At this overall level, there is

Table 2.1   The Nigerian Labor Force, Comparison of NLSS and GHS

	NLSS	GHS
Population aged 15–65 not in schooling	41,562	42,379
Labor force	31,366	31,862
percentage	*73.9*	*77.0*
Not in labor force	10,193	10,517
percentage	*26.1*	*23.0*
Employed	31,051	31,042
percentage	*98.9*	*97.0*
Unemployed	315	820
percentage	*1.1*	*3.0*

Note: Top row is frequency; bottom row is column percentage. For both the NLSS and the GHS, the percentage points in this study are weighted using household weights provided by the Nigerian Office of Statistics. As a result, the absolute numbers (the sample sizes) and values expressed as percentages do not necessarily correspond.

broad agreement between the numbers from the NLSS and the GHS. The GHS for 2004 shows that the proportion of the population aged 15 to 65 not in school and defined as out of the labor force is 23 percent, while the NLSS shows 26 percent. While the measured unemployment rate in the GHS data, at 3 percent, is much higher than that from the NLSS, at 1 percent, it is clear that for these national averages, unemployment as conventionally measured is very low.

Table 2.2 breaks down this number by gender, and table 2.3 does so by sector. It is clear that the two sources give very different numbers. In table 2.2, the NLSS data show 16 percent of men and 35 percent of women as out of the labor force, while the GHS data for 2004 show 4 percent of men and 39 percent of women. The breakdown by sector in table 2.3 also produces major differences. In the NLSS data, 30 percent of those in urban areas are classified as out of the labor force, while the GHS data show 17 percent—a substantial difference. The proportion out of the labor force in urban areas is higher than in the rural sector in the NLSS data, while the opposite is true for the GHS data.

What accounts for these differences, and what are their implications for measures of unemployment and joblessness in Nigeria? The most likely explanation lies in the design of the questionnaires. The NLSS asks individuals directly about their income-earning activities. The GHS asks in one question whether the respondent was doing something or, in effect, doing nothing. Recall the following options for responding to the question "What

Table 2.2   Labor Force Status by Gender as Frequency and Percentage of Population Aged 15 to 65, Not in School

	Female	Male	Total
NLSS			
Sample	21,878	19,684	41,562
Labor force	14,248	17,118	31,366
	64.7	*84.0*	*73.9*
Unemployment	215	100	315
(conditional on being in the labor force)	*1.6*	*0.7*	*1.1*
Not in labor force	7,628	2,565	10,193
	35.3	*16.0*	*26.1*
GHS			
Sample	22,934	19,445	42,379
Labor force	13,097	18,765	31,862
	60.9	*96.2*	*77.0*
Unemployment	368	452	820
(conditional on being in the labor force)	*3.2*	*2.9*	*3.0*
Not in labor force	9,837	680	10,517
	39.1	*3.8*	*23.0*

Sources: Nigeria Living Standards Survey 2003 –04; General Household Survey 2004.
Note: Numbers in italic are percentages.

Table 2.3   Labor Force Status by Rural and Urban Sectors, as Frequency and Percentage of Population Aged 15 to 65, Not in School

	Rural	Urban	Total
NLSS			
Sample	32,079	9,483	41,562
Labor force	24,636	6,731	31,366
	76.6	*70.4*	*73.9*
Unemployment	221	94	325
(conditional on being in the labor force)	*0.9*	*1.4*	*1.1*
Not in labor force	7,443	2,750	10,193
	23.4	*29.6*	*26.1*
GHS			
Sample	33,175	9,204	42,379
Labor force	24,415	7,447	31,862
	74.8	*83.1*	*77.0*
Unemployment	501	319	820
(conditional on being in the labor force)	*2.6*	*4.1*	*3.0*
Not in labor force	8,760	1,757	10,517
	25.3	*16.9*	*23.0*

Sources: Top panel, Nigeria Living Standards Survey 2003–04; bottom panel, General Household Survey 2004.
Note: Numbers in italic are percentages.

Table 2.4   Labor Force Status as Frequency and Percentage of Population, Aged 15 to 65, Not in School

	1999	2004	2006	Total
Labor force status				
Not in the labor force	17,415	10,517	10,104	38,036
	25.3	*23.0*	*25.2*	*24.5*
In the labor force	48,914	31,862	25,626	106,402
	74.7	*77.0*	*74.8*	*75.5*
Total sample	66,329	42,379	35,730	144,438
	100	*100*	*100*	*100*
Unemployment status				
Employed	48,003	31,042	25,081	104,126
	97.8	*97.0*	*97.4*	*97.4*
Unemployed	911	820	545	2,276
	2.2	*3.0*	*2.6*	*2.6*
Total sample	48,914	31,862	25,626	106,402
	100	*100*	*100*	*100*

Source: General Household Survey 1999–2006.
Note: Numbers in italic are percentages.

was your main job in the last week?" used in the GHS to identify economic activity:

- Worked for pay
- Got job but did not work
- Worked for profit
- On attachment but did not work
- Apprenticeship
- Stayed home
- Went to school
- Did nothing

If women regard their main job as "keeping home" and men are reluctant to reply "doing nothing," then this approach is going to produce quite a different gender breakdown than the NLSS, which infers inactivity from direct, and sequenced, questions as to the form of the economic activity. In other words, the measure obtained for how many women are out of the labor force will depend on whether one asks first "Are you working on a family farm?" (the NLSS approach) or "Is your main job keeping home?" (the GHS approach).

While the numbers for those classified as out of the labor force differ substantially by gender between the NLSS and the GHS, the patterns for unemployment are similar, with both data sources giving a higher unemployment rate for women than for men and for urban over rural areas.

The opportunity to compare across questionnaires at the same point in time is unusual, so the fact that they have produced such different gender patterns suggests caution in using such data to infer the answer to the question: if more jobs were available, who would take them? Before that question can be addressed, a clearer picture is needed regarding what the data can reveal as to the nature of the jobs that are currently available.

Types of Employment

After defining who is in the labor force, the next concern is how jobs are to be defined. In places where most jobs are not wage jobs—this is the case in most African countries, including Nigeria—it is far from obvious how the notion of a job should be interpreted from the data. It seems clear from much of the discussion about the lack of jobs for the new secondary education graduates that jobs are defined as wage jobs. The study will return to this point once the data have been used to establish which types of jobs can be measured from the surveys.

In Haywood (2007), four categories of jobs were identified from the NLSS: family agriculture, nonagriculture selfemployment, non-agriculture unpaid family work, and wage employment. Wage employment was then subdivided into three categories: the private sector (including cooperatives), the public sector, and nongovernmental organizations (NGOs) and international organizations. These job definitions were suggested by how the questionnaire was organized.

This study seeks to make the jobs identified from the GHS as comparable as possible to those from the NLSS, using three dimensions from the questionnaire. The first is the industry in which the individual worked. The second is his or her answer to the question, "What was your main job in the last week?" The third is his or her answer to the question about employment status, which had the following options:

- Employer
- Employee
- Own account worker

- Member of producer cooperative
- Unpaid family worker
- Other

This study identifies the job as being "family agriculture" if the industry is classified as agriculture, fishing, or forestry and the main job is classified as "worked for profit." Family agriculture also includes those who did not identify themselves as working for profit but gave their employment status as "employer" or "own account worker."

A job is identified as being a "wage job" if either of the following are true:

- The main job in the previous week is reported as "worked for pay."
- The main job in the previous week is reported as "got job but did not work," or "on attachment but did not work," or "did nothing" and the employment status is given as "employee."

As already noted, the job of "apprenticeship" can be identified directly, because it is an occupational choice for "what was your main job in the last week?"

A job is identified as being "self-employed nonagriculture" if the sector given is other than agriculture, fishing, or forestry and the answer to the question about main job in the last week is given as "worked for profit." The job is also identified as "self-employed nonagriculture" if the main job of the last week is given as "got job but did not work" and the employment status is identified as "own account worker."

Nonagricultural unpaid workers are identified as those who do not work in agriculture, fishing, or forestry and who give their employment status as "unpaid family worker."

Table 2.5 presents the data from the NLSS as reported in Haywood (2007). Tables 2.6 and 2.7 show the breakdown of GHS data for 1999, 2004, and 2006 for the categories of employment, organized to be as comparable as possible with those from the NLSS. Table 2.6 shows the percentages as a proportion of the population and is thus directly comparable for 2004 to the second column of table 2.5. Table 2.7 shows the same breakdown as a percentage of the labor force and, again for 2004, is directly comparable to the first column of table 2.5. Attention is confined to a comparison between the NLSS and the GHS data for the population aged 15 to 65 and not in school; that is, table 2.5, column 2; and table 2.6.

Table 2.5   Types of Employment, NLSS

	Percentage of the labor force	Percentage of the population	Number in sample
Family agriculture	51.3	37.8	19,505
Nonagricultural self-employed	30.0	22.1	6,796
Nonagricultural unpaid family work	3.4	2.5	1,213
Wage employment	14.3	10.4	3,292
Unemployed	1.1	0.8	315
Not in the labor force	–	26.3	10,193
Total	100	100	41,314

Source: Nigeria Living Standards Survey 2003–04.

Table 2.6   Types of Employment as Frequency and Percentage of the Population, GHS

	1999	2004	2006	Total
Family agriculture	22,116	16,780	14,441	53,337
	30.8	36.6	37.8	35.2
Nonagricultural self-employed	12,656	8,762	6,499	27,917
	24.1	25.8	22.9	24.2
Nonagricultural unpaid family work	1	34	21	56
	0	0.08	0.06	0.05
Wage employment	9,006	3,724	3,127	15,857
	15.0	10.4	10.0	11.7
Apprenticeship	1,111	421	572	2,104
	2.1	1.1	1.9	1.7
Unemployed	911	820	545	2,276
	1.7	2.4	1.9	2.0
Not in the labor force	17,415	10,517	10,104	38,036
	26.4	23.7	25.5	25.2
Total	63,216	41,068	35,309	139,583
	100	100	100	100

Source: General Household Survey 1999–2006.
Note: Numbers in italic are percentages.

Both data sources agree that employment continues to be dominated by the agriculture sector, with 38 percent reported in the NLSS and 37 percent in the GHS. Furthermore, both data sources agree that the second-most important source of employment is nonagriculture self-employment, with very similar proportions of 22 percent and 26 percent in the GHS and NLSS, respectively.

Both the NLSS and GHS data for 2004 show that between 60 and 62 percent of the population aged 15 to 65 and not in school are self-employed. Both sources are in almost exact agreement as to the extent of

Table 2.7   Types of Employment as Frequency and Percentage of the Labor Force, GHS

	1999	2004	2006	Total
Family agriculture	22,093	16,777	14,418	53,288
	41.9	47.9	50.7	47.1
Nonagricultural self-employed	12,656	8,762	6,499	27,917
	32.8	33.8	30.7	32.4
Nonagricultural unpaid family work	1	32	3	36
	0.00	0.09	0.01	0.03
Wage employment	8,887	3,724	3,127	15,738
	20.1	13.6	13.5	15.5
Apprenticeship	1,111	421	572	2,104
	2.8	1.4	2.5	2.2
Unemployed	911	820	545	2,276
	2.3	3.2	2.6	2.7
Total	45,659	30,536	25,164	101,359
	100	100	100	100

Source: General Household Survey 1999–2006.
Note: Numbers in italic are percentages.

agricultural and nonagricultural self-employment. The same is true for wage employment. Both the NLSS and the GHS data show that in 2004, 10 percent of the population had wage jobs, which translates into 14 percent of the labor force (tables 2.5–2.7).

Unemployment is higher in the GHS data for 2004 than in the NLSS data, while the NLSS identifies more people as nonagricultural unpaid family workers than does the GHS. These small differences almost certainly reflect the design of the questionnaires. They do not, however, affect the broadly similar pattern from both data sources of a labor market characterized by 60 percent self-employment, 25 percent out of the labor force, 10 percent wage employment (where apprentices are included with wage employees), and 5 percent unemployed or unpaid. It is important to stress that these are rounded numbers, which are designed to show that the second-most important aspect of the labor market is the extent of measured inactivity.

So far, this study has focused on the similarities and differences that emerge from a comparison of the NLSS with the GHS for 2004. The GHS data can be used to extend the analysis by looking at changes over time. It has already been noted that the magnitudes of these types of employment and nonemployment may be sensitive to how the questionnaire is designed. The advantage of the GHS is that over the period 1999 to 2006, while it underwent an extension in terms of the questions that were asked, there were only minor changes to some of the categories used, and the overall structure of the questionnaire remained unchanged.

In discussions of employment policy in Nigeria, it is frequently asserted that insufficient numbers of jobs are being created. The rather striking finding from table 2.6 is that the proportion of the population aged 15 to 65 (where those in full-time education continue to be excluded) with a wage job declined from 15 percent in 1999 to 10 percent in 2006. The share of those classified as nonagriculture self-employed remained broadly constant at 23 to 24 percent. The category that saw a major increase in its share of the population was family agriculture, which rose from 31 percent to 38 percent.

This pattern of changes in the structure of the labor force is at variance with that observed in most of Sub-Saharan Africa in the 1990s. Figure 2.1 shows, using data from Kingdon, Sandefur, and Teal (2006), the pattern of change in the labor markets of five African economies. In three—Ghana, Tanzania, and Uganda—there is explosive growth in nonagricultural self-employment relative to wage employment. In the case of the other two—urban Ethiopia and South Africa—the measured unemployment rate rises substantially over the period. The data are based on a breakdown of the labor force; the comparable numbers for Nigeria are set out in table 2.7.

Figure 2.1   Trends in Nonagricultural Employment
(absolute number of workers, thousands)

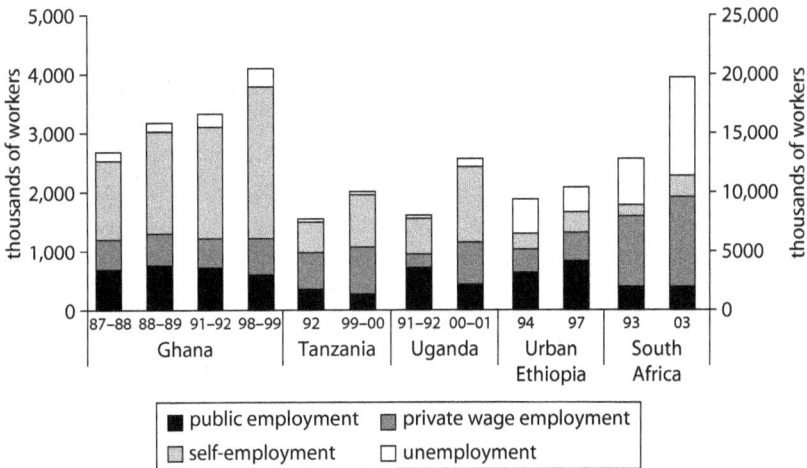

Source: Kingdon, Sandefur, and Teal 2006.

It should be remembered that the periods over which the changes are being measured are not the same. With that caution, the differences are striking. In Ghana, Uganda, and Tanzania, the proportion of the labor force working in family agriculture over the 1990s declined (Kingdon, Sandefur and Teal, 2006)—in the case of Tanzania, dramatically so, from 80 percent to 70 percent of the labor force. This contrasts with a rise in those working in family agriculture in Nigeria. Whereas in urban Ethiopia and South Africa, the rapid rises in the labor force led to increased unemployment, there was virtually no change in the measured unemployment rate in Nigeria, as measured in the labor force surveys.

Table 2.7 shows that as a percentage of the labor force, unemployment was 2.3 percent in 1999 and 2.6 percent in 2006. It is also clear from table 2.6 that there was virtually no change in the proportion of the population aged 15 to 65 and not in school who were classified as out of the labor force.

The implication of these figures is that over the period 1999 to 2006, the most important structural changes in Nigeria's labor force were a shift into agricultural employment and a shift out of wage employment. In 1999, wage employment was 20.1 percent of the labor force (table 2.7), compared with 13 percent for Ghana and Uganda and 7 percent for Tanzania for the same period (Kingdon, Sandefur, and Teal 2006). By 2006, wage employment in Nigeria had decreased to 13.5 percent.

Such a major shift in employment between agriculture and wage earning opportunities clearly ties in with the divide between the rural and urban sectors, which is reported in table 2.8. The patterns already observed across the national data are repeated within the urban and rural sectors.

In the urban sector, the share of the population in family agriculture and out of the labor force increases, and the share of the population in either wage employment or nonagricultural self-employment declines. These falls in share are not large, on the order of 2 to 3 percent, but it is important that they are falling rather than rising. This broad pattern is repeated in the rural sector, although here the decline in wage employment is substantial, from 11 percent to 7 percent of the population. Across both the urban and the rural sectors, the proportion of the population in apprenticeship or classified as unemployed changes little over this period.

The data in table 2.8 are based on the population aged 15 to 65 and not in full-time education. If there is an increasing problem in finding jobs, this will be apparent in the youth labor market.

Table 2.9 repeats the breakdown of the data from table 2.8 but now confines the sample to those aged 15 to 25, still excluding those in full-time education. The patterns of declining earning opportunities in both

Table 2.8   Types of Employment as Frequency and Percentage of the Population, Aged 15 to 65, Excluding Those in Full-time Education

	1999	2004	2006	Total
Urban				
Family agriculture	1,511	754	967	3,232
	7.9	6.5	10.6	8.3
Nonagricultural self-employed	5,920	4,162	2,748	12,830
	44.9	50.2	44.9	46.7
Nonagricultural unpaid family work	0	7	5	12
	0.00	0.04	0.07	0.04
Wage employment	3,010	1,882	1,340	6,232
	23.3	21.0	19.3	21.2
Apprenticeship	362	139	194	695
	3.3	1.6	3.4	2.8
Unemployed	362	139	194	695
	2.7	3.5	3.5	3.2
Not in the labor force	2,909	1,757	1,573	6,239
	18.0	17.2	18.3	17.8
Total	14,059	9,020	7,016	30,095
	100	100	100	100
Rural				
Family agriculture	20,605	16,026	13,474	50,105
	40.8	48.2	46.7	45.5
Nonagricultural self-employed	6,736	4,600	3,751	15,087
	15.0	16.4	15.6	15.7
Nonagricultural unpaid family work	1	27	16	44
	0.00	0.08	0.06	0.04
Wage employment	5,996	1,842	1,787	9,625
	11.4	6.3	7.0	8.0
Apprenticeship	749	282	378	1,409
	1.5	0.9	1.4	1.3
Unemployed	564	501	3561	1,421
	1.3	2.0	1.5	1.6
Not in the labor force	14,506	8,760	8,531	31,797
	30.1	26.2	27.9	27.9
Total	49,157	32,038	28,293	109,488
	100	100	100	100

Source: General Household Survey 1999–2006.
Note: Numbers in italic are percentages.

nonagricultural self-employment and wage employment are now much more accentuated. For those located in urban areas, wage employment as a share of the population fell by nearly half, from 14 percent to 9 percent of the population, while nonagricultural self-employment declined from 28 percent to 24 percent. In rural areas, wage employment practically

Table 2.9   Types of Employment as Frequency and Percentage of the Population, Aged 15 to 25, Excluding Those in Full-time Education

	1999	2004	2006	Total
Urban				
Family agriculture	124	88	121	333
	4.0	3.7	5.5	4.3
Nonagricultural self-employed	746	559	317	1,622
	28.0	34.8	23.7	28.9
Nonagricultural unpaid family work	0	5	3	8
	0.00	0.16	0.24	0.13
Wage employment	389	146	108	643
	13.5	9.1	9.3	10.7
Apprenticeship	338	117	151	606
	11.7	6.8	11.4	10.2
Unemployed	265	211	92	568
	9.1	11.6	8.4	9.7
Not in the labor force	1,008	620	550	2,178
	30.8	33.5	37.5	33.8
Total	2,870	1,746	1,342	5,958
	100	100	100	100
Rural				
Family agriculture	2,008	2,890	2,138	7,036
	16.9	34.0	31.1	28.0
Nonagricultural self employed	923	1,076	623	2,622
	9.5	15.3	12.0	12.4
Nonagricultural unpaid family work	1	22	12	35
	0.01	0.26	0.15	0.15
Wage employment	1,954	175	175	2,304
	15.4	2.7	3.2	6.6
Apprenticeship	623	210	254	1,087
	5.5	2.9	4.5	4.2
Unemployed	445	352	249	1,046
	4.4	5.9	4.3	4.9
Not in the labor force	5,266	2,997	3,115	11,378
	48.2	38.9	44.8	43.8
Total	11,220	7,722	6,566	25,508
	100	100	100	100

Source: General Household Survey 1999–2006.
Note: Numbers in italic are percentages.

disappeared, declining from 15 percent to 3 percent of the population. In the urban sector, there were increases in the proportion of the population in family agriculture and out of the labor force. In the rural sector, there was a near doubling of those working in family agriculture.

In 2006, for young people between ages 15 and 25 and not in full-time education, only 33 percent of those in the urban sector had a job in the form of wage or non-agricultural self-employment. In the rural sector, the comparable number was 15 percent. In summary, if a job meant non-farm employment, either in the form of a wage job or nonagricultural self-employment, only 19 percent of those aged 15 to 25 had a job.

Types of Wage Jobs

As shown above, the proportion of the workforce who are in wage jobs is low and has been declining over the period 1999 to 2006. What can be said about the divide within wage jobs between the public and private sectors? Table 2.10, taken from Haywood (2007), provides the breakdown of types of wage jobs that can be identified from the NLSS. In that survey, it is possible to distinguish clearly between the public and private sectors, although, as discussed in Haywood (2007), there are some discrepancies in the way questions were answered.

In this classification, there is some uncertainty as to the distinction being drawn between private and public companies. As a direct comparison with the NLSS does not appear possible, table 2.11 shows the changes in employment across the categories identified from the GHS.

The GHS survey gives the following categories of wage employment:

- Private company
- Public company
- Parastatal
- Ministry
- Other

There are substantial differences across the data sets, which are almost certainly due to differences in how the questionnaires identify categories

Table 2.10   Types of Wage Employment

	Percentage of the wage labor force	Number in sample
Private sector (including cooperatives)	21.6	652
Public sector	62.1	2,235
NGO, international organization	9.8	405
Total	100	3,292

Source: Haywood 2007, based on Nigeria Living Standards Survey 2003–04.

Table 2.11   Types of Wage Employment as Frequency and Percentage of the Population, 1999, 2004, and 2006

	1999	2004	2006	Total
Parastatal, ministry	2,689	1,638	1,426	5,753
	48.6	42.2	45.6	45.4
Private company	625	637	407	1,669
	17.0	20.5	18.0	18.6
Public company	553	394	180	1,127
	11.6	12.0	6.9	10.2
Other	1,199	966	836	3,001
	22.8	25.2	29.6	25.9
Total	5,066	3,635	2,849	11,550
	100	100	100	100

Source: General Household Survey 1999–2006.
Note: Top row is the frequency; bottom row is the column percentage.

within wage employment. However, even if the GHS classifications are accepted, the public sector is at least 50 percent of wage employment. On the basis of the NLSS data, this may well be a substantial underestimate. Because wage employment was only 13.5 percent of the labor force in 2006, these numbers imply a private wage employment sector of 7 percent or less. While this number may appear very low, it is not dissimilar to that found in Ghana and Uganda, and reflects the continuing domination of the public sector in employment in many African countries (Kingdon, Sandefur, and Teal 2006).

Incomes Across Sectors

The following provides an overview of the principal earnings differentials in the Nigerian labor market, based on individual incomes from the NLSS and the GHS surveys.

In the NLSS data, earnings include workers' wages and monetized estimates of the value of allowances. In practice, allowances are very small compared to direct incomes (wages, trading, or vending gains). In Haywood (2007), different sources of income were combined. Average monthly earnings were   15,619, or around US$94. Table 2.12, taken from Haywood (2007), provides an overview of earnings for 2004 from the NLSS.

The approach in the GHS to measuring incomes is very different from that in the NLSS. A single question was asked of all those who reported having a job: "Income in the last month from all jobs and including all

Table 2.12   Average Monthly Earnings per Worker

	Average earnings	Standard deviation	Observations
Naira (2003 prices)	15,619	27,191	13,529
U.S. dollars	94.10	194.20	13,529
By geography (US$)			
Rural sector	69.50	151.90	9,269
Urban sector	114.60	221.50	4,260
By gender (US$)			
Female workers	65.60	136.90	5,008
Male workers	112.50	221.50	8,521
By schooling (US$)			
No schooling	58.20	142.90	78
Some primary schooling	64.70	160.70	760
Primary schooling	74.40	144.70	3,129
Middle schooling	112.40	228.40	135
Postsecondary schooling	121.80	184.70	234
University education	256.00	332.40	593

Source: Haywood 2007, based on Nigeria Living Standards Survey 2004.

allowances?" Table 2.13 reports the answers to this question for each of the main employment categories identified from the data:

- Family agriculture
- Nonagriculture self-employed
- Wage job

Table 2.13 reports mean earnings in real naira (using 2003 prices). The first point to note is how similar the figure for 2004 is to that given in the NLSS, as reported in table 2.12. The NLSS data report an average earnings figure of   15,619. Deflating this to 2003 prices results in a figure of   9,373. The GHS data for 2004 give a figure of   9,739 (2003 prices).

While Haywood (2007) explores the differences across earnings from the NLSS data, here the question asked is how earnings have changed over time. Table 2.13 reports mean earnings over the period, again in real naira prices. The mean of log earnings is also given. This value is informative, as it will typically be closer to median earnings (since the distribution is close to log normal).

Table 2.13   Mean Monthly Earnings and Education by Employment Type

	1999	2004	2006	Average
Earnings in naira (2003 prices)				
Family agriculture	4,573	8,219	8,851	6,327
Nonagricultural self-employed	6,065	9,174	9,049	7,483
Wage job	9,924	16,437	12,362	12,539
Total	5,785	9,739	9,427	7,577
Ln (earnings in naira, 2003 prices)				
Family agriculture	8.06	8.57	8.58	8.30
Nonagricultural self-employed	8.34	8.72	8.70	8.51
Wage job	8.86	9.43	9.07	9.09
Total	8.26	8.75	8.69	8.48
Years of education				
Family agriculture	2.7	3.5	3.5	3.2
Nonagricultural self-employed	5.6	6.3	6.3	6.0
Wage job	9.8	10.8	10.8	10.4
Total	4.6	5.4	5.2	5.0

Source: General Household Survey 1999–2006.
Note: Ln = logarithm.

The finding from table 2.13 is that average earnings increased nearly 62 percent over this period, from   5,800 to   9,400 per month (2003 prices). Further, this rise has been highest for those in the poorest sector, namely family agriculture, where earnings have nearly doubled.

Those in wage jobs, while still having by far the highest earnings, have seen a rise of only 34 percent. As a result of this higher rate of growth of earnings for family agriculture, the gap between wage employment and earnings from family agriculture declined from 2.2 to 1.4 over the period 1999 to 2006—a quite remarkable fall.

The final panel of table 2.13 shows the average years of education across the three employment types. Over the period 1999 to 2006, the average years of education of those in these employment categories increased by 13 percent. This increase was highest for those in family agriculture. The gap between the average education level of those in wage employment relative to those in family agriculture declined. However, it remained significant, with the average level of education for those in wage jobs in 2006 three times the level of education for those in agriculture.

Table 2.14 repeats the breakdown from table 2.13, but uses U.S. dollars rather than naira. Because the naira has appreciated over this period, the rise in U.S. dollar–denominated prices is larger than that in real naira—in fact, almost twice as large. This much larger increase in incomes in U.S. dollar terms, rather than in domestic prices, implies that

Table 2.14   Mean Monthly Earnings by Employment Type

	1999	2004	2006	Average
Earnings in U.S. dollars				
Family agriculture	27.00	70.00	98.00	50.00
Nonagricultural self-employed	35.00	80.00	103.00	59.00
Wage job	57.00	143.00	142.00	99.00
Total	34.00	84.00	106.00	60.00
Ln (earnings in U.S. dollars)				
Family agriculture	2.92	3.81	4.08	3.36
Nonagricultural self-employed	3.19	3.98	4.23	3.58
Wage job	3.71	4.69	4.60	4.17
Total	3.12	4.00	4.20	3.55

Source: General Household Survey 1999–2006.
Note: Ln = logarithm.

labor costs are becoming increasingly uncompetitive in the international market. In the context of labor-intensive manufacturing exports, labor costs are important.

While systematic data comparing wage rates are scarce, wages of US$50 per month have been cited for China. As table 2.14 shows, by 2006 average wages were US$142 per month. These are very high wages for jobs in very poor countries.

Tables 2.15 and 2.16 report a similar breakdown for jobs within wage employment. Those jobs classified as "other" are, by far, the least well paid of those in the wage sector, having earnings of 75 percent of the mean in 2006. However, all categories saw very substantial increases in earnings over this period, and the differences across the types of wage employment were small. In 2006, those working in parastatals and government agencies earned, on average, US$174 per month. Years of education were also highest in this category, and by 2006 had risen to an average of 12.2 years.

Given the possibility of observing these incomes over time, some questions can be asked about the extent to which education impacts both earnings and the probability of getting a job.

Mincerian Earnings Equations

The descriptive statistics presented so far appear to show very substantial rises in earnings across all types of employment. This section uses the Mincerian earnings function to ask whether these rises were the result of increases in the returns to education, or reflected underlying growth factors in the economy.

Table 2.15   Mean Monthly Earnings in Naira by Education and Type of Wage Job

	1999	2004	2006	Average
Earnings in naira (2003 prices)				
Parastatal, ministry	11,346	19,193	14,449	14,328
Private company	8,819	13,379	12,165	11,251
Public company	11,413	16,367	12,321	13,363
Other	6,839	14,009	9,429	9,935
Total	9,975	16,497	12,432	12,659
Ln (earnings in naira, 2003 prices)				
Parastatal, ministry	9.02	9.64	9.27	9.26
Private company	8.83	9.21	9.08	9.03
Public company	9.10	9.46	9.19	9.24
Other	8.53	9.21	8.71	8.81
Total	8.88	9.43	9.07	9.11
Years of education				
Parastatal, ministry	10.9	12.0	12.2	11.6
Private company	9.2	9.6	10.0	9.5
Public company	10.7	10.5	11.5	10.8
Other	7.9	9.6	8.2	8.6
Total	10.0	10.8	10.7	10.4

Source: General Household Survey 1999–2006.
Note: Ln = logarithm.

Table 2.16   Mean Monthly Earnings in U.S. Dollars by Education and Type of Wage Job

	1999	2004	2006	Average
Earnings in US$				
Parastatal, ministry	66	167	166	111
Private company	51	117	141	92
Public company	66	143	141	102
Other	39	122	107	81
Total	58	144	143	100
Ln (earnings in US$)				
Parastatal, ministry	3.86	4.90	4.80	4.32
Private company	3.68	4.47	4.62	4.15
Public company	3.94	4.72	4.72	4.31
Other	3.38	4.46	4.23	3.92
Total	3.73	4.69	4.60	4.31

Source: General Household Survey 1999–2006.
Note: Ln = logarithm.

Table 2.17 reports, in column (1), an equation that controls only for sector and year but not for the different human capital attributes of the worker. Earnings rose by 54 percent from 1999 to 2006 and, on average over the period, a wage earner received twice the income of the farmer and 75 percent higher earnings than the nonagricultural self-employed.

Table 2.17   Income as a Function of Gender, Age, and Education

	(1) Basic equation	(2) Pooled equation	(3) Wage job	(4) Nonagricultural self-employed	(5) Farmer
Male		0.42***	0.19***	0.55***	0.38***
		(0.01)	(0.02)	(0.01)	(0.01)
Age		0.05***	0.07***	0.05***	0.05***
		(0.00)	(0.00)	(0.00)	(0.00)
Age_sq		−0.05***	−0.07***	−0.04***	−0.04***
		(0.00)	(0.01)	(0.00)	(0.00)
Primary		0.18***	0.28***	0.27***	0.12***
incomplete		(0.04)	(0.10)	(0.08)	(0.05)
Primary complete		0.23***	0.28***	0.28***	0.20***
		(0.01)	(0.04)	(0.01)	(0.01)
Second reached		0.40***	0.55***	0.47***	0.29***
		(0.01)	(0.03)	(0.01)	(0.01)
Postsecondary		0.80***	0.93***	0.77***	0.59***
		(0.01)	(0.03)	(0.03)	(0.04)
Urban		0.19***	0.15***	0.21***	0.14***
		(0.01)	(0.01)	(0.01)	(0.02)
Dum_04	0.48***	0.45***	0.48***	0.34***	0.51***
	(0.01)	(0.01)	(0.01)	(0.01)	(0.01)
Dum_06	0.43***	0.44***	0.17***	0.35***	0.57***
	(0.01)	(0.01)	(0.02)	(0.02)	(0.01)
Wage	0.56***	0.16***			
	(0.01)	(0.01)			
Farmer	−0.21***	−0.19***			
	(0.01)	(0.01)			
Constant	8.30***	6.67***	6.49***	6.67***	6.58***
	(0.01)	(0.03)	(0.10)	(0.06)	(0.05)
Observations	73,115	73,115	10,435	23,303	39,377
R-squared	0.15	0.28	0.30	0.29	0.16

Source: Authors' calculations.
Note: Ln = logarithm; real naira earnings 2003 = 100.
*** = $p < 0.01$.

Table 2.17, column (2), adds controls for a range of human capital and other worker attributes. Rather remarkably, this scarcely affects the time dummies measuring the underlying growth of earnings. The most important finding here is that the effect of controls for human capital reduces the earnings differential between those with a wage job and farmers to 42 percent, and the differential between those with a wage job and the nonagricultural self-employed to only 17 percent. These are rather small differentials.

Table 2.17, columns (3) to (5), show the earnings functions for each employment category separately. It must be stressed that these are simply descriptive statistics that do not allow for the problems posed by selection into these occupations. Several important aspects of the data are revealed by this decomposition.

First, with these controls for human capital, the rise in earnings is still highest for farmers, who saw an increase of 77 percent in contrast to a rise of only 19 percent for wage employees. The findings from the basic descriptive statistics continue to hold once the study controls for human capital, gender, and location in an urban area. Those with the lowest earnings see the largest rise in earnings, thus closing the gap between wage earners and farmers. Second, there is a hierarchy in the returns to education in which farmers are the lowest, the nonagricultural self-employed are higher, and wage earners are the highest. In broad terms, at nearly every level of education, the return is twice as high for the wage earner as for the farmer. Third, the gender differential in earnings is lowest for those with a wage job, at 20 percent; this differential more than doubles to 46 percent for farmers and increases to 73 percent for the nonagricultural self-employed. As it has been shown that wage employment is declining relative to farming, these differentials imply an increase in the average differential in the economy. Fourth, the concave age earnings profile appears to be remarkably similar across the three occupations.

The two most important differences across the three sectors are in the returns to education and the gender differential. These findings with respect to education are clearly consistent with the notion that education pays off more in wage employment. Before turning to the factors that determine whether a worker has a wage job, table 2.18 tests for whether the returns to education have been changing within the three occupations. In table 2.18, each of the education categories identified from the GHS data is interacted with a dummy for the years 2004 and 2006. This allows a deduction of how the returns to education vary with the level of education, and how the returns have changed over this period.

Table 2.18 shows two key findings. First, the returns to education are convex with respect to level; that is, the returns increase with the level of education. Second, the returns to education have been falling over this period and for wage employees, these falls have occurred at all levels of education.

The convexity is clear for all three sectors. For wage employees in 1999, the Mincerian return to completing primary education was a 7 percent

Table 2.18   Income as a Function of Gender, Age, and Education, with Returns to Education over Time

	(1) Wage job	(2) Nonagricultural self-employed	(3) Farmer
Male	0.19***	0.55***	0.38***
	(0.02)	(0.01)	(0.01)
Age	0.07***	0.05***	0.05***
	(0.00)	(0.00)	(0.00)
Age_sq	−0.07***	−0.04***	−0.04***
	(0.01)	(0.00)	(0.00)
Primary incomplete	0.67***	0.33	0.05
	(0.21)	(0.27)	(0.11)
Primary complete	0.41***	0.26***	0.24***
	(0.05)	(0.02)	(0.01)
Second reached	0.70***	0.46***	0.36***
	(0.05)	(0.02)	(0.02)
Postsecondary	1.07***	0.75***	0.72***
	(0.05)	(0.04)	(0.06)
Urban	0.15***	0.21***	0.13***
	(0.01)	(0.01)	(0.02)
Dum_04	0.79***	0.27***	0.54***
	(0.06)	(0.02)	(0.01)
Dum_06	0.49***	0.43***	0.63***
	(0.09)	(0.03)	(0.02)
Primary_incomplete_Dum04	−0.43	0.01	0.01
	(0.30)	(0.30)	(0.14)
Primary_complete_Dum04	−0.31***	0.11***	−0.07***
	(0.07)	(0.03)	(0.02)
Second_reached_Dum04	−0.37***	0.08***	−0.10***
	(0.07)	(0.03)	(0.03)
Postsec_Dum04	−0.33***	0.09	−0.18**
	(0.07)	(0.06)	(0.09)
Primary_incomplete_Dum06	−0.83***	−0.19	0.08
	(0.25)	(0.29)	(0.13)
Primary_complete_Dum06	−0.38***	−0.09**	−0.12***
	(0.11)	(0.04)	(0.03)
Second_reached_Dum06	−0.33***	−0.12***	−0.20***
	(0.10)	(0.04)	(0.04)
Postsec_Dum06	−0.35***	−0.14	−0.30**
	(0.10)	(0.09)	(0.12)
Constant	6.35***	6.68***	6.55***
	(0.10)	(0.06)	(0.05)
Observations	10,435	23,303	39,377
R-squared	0.31	0.29	0.16

Source: Authors' calculations.
Note: Ln = logarithm; real naira earnings 2003 = 100.
*** = $p < 0.01$, ** = $p < 0.05$.

higher annual income, while for those who achieved a postsecondary level, the return from secondary to postsecondary was 13 percent, or nearly twice as high. For those who worked in self-employment, either in farming or urban, the average returns were lower, but were again higher at higher levels.

The falls in the returns to education also occurred for all three sectors. For those reaching secondary level, the returns over this period fell by 10 to 30 percent. The implication is that the increases in incomes between 1999 and 2006 were highest for those with no education. For these workers, wage incomes rose by 80 percent, incomes from non-farm self-employment rose by 42 percent, and farm incomes doubled.

It is clear from these tables that the pattern of income growth over this period in Nigeria favored those in low-paying sectors, in particular farmers, and within these sectors those who were poorest, that is, those with the lowest levels of education.

Finally, in this section, table 2.19 presents a simple linear probability model for wage jobs. The model confirms that there has been a substantial decline in the probability of obtaining a wage job for any given level of education and that higher levels of education are now needed to obtain a wage job.

Nonparticipation in the Nigerian Labor Market

It has been shown that of the working-age population 15 to 65 years and not in school, 26 percent are found to be out of the labor force in the NLSS, meaning that they appear to be neither working nor looking for work. This final section of the study seeks to shed some light on their characteristics. Nonparticipants can be subdivided into two demographically distinct groups based on gender and age. Within these groups, religious faith and geography are also important.

Demographics

Those not participating in the labor market are predominantly young, female, and more highly educated. These tendencies, shown in tables 2.20 and 2.21, are also valid conditionally, with each factor (age, gender, years of education) independently increasing the probability of being out of the labor force (Kingdon, Sandefur, and Teal 2006).

Furthermore, there appear to be two very distinct groups of persons out of the labor market: first, unmarried young men, often living with their parents and with above-average education, and second,

Table 2.19   A Linear Model of the Probability of Getting a Job

	(1) Wage	(2) Wage
Male	0.01***	0.01***
	(0.00)	(0.00)
Age	−0.01***	−0.01***
	(0.00)	(0.00)
Age_sq	0.01***	0.01***
	(0.00)	(0.00)
Primary_incomplete	0.09***	0.09**
	(0.02)	(0.04)
Primary_complete	0.04***	0.03***
	(0.00)	(0.00)
Second_reached	0.15***	0.16***
	(0.00)	(0.01)
Postsec	0.64***	0.63***
	(0.01)	(0.01)
Dum_04	−0.10***	−0.11***
	(0.00)	(0.00)
Dum_06	−0.10***	−0.10***
	(0.00)	(0.00)
Primary_incomplete_Dum04		0.01
		(0.05)
Primary_complete_Dum04		0.02***
		(0.01)
Second_reached_Dum04		−0.01
		(0.01)
Postsec_Dum04		0.01
		(0.01)
Primary_incomplete_Dum06		−0.02
		(0.05)
Primary_complete_Dum06		0.00
		(0.01)
Second_reached_Dum06		−0.02**
		(0.01)
Postsec_Dum06		0.04***
		(0.01)
Constant	0.31***	0.31***
	(0.01)	(0.01)
Observations	96,943	96,943
R-squared	0.21	0.21

Source: Authors' calculations.
Note: Wage = 1 if wage job, otherwise zero. Robust standard errors are in parentheses.
*** = $p < 0.01$.

Table 2.20   Characteristics of Nonparticipants by Gender and Age
(percent)

	Female	Male	Overall
15–19 years	17.21	38.84	23.50
20–24	20.16	33.22	23.96
25–29	17.83	14.99	17.00
30–39	22.74	5.88	17.84
40–49	12.31	1.56	9.18
50–59	6.21	2.39	5.10
60–65	3.55	3.13	3.43
Total	100	100	100

Source: Authors' calculations.
Note: Women are 70.91 percent and men are 29.09 percent of nonparticipants, based on 10,193 respondents.

Table 2.21   Characteristics of Nonparticipants by Gender and Education
(percent)

	Female	Male	Overall
Koranic	9.03	3.05	7.3
University	1.28	5.82	2.59
Postsecondary	0.92	2.16	1.28
Secondary	21.96	50.93	30.35
Middle school	0.85	1.25	0.97
Primary	12.91	19.21	14.74
Some primary	2.67	2.19	2.53
None	50.38	15.39	40.25
Total	100	100	100

Source: Authors' calculations.
Note: Women are 70.91 percent and men are 29.09 percent of nonparticipants, based on 7,470 respondents.

married and unmarried women of all ages, especially of Muslim faith. Table 2.22 compares participation rates along key categories, while tables 2.23 through 2.25 compare family arrangements across participants and nonparticipants.

The average age of men not in the labor force is 23 years compared to 40 years for those in the labor market. For the population of young men, household sizes are typically much larger when they are out of the labor force, suggesting that young men may be benefiting from the household services of their parents. By contrast, the differences in household size and age between women in and outside the labor force are less marked.

Table 2.22   Participation Rates by Gender, Geographical Sector, and Religion
(percent)

	Women out of labor force		Men out of labor force	
	Muslim	*Christian*	*Muslim*	*Christian*
Urban	45.0	28.5	18.6	22.4
Rural	47.5	21.5	8.2	13.4

Source: Authors' calculations.
Note: Ninety-eight percent of nonparticipants are Muslims or Christians. Others dropped here.
Sample size = 10,029.

Table 2.23   Marital Status of Participants and Nonparticipants by Gender
(percent)

	Women		Men	
	Out of labor force	*In labor force*	*Out of labor force*	*In labor force*
Married	76.17	79.64	8.77	76.20
Unmarried	23.83	20.36	91.23	23.80
Total	100	100	100	100

Source: Authors' calculations.
Note: Sample size = 10,029.

Table 2.24   Household Sizes of Participants and Nonparticipants by Gender

	Women		Men	
	Out of labor force	*In labor force*	*Out of labor force*	*In labor force*
Average household size (persons)	2.95	2.33	4.00	2.25

Source: Authors' calculations.
Note: Sample size = 10,029.

Only a very small proportion of those not in the labor force has ever worked—of about half of the group that answered this question, only around one percent identified themselves as having previously worked. Of the few who stated their previous occupation, both men and women were mostly in agriculture, with smaller fractions working as manual laborers and in jewelry. Men also often gave "studies" and "retirement" as previous occupations, while women often gave "housekeeping," presumably contrary to the intention of the question about previous work experience. For men, the amount of time spent on housekeeping was much

Table 2.25   Relationship to Household Head of Participants and Nonparticipants by Gender
(percent)

	Women		Men	
	Out of labor force	In labor force	Out of labor force	In labor force
Head of household	1.47	15.72	8.44	83.64
Spouse of household head	66.03	72.46	0.09	0.07
Child of household head	22.76	6.86	78.36	13.67
Brother or sister of household head	2.13	1.19	4.90	1.50
Other relative (parent, uncle, etc.)	<10.00	<4.00	<4.00	<1.00

Source: Authors' calculations.
Note: Based on question s1q3 of Nigeria Living Standards Survey 2003–04.

lower (table 2.26). These answers give some indication as to the typical situation of those out of the labor force.

Activities of Persons Outside the Labor Force
Since the NLSS questionnaire asks certain questions only of people in the labor force, relatively little is known about the activities of labor force nonparticipants.

One area that the questionnaire investigates relates to the housework in which individuals engage. Table 2.27 shows that the reported investment in the ten most common housekeeping activities is considerable for those out of the labor market, particularly for women.

The large difference between men's and women's investment in household chores may lead to the conclusion that women are staying at home to tend to housekeeping. Table 2.27 gives the average time spent on the ten most common tasks aggregated from table 2.26, and compares the investment by gender for participants and nonparticipants in the labor market. From this table, it does not appear that labor market participation influences the amount of time spent on these housekeeping tasks, either for men or for women.

Other Issues
Participation rates seem not to be significantly affected by migration or illness, although inconsistent replies may result in slight measurement errors.

Migration. While persons out of the labor force are slightly less likely to have migrated from another area, the differences are small and

Table 2.26 Household Activities of Nonparticipants by Gender, 10 Most Common Chores

	Women out of labor force		Men out of labor force	
	Have you spent any time in the past 7 days on…? (percentage answering yes)	How much time, including travel time, did you spend on…in the last week? (hours last week)	Have you spent any time in the past 7 days on…? (percentage answering yes)	How much time, including travel time, did you spend on…in the last week? (hours last week)
Fetching firewood for the household	21.0	6.04	17.8	5.12
Fetching water	46.3	5.47	43.2	4.11
Ironing clothes for the household	17.0	3.88	44.6	3.48
Taking care of children in the household	49.2	21.66	8.3	7.15
Sweeping for the household	70.1	5.50	35.4	3.43
Disposing of garbage for the household	26.1	4.29	25.5	3.27
Preparing meals for the household	73.6	12.29	19.9	5.38
Marketing or shopping for the household	25.3	6.17	18.0	5.31
Running errands for the household	23.3	5.01	32.1	4.30
Washing dishes for the household	62.6	5.37	28.2	3.82

Source: Authors' calculations.
Note: Based on questions s4iq1-s4iq24 of Nigeria Living Standards Survey 2003–04. Sample size = 10,193, aged 15 to 65, not in school and not in the labor market.

Table 2.27   Average Hours Worked Last Week by Gender, 10 Most Common Chores

	Women		Men	
	Out of labor force	In labor force	Out of labor force	In labor force
Hours spent on ten chores last week	35.19	36.89	11.36	13.35

Source: Authors' calculations.
Note: Based on questions s4iq1-s4iq24 of Nigeria Living Standards Survey. Sample size = 51,107, aged 15 to 65 and not in school, of which 10,193 not in the labor market.

become insignificant when controlling for the more important factors mentioned above.

Illness. There is no higher incidence of illness or injury in the population of nonparticipants compared to the labor force. Thus, illness, does not appear to be a significant cause of nonparticipation. Furthermore, workers without jobs are only rarely prevented from job searching as a result of illness or injury; therefore, those out of the labor force are unlikely to be unemployed people too ill to search for jobs.[2] The rate of illness is similar in all groups, so selection is likely to be of little importance overall.

Measurement error. A small proportion of the sample who reply inconsistently may be individuals attending school or working. The definition of the labor force is based on a question relating to work engaged in over the past 12 months. A similar question relating to a subset of this period—the last 7 days—should, however, be answered equally by persons outside the labor market. Of the respondents (two thirds of nonparticipants), 4 percent of men replied that they worked in the last 7 days (agriculture, jewelry, and manual labor being the most common cases). For women, the rate of inconsistent replies is around 2.5 percent. Conservatively attributing these cases to the working population gives an average rate of nonparticipation for the working-age population in the economy of more than 20 percent.

Notes

1. There were minor changes in the design of the questionnaire over the period from 1999 to 2006. In 1999 and 2004, an additional category, "community/ voluntary work," was identified as a wage job if the respondent also gave

"employee" or "member of a producer cooperative" as his or her employment status.

2. Around 10 percent of the sample reported suffering from illness (the proportion of ill in the labor force is almost identical at 10.38 percent), with half of the ill stating that they stopped their usual activities as a result. While one third of sufferers reported stopping their activities for fewer than three days, one third reported stopping for more than a week. Illness might, therefore, have prevented some of these individuals (5 percent of those out of work) from searching for employment, causing them to be unemployed.

CHAPTER 3

Growth, Employment, and Industry in Nigeria

Markus Eberhardt and Francis Teal

Overview

The pattern of growth in Nigeria has not focused on the industrial sector, but on agriculture and self-employment. Such activities are dominated by small-scale enterprises; since farms are small and most self-employment is own employment, the number of the self-employed who run their own businesses is a small percentage of total self-employment. As the recent past has demonstrated, such activities can provide increased incomes, but this pattern of growth is constrained by three closely related factors. The first factor is the low level of productivity that characterizes these sectors. The second is that, because the activities are small scale, the opportunities for investment in them is limited. The third is that demand is driven by the domestic market rather than exports. The key to successful acceleration of Nigeria's growth is to address issues of low productivity. Further, if the patterns that have been observed in rapid-growth economies are to be repeated, larger-scale enterprises will be needed and must be directed to the export market. The comparative review section of this chapter demonstrates that this export orientation has been followed in industry, but argues that the size of the enterprises and their export orientation—rather than the sector—may be the key to growth.

That section also outlines why larger enterprises and export orientation will be crucial to the longer-run sustained growth of the Nigerian economy.

Policy success has, to date, been concentrated on the domestic market. This book proposes ways that Nigeria can build on that policy success, leading to a second phase that extends Nigeria's access to regional markets, and from there builds competitiveness in the international market. This approach is taken because of the need, in the long run, to create wage jobs. The absence of wage jobs is the key to understanding why Nigerians feel there are no jobs, while the data show that employment has been rising with the growth of the labor force. In the minds of Nigerians, particularly those who are young and better educated, jobs mean wage jobs.

Why focus on wage jobs when income has been growing without any expansion in such jobs? The issue is the incomes available from the jobs. Wage jobs, in an African context, represent the only way that incomes can rise for the unskilled; therefore, income growth for the unskilled will be limited without a sustained expansion of wage jobs in larger enterprises. The next section provides an overview of this issue of job creation in the context of the size of firms, drawing on data from Nigeria's manufacturing sector. Following that, the comparative review section provides evidence from comparative cross-country data as to how countries able to enter the international markets via exports have fared over the period from the 1970s to 2003. The question for Nigeria in the medium term as to whether exports are essential is then considered. A final section provides an overview of which sectors will provide which types of jobs.

Job Creation, Wages, and Firm Size

The data presented in chapter 2 of this volume show how, by conventional measures, unemployment rates can be low yet jobs scarce. This apparent paradox is due to the insufficient income provided by many jobs, particularly jobs available for young Nigerians. So the policy problem is not simply to create jobs, but to create the types of jobs that Nigerians want.

What are the characteristics of such jobs? Typically, good jobs are described as those that provide good pay, working conditions, promotion prospects, and security. Within the wage labor market in Africa, such jobs have traditionally been associated with the public sector. Broadly speaking, across almost all countries in Sub-Saharan Africa, there has been a failure to create good jobs in the private sector. This report focuses on the underlying causes of this failure and how industrial policy can be used to address the problem.

In Sub-Saharan Africa in the last decade, most job creation has been in the self-employment sector, particularly in urban areas (figure 3.1). Nigeria is no exception to this general trend. The inadequate growth in wage jobs has important implications for a range of policy issues. With the expansion of education, the number of formal sector jobs is failing to keep pace with the growth of school leavers. Increasingly higher levels of education are perceived as necessary to get a job. An expansion of education without an expansion of jobs for the newly educated is a recipe for social unrest.

Policy needs to focus not only on creating jobs, but also on creating higher-wage jobs. If those making a marginal living in the self-employed sector could be absorbed into a higher-paying wage sector, this would be a powerful mechanism for expanding incomes for the poorest. It is a mechanism that is powerfully driving the growth of the Chinese economy at present and is conspicuously absent in Nigeria and most African countries, as will be shown in the next section. Developing a high-wage job-creation machine needs to be a central policy objective. The extent to which wages are related to firm size is illustrated in figure 3.2, which shows how the earnings of younger workers currently entering the labor market vary depending on the size of firm in which they work. Wages for the young worker in a micro firm are about US$22 per month, compared with US$35 per month for those in larger firms—a 50 percent differential.

Figure 3.1   Where Do Jobs Get Created?

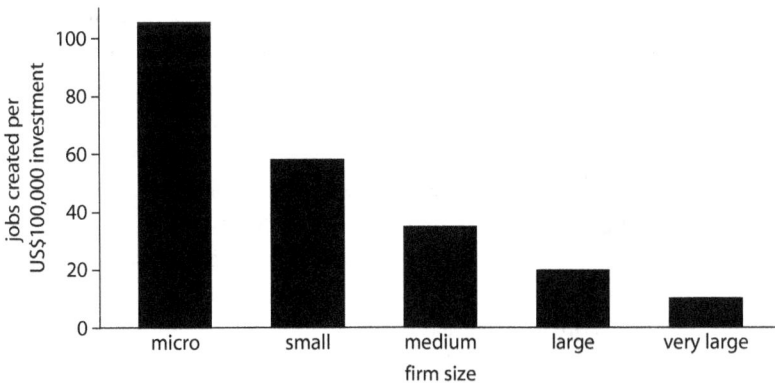

Source: Malik and Teal 2008.
Note: A microfirm is one employing less than 6 workers, small is 6 to 20, medium is 21 to 75, large is 76 to 199, and very large is greater that 200.

Figure 3.2   Where Do Better Jobs Get Created?

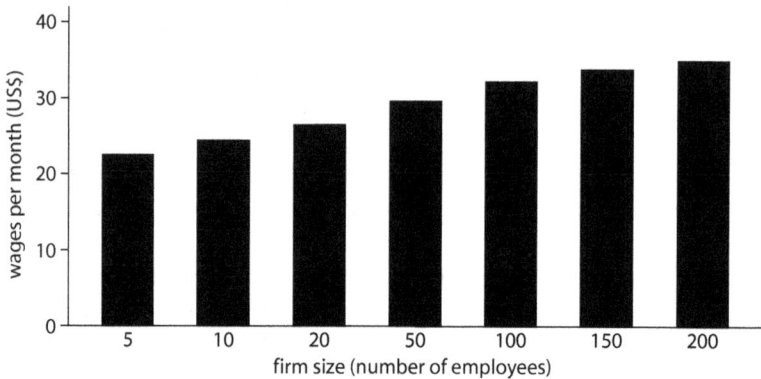

Source: Malik and Teal 2008.
Note: The wages are calculated over the period 2000 to 2004 for an unskilled male worker aged 20 with 9 years of education and just starting out in the labor force.

In summary, microfirms and small firms are good at creating jobs but not good at producing higher-paying jobs. This is the key policy problem in the area of wage jobs. Where such jobs are being created, they are low-wage jobs, because they are concentrated in the small-scale sector serving the domestic market. It is not that job creation in smaller firms should be discouraged, but that policy needs to ensure that growth can move beyond this stage. The next section considers how this has been done in other countries.

Nigeria's Production and Exports in a Comparative Context

This section sets Nigeria's industrial production and exports in a comparative context. It begins by showing how employment in manufacturing within countries has changed over recent decades in the context of three types of manufacturing: first, resource-based sectors (food and wood production will be used as representative examples later in the section); second, low-tech, labor-intensive sectors (apparel and footwear will be used); and, finally, medium- and high-tech sectors (machinery, electric machinery, electronics will be considered). Both production and export for these types of manufacturing will be examined. The final part of this section examines comparative data for the service sector.

The Global Share of Employment in Manufacturing
The data on employment in manufacturing—taken from the United Nations Industrial Development Organization (UNIDO 2004) and

Nicita and Olarreaga (2007) throughout this section—have been arranged according to five stylized groups of countries, based on growth performance (above and below median growth) over the 1970–2003 time horizon. The data show sector employment for an early period (1970–84) and a late period (1985–2003) in each country grouping.

Table 3.1 shows that Nigeria has expanded manufacturing employment in the low-, medium-, and high-tech sectors, while the resource-based manufacturing sectors have contracted. Nigeria's share of employment in the labor-intensive, low-tech manufacturing sectors at the end of the period is comparable to that of the group of fast-growing low-income countries (LICs). For comparative purposes, data have been chosen where coverage for Nigeria is relatively limited. While use of additional, more up-to-date Nigerian data sources for the manufacturing employment figures may lead to a more complete picture, earlier research (Malik and Teal 2008) suggests that the essential trends are captured by the figures presented.

The distribution of workers within an economy can indicate a sector shift of concentration; however, it would not account for overall expansion or contraction of manufacturing employment. To assess this, one must use a measure for relative employment across the country groupings and sectors .

Table 3.2 shows that for a number of slow-growing LICs, including Nigeria,[1] the share of global manufacturing employment has remained small, whereas some fast-growing countries, including China and Vietnam, have expanded their share quite dramatically. In all three sector groups, these countries virtually doubled their share over the period analyzed, thus creating employment on a considerable scale. Since this shift might have been driven by China, the analysis was redone (second panel of table 3.2) to see whether the patterns would still hold if China were excluded from the analysis. With the exclusion of China, the new analysis showed that the global share of manufacturing employment in slow-growing LICs is still negligible and stagnant, whereas the share for fast-growing LICs virtually doubles in each of the three sector groups.

In relative terms, therefore, a significant global shift of manufacturing employment to LICs has taken place, and the process is dominated, but not entirely driven, by China's manufacturing employment expansion.

An Analysis of Production Intensity in Manufacturing

Again, the focus is on three sector groups—resource-based, low-tech, and medium- and high-tech sectors—and on charting of the evolution of production intensity over time. Production intensity is defined as the share of an economy's manufacturing value-added (MVA) that is located within a

Table 3.1 Within-Country Share of Employment in Manufacturing, 1970–84 and 1985–2003

Period	UNIDO-CIP production classification	Slow-growing LIC		Nigeria		Fast-growing LIC		Fast-growing LIC, excluding China		Slow-growing MIC	
		Share of labor %	Median value	Share of labor %	Median value	Share of labor %	Median value	Share of labor %	Median value	Share of labor %	Median value
1970–85	Resource-based	47.3	2,240	37.0	140	42.8	2,000	43.8	1,920	41.5	3,690
1985–2003		50.0	1,330	24.9	70	36.6	2,580	37.9	2,390	40.0	4,010
1970–85	Low-tech	35.3	1,760	41.2	112	34.9	1,600	35.4	1,536	31.9	2,952
1985–2003		29.7	1,060	48.7	56	42.9	2,064	44.3	1,912	30.1	3,208
1970–85	Medium- and high-tech	13.7	2,190	20.0	140	15.7	2,000	15.1	1,920	23.1	3,690
1985–2003		18.5	1,290	26.4	70	13.7	2,580	12.1	2,390	24.5	4,010

Source: UNIDO 2004; Nicita and Olarreaga 2007.

Note: CIP = competitive industrial performance; LIC = low-income country; MIC = middle-income country. For Nigeria, second period employment data from 1991–96. Lighter shading shows increases of at least 2 percent; darker shading shows decreases of at least 2 percent.

Table 3.2   Global Share of Employment in Manufacturing, 1970–84 and 1985–2003
(percentage)

Period	UNIDO-CIP production classification	Share of labor (%)				
		Slow-growing LICs %	Fast-growing LICs %	Slow-growing MICs %	Fast-growing MICs %	OECD countries %
1970–84	Resource-based	0.9	21.3	9.8	13.0	29.5
1985–2003		0.7	41.7	5.9	11.4	25.2
1970–84	Low-tech	0.7	18.4	8.7	15.7	31.0
1985–2003		0.6	43.7	5.5	14.1	26.0
1970–84	Medium- and high-tech	0.2	21.2	4.7	9.9	33.9
1985–2003		0.1	38.3	2.8	10.2	34.0
Excluding China:						
1970–84	Resource-based	1.0	10.3	11.1	14.9	33.6
1985–2003		0.8	17.0	8.3	14.8	36.5
1970–84	Low-tech	0.8	9.0	9.5	17.4	34.3
1985–2003		0.7	17.3	7.1	19.5	34.9
1970–84	Medium- and high-tech	0.2	4.9	5.5	12.0	40.9
1985–2003		0.2	8.0	4.4	14.7	50.7

Source: UNIDO 2004; Nicita and Olarreaga 2007.
Note: We report the average share of global employment in each of the country groups reviewed. These numbers do not add up to 100 percent, as some emerging market and other economies are not considered in any of the five groupings.
CIP = competitive industrial performance; LIC = low-income country; MIC = middle-income country; OECD = Organisation for Economic Co-operation and Development. Lower panel excludes China. Lighter shading shows increases of at least 2 percent; darker shading shows decreases of at least 2 percent. Medians are preferred since the distribution of averages in each category is likely to be skewed.

specific sector compared to the world average. In the following figures, this intensity has been expressed in percentage terms: 100 percent production intensity for a country group in, for example, food products indicates that it has the same industrial focus on food production as an average country in the world. A lower value, say 50 percent, would indicate that this sector plays a less important role in overall manufacturing in this country group than it does for an average country. Since the sector production data for Nigeria in our dataset are limited, values for Nigeria and other slow-growing LICs are presented as one group and contrasted with those for the group of fast-growing LICs (figure 3.3).

In reviewing these findings, a number of issues should be noted. First, the overall levels of MVA in Nigeria are very low compared to other LICs. For 1994–2003, Nigeria had, on average, only US$15.60 per capita MVA and an MVA-in-GDP share of 3.9 percent, compared with around US$23.70 per capita MVA and a share of 8.8 percent in all other LICs (U.S. dollars,

Figure 3.3   Evolution of Production Intensity for Countries Like Nigeria and More Successful Countries

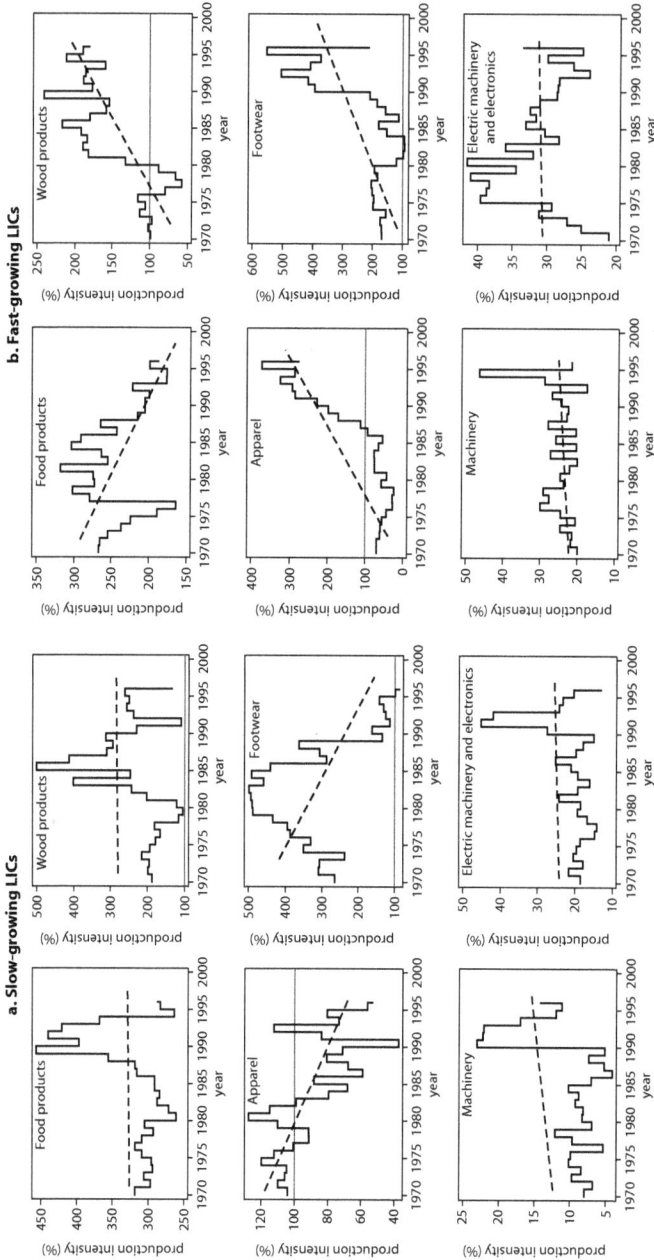

a. Slow-growing LICs

b. Fast-growing LICs

Source: Authors' calculations.

Note: Panel (a) represents countries similar to Nigeria; panel (b) represents countries much more successful than Nigeria.

year 2000 values). Second, the production intensity for the slow-growing LICs presented should not necessarily be compared with the world average (100 percent) but with the intensity of the successful LICs, which have grown dramatically over the past decades. Third, China is excluded from the following analysis so as not to make the findings dependent on the most outstanding success story of the past decades. The inclusion or exclusion of China does not, however, change the patterns described.

The graphs in figure 3.3 plot the intensity (on the vertical axis) over time (on the horizontal axis) and add a rough indication of the overall trend of evolution (dashed line).

At first glance, although the trajectories for the resource-based sectors (with food and wood production as representative examples) are very different between the two country groups, they nevertheless tell the same story of high concentration (values far in excess of 100 percent). The story, however, differs for the low-tech, labor-intensive sectors (apparel and footwear, for example), where the successful LICs in the panel (b) have dramatically increased their intensity, whereas in the slow-growing LICs in panel (a) intensity declined over time. For the medium- and high-tech sectors (machinery, electric machinery, and electronics are the representative sectors), the patterns look very similar across the two panels, with relatively limited change in production intensity over time and intensity levels of around 10 to 40 percent of world average. This suggests the comparatively high skill requirements of production in these sectors. A production-intensity graph for middle-income countries, for instance, would show that the successful countries among these groups have considerably expanded their production intensity in this sector group.

An Analysis of Export Intensity in Manufacturing
This section turns from production to exports. The analysis of export intensity can make use of data for Nigeria, which are available for the entire period studied. Export intensity in a sector expresses a country's share of manufacturing exports in that sector, vis-à-vis total manufacturing exports, expressed in relative terms against the world average. Again, it might be beneficial to put Nigerian exports into the context of the LIC country average: for 1994–2003, the former amounted to around US$2.10 per capita, whereas the average LIC exports per capita were US$8.00. The share of manufacturing exports in total exports accounts for around 2 percent in Nigeria, in contrast to almost 17 percent in other LICs. The graphs in figure 3.4 benchmark Nigeria against fast-growing LICs.

Figure 3.4 Evolution of Export Intensity for Nigeria and More Successful Countries

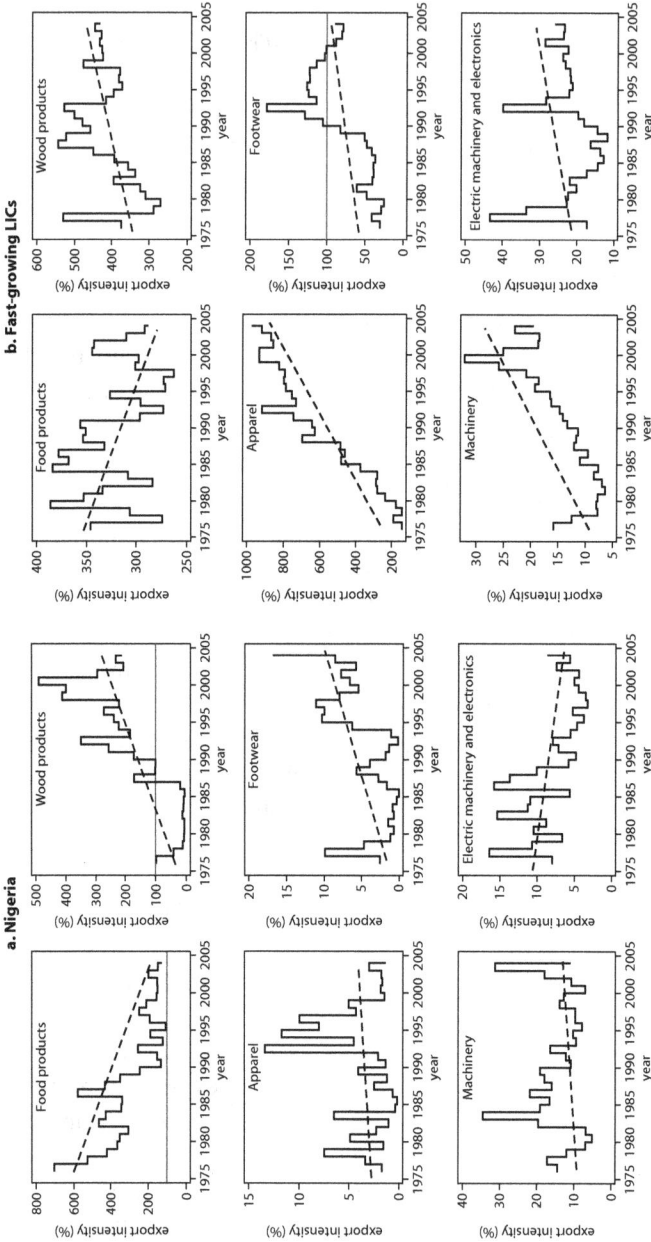

a. Nigeria

b. Fast-growing LICs

Source: Authors' calculations.
Note: Panel (a) represents Nigeria; panel (b) represents countries much more successful than Nigeria.

The patterns are not dissimilar to those in the production case: Nigeria has a relatively strong concentration on exports of resource-based manufactures such as food and wood products, which is also the case in the fast-growing LICs. The differences in the low-tech product exports are, however, particularly striking: Nigeria's export intensity in these products has remained relatively unchanged, whereas the export growth in the fast-growing LICs has largely been achieved through apparel and footwear export production. In the medium- and high-tech sectors, the field is again dominated by the MICs (not presented), whereas export intensity in the LICs has been relatively stable over time.

Not all exports are alike: products such as apparel, footwear, and electronics are competing with global exports and are thus competitive based on low price, sound logistics, and other elements of a functioning supply chain. In contrast, many food products only compete in the regional arena due to differences in taste.

Thus, in relative terms, a significant global shift of manufacturing employment to LICs has taken place, a process which is dominated, but not entirely driven, by China's manufacturing employment expansion.

The changes in production shown in figure 3.3 are reflected in the export patterns shown in figure 3.4. These changes are particularly clear for the apparel sector, which is the most labor-intensive of all sectors. It is this labor-intensive production sector driven by global exports, (for example, in apparel or footwear) that has *not* characterized the slow-growing economies, many of them—including Nigeria—in Africa. The sectoral composition of Nigeria's exports explains why growth has not been linked to wage jobs. The reasons why sectors that create many jobs are linked to export, not domestic markets, are discussed below.

The figures of absolute manufacturing exports and share of manufacturing in total exports given at the beginning of this section are an indicator of the gap between actual and potential manufacturing exports. Nigerian manufacturing exports for 1994–2003 were around US$2.10 per capita, or one quarter the LIC average. In other words, a fourfold increase in exports would take Nigeria to the average.

There are many reasons, however, why entering the international market for low-skill manufactures is unlikely to be a viable strategy for Nigeria in the short term. The link between growth and jobs is not necessarily the fact that these exports are manufactures; it is that they are labor intensive and from larger-scale enterprises. The link between scale to labor intensity is important. The key to better-paying jobs is the productivity of the enterprise, and the evidence for Africa generally, and for

Nigeria specifically, points to higher productivity being associated with larger-scale enterprises.

The Importance of the Services Sector for Economic Growth

A standard approach to economic development would typically chart the transition from a developing to a developed country in three stages. In the first stage, labor moves out of agriculture and into manufacturing (initially into labor-intensive activities). In the second stage, the country's manufacturing sophistication rises, shifting labor into more capital-intensive sectors. In the third stage, workers move from manufacturing into service sector jobs, for example, in the high-skill financial services sector.

Over the past decade, this viewpoint, however, has been challenged by the development experience of a small number of LICs, primarily India, but also the Philippines, and to a certain extent China (Bryson 2007). These countries developed considerable expertise and, most importantly, employment in relatively skill-intensive service-sector activities such as programming or other information technology (IT) services, accountancy services, call centers, and other communications-related services (Hermelin and Rusten 2007). One crucial element of this type of activity is that the "off-shoring" of service activities from developed country markets to developing countries has been made possible by the application of new technologies and new ways of organizing service production systems. Further, contrary to the first global shift of manufacturing activities from developed countries to emerging and developing economies in the 1990s (Dicken 1992), this second global shift in services is being determined by the education and language abilities of service workers and not by sound logistics, low wages, and other production costs alone. A final element is that firms engaging in these activities generally deliver mass-produced services, making extensive use of new equipment and operating procedures, which render these types of services comparatively capital intensive. It is thus not surprising that India, endowed with skilled graduates, low wages relative to those in developed countries, and a large English-speaking population, has developed an IT sector. India has emerged as the most popular off-shoring destination for North American and European countries: every year, India produces 2 million university graduates, most of whom have been taught in English (Bryson 2007).

While India's emergence as the personification of a "new international division of service labor" was sudden (around the year 2000, call centers did not exist in India, whereas by 2004 the industry already employed almost 100,000 workers), the reasons for this rise are very clear and identifiable. The 2004 *World Investment Report* (WIR), published by the United Nations Conference on Trade and Development (UNCTAD), presents a wealth of information about this second shift, particularly about the Indian experience.

Only a small proportion of service activities has been involved in the second global shift. The skills and IT requirements, together with the need for a geographical location that can serve both the U.S. and European markets on a 24-hour basis, effectively limit the number of successful candidates (Bryson 2007). It is therefore important not to overstate the significance of this shift for developing country industrial policy: the WIR (2004) lists a single foreign direct investment (FDI) project linked to services exports in Nigeria for the 2002–03 period, out of a total of 799 projects in developing countries, including call centers, shared service centers, IT services, and regional offshore headquarters (the WIR provides no data on the investment of domestic firms).

However, within the overall services sector—wholesale and retail trade; restaurants and hotels; transport and storage; communications; finance, insurance, real estate, and business services; and community, social, and personal services, according to the International Labor Organization's *Key Indicators of the Labor Market* (ILO 2007b)—the vast majority of activities are still based on traditional face-to-face work. In LICs, this type of low-skill service activity is characterized by relatively low productivity because it is difficult to substitute with machines and is located in small-scale enterprises (Bryson 2007).

The distinction within the services sector between skilled and unskilled workers is important. The service sector can be divided into three sections: first, the traditional labor-intensive services sector (retail, transport, repair), which is low skill; second, the skill-intensive services sector (banking, finance, insurance); and third, the traded services sector (off-shoring), which is medium skill. Data on the services sector are patchy at best, particularly in the developing country context. Most of the data reported do not distinguish these three subsectors consistently across countries, and general statements need to be interpreted with this in mind. As noted in ILO (2007b), "The services-producing sectors can provide many opportunities for productive employment; however, employment in services ranges from well-paid salaried jobs of highly skilled workers enjoying adequate working conditions, to subsistence trade activities that are widespread on the streets in the developing world. Many workers in the latter situation may be underutilized even if they are working excessive hours battling for a meager income."

The ILO report (2007b) states that global employment in the tertiary sector rose from 37 percent in 1996 to 42 percent in 2006, thus exceeding employment in agriculture for the first time (agricultural employment accounted for 42 percent in 1996 and 36 percent in 2006, with industry relatively stable at 21 percent). Table 3.3 shows a breakdown of the structural change within broad regional and income categories. It seems that a shift toward services is noticeable over the ten-year period in virtually all regions. Note, however, that the sample for Sub-Saharan Africa is made up of only six countries (South Africa, Botswana, Namibia, Madagascar, Tanzania, and Ethiopia) and that the trends are likely to be dominated by the South African experience. Employment data for services in Africa, like that for manufacturing, are sparse, and it is difficult to draw reliable conclusions from the ILO (2007b) analysis.

Given the limited number of data points for service-sector employment in LICs, only very few examples of labor productivity growth in these economies can be provided. Data availability is constrained to those in the ILO (2007b) report; these data are presented in table 3.4.

Table 3.3   Changes in Industrial Structure Over the Past Decade
(share of employment)

	Agriculture		Industry		Services	
	1996	*2006*	*1996*	*2006*	*1996*	*2006*
World	41.9	36.1	21.1	21.9	37.0	42.0
Developed economies and EU	6.2	4.2	28.5	24.7	65.3	71.2
Central and Southeast Europe (non-EU) and CIS	27.2	20.3	28.7	25.8	44.1	53.8
East Asia	48.5	40.9	24.3	25.6	27.2	33.5
Southeast Asia and the Pacific	51.0	45.4	16.5	18.6	32.5	36.0
South Asia	59.7	49.4	15.2	21.0	25.1	29.6
Latin America and the Caribbean	23.1	19.6	20.7	20.8	56.1	59.6
North Africa	36.5	34.4	19.8	20.0	43.7	45.6
Sub-Saharan Africa	74.4	65.9	7.5	10.0	18.1	24.1
Middle East	21.2	18.1	25.2	25.6	53.7	56.3

Source: ILO 2007b.
Note: CIS = Commonwealth of Independant States; EU = European Union. Figures for 2006 are estimates. Lighter shading shows increases of at least 2 percent; darker shading shows decreases of at least 2 percent.

Table 3.4   Average Growth of Value-Added per Person Employed in Services, 1980–2005, to Other Sectors

	Total economy	Agriculture	Manufacturing	Services Transport, communications	Services Retail, tourism
India	3.7	1.5	3.4	4.6	n/a
Indonesia	2.1	2.3	3.6	0.3	1.3
Mexico	−0.1	1.5	0.7	0.5	−2.6
Brazil	−0.1	3.6	−0.9	−1.1	−3.4
Korea, Rep. of	4.7	7.4	6.3	5.4	3.4
Taiwan, China	4.1	—	4.7	5.9	4.3

Source: ILO 2007b.

Note: — = not available. Agriculture includes forestry and fisheries.

Table 3.4 shows that India's average growth rate in transport and communication services, at 4.6 percent, trumps that of agriculture and manufacturing in the 1980–2005 period. This development is dominated by the phenomenal expansion of IT and communication services over the past decade. MICs such as Indonesia, Mexico, and Brazil, arguably endowed with a sizeable population of appropriately skilled workers, have not been able to expand productivity in their services sectors, or if they have, the growth rates have lagged far behind those achieved in manufacturing. Only in Taiwan, China, have parts of the services sector improved productivity faster than the manufacturing sector.

Data from the World Bank's World Development Indicators database can be used to compute averages for service sector-related output developments over the 1994–99 and 2000–06 periods. Since the employment data are missing for many countries, population data are used, which makes the measures somewhat crude indicators of labor productivity. In table 3.5, the figures for Nigeria are compared with those for other LICs and also with China, India, and the averages for MICs and high-income countries (HICs).

Table 3.5 shows that Nigeria lags behind other LICs in terms of the importance of the services sector: the share of service sector value-added (VA) in GDP is around 20 percent, compared with around 40 percent in other LICs and even higher shares in MICs and HICs. Nigeria's per capita VA from services is around US$80, whereas other LICs earn around US$120–130 per capita. Growth in services VA per capita changed from −0.6 percent per year in the earlier period to +4.2 percent in the later period, exceeding the rates for typical LICs but lagging the productivity

Table 3.5   Services in Nigeria and Other Countries
(median values)

Variable	Unit	Nigeria	Other LICs	India	China	MICs	HICs
1994–2000							
GDP per capita	Real US$ (2000)	365	299	393	716	1,984	18,715
Services VA per capita	Real US$ (2000)	79	122	176	297	1,012	12,477
Growth in services							
VA per capita	%	−0.6	1.7	6.7	8.0	2.7	2.8
Growth in services	%	2.3	5.0	8.3	9.8	4.7	3.4
Services VA–share							
of GDP	%	21.7	41.9	47.1	34.4	56.4	66.5
Services trade–							
share of GDP	%	15.2	14.5	5.3	5.5	18.1	16.7
Since 2000							
GDP per capita	Real US$ (2000)	396	345	511	1,209	2,142	22,699
Services VA per capita	Real US$ (2000)	85	136	233	450	1,121	14,451
Growth in services							
VA per capita	%	4.2	2.8	5.6	8.8	3.2	2.3
Growth in services	%	6.9	5.6	8.4	10.2	4.9	3.2
Services VA–share							
of GDP	%	24.2	44.2	52.9	40.7	58.8	69.0
Services trade–share							
of GDP	%	13.1	15.4	8.1	6.2	19.4	19.2

Source: World Development Indicators database.
Note: Other LICs: 43 countries; MICs: 76 countries; HICs: 36 countries. The data represent medians within each of the country groupings and time periods indicated. All estimates are statistically significantly different from zero at the 1 percent level, with the exception of growth in services for Nigeria.

growth witnessed in China and India. Given Nigeria's lower per capita VA from the service sector, these growth rates may just represent Nigeria catching up with the level of other LICs. The Chinese experience suggests that service sector productivity growth may be higher when there is strong manufacturing growth performance (China's per capita manufacturing VA growth averaged around 10 percent per year in the past decade). Productivity comparisons across the service and manufacturing sectors are difficult, as much service sector activity in Nigeria is trading, where incomes accrue to the self-employed.

Where there are data across incomes from wages and the self-employed, the results show that wages in small firms are lower than the incomes available from self-employment (Sandefur, Serneels, and Teal 2006). However, once enterprises start to grow, incomes from wage employment become substantially larger.

The distinction drawn above between those parts of the service sector that are skill intensive and those that are not is also important in terms of assessing the income consequences of the creation of employment opportunities. If these employment opportunities are relatively skill intensive, then the incomes will reflect, in part, the returns from those skills. The Otigba computer cluster, one of the case studies on clusters in Africa presented in Oyelaran-Oyeyinka and McCormick (2007), provides an example of successful and relatively skill-intensive service sector growth (see chapter 4 of this book). The data indicate that growth is driven by new firms entering the cluster and not by existing firms increasing in size. In comparison to other firms in Africa, export levels for firms in the cluster, at 25 to 39 percent, are very high. While most of these exports appear to be within the West Africa region, the case study illustrates the general theme of this section that export markets provide a source of demand growth that is not provided by exclusive reliance on the domestic market.

It is clear that skilled service sector exports offer employment opportunities for the rapidly growing number of more highly educated Nigerians. The regional export market probably offers more opportunities in the short run than the international market, where competition will be more intense. However, it is also clear that this is not a market segment that can absorb a large number of the unskilled. The sector that does not absorb them is the traditional services sector, and both its market orientation and the scale of its enterprises ensure that incomes in that sector remain low. The next section turns to a more general consideration of the issues raised by the differences in growth rates possible between the domestic and export sectors.

Notwithstanding the need to create a basis for export-led growth over the long term, Nigeria's significant comparative cost disadvantage, emanating from poor physical infrastructure and other shortcomings in the business environment, will likely limit prospects for strong export growth over the short to medium term. This suggests that an appropriate thrust for Nigeria's current growth strategy is a continued focus on capturing a growing share of the domestic market. Since 2001, growth has been stimulated by domestic demand largely driven by foreign inflows, which indicates that the prospects for growth to continue being driven by these factors are favorable, particularly if measures are taken to promote growth in selected promising value chains (see chapter 4 of this book). While growth may continue to rely on the domestic market in the short to medium term, it will be essential even during this phase to implement policies aimed at developing Nigeria's export potential. The success of the Otigba cluster suggests that such potential exists even in the current rather difficult circumstances and that it could be further developed if selective targeted measures are implemented to improve the business environment.

The Link between Wage Jobs and Structural Change

Improved economic performance in Africa is not confined to Nigeria. Until the economic crisis of late 2008, Africa was experiencing much improved growth rates. However, as the analysis has shown, this much-improved performance in Nigeria has not been associated with the kind of structural transformation—from an economy based on small-scale rural and urban self-employment to one based on larger-scale, often industrial firms—that has characterized the rapid growth of economies over the last 30 years. In this respect, Nigeria is a rather extreme example of a process of growth without structural change. Associated with this form of growth has been the lack of wage jobs. This suggests that the two may well be linked.

The lack of structural change and the lack of wage jobs are linked through the way income growth translates into demand. As incomes rise, demand shifts away from food and basic goods to manufacturing and services. In the case of Nigeria's growth path (and to only a slightly lesser extent, Africa more generally), domestic income growth has driven domestic demand for manufacturing and services. The domestic response is through small-scale activities in either the rural or the urban sectors. Such a growth path does produce goods and jobs; however, the jobs are low-paying and dominated by self-employment. The reason is that the investment necessary to raise labor productivity, and therefore wages, is not occurring given that growth is through small-scale activities where investment does not occur. Larger enterprises in Africa are far more capital intensive, and this capital intensity is the key to higher wages.

Such an analysis suggests two questions. Why does investment not occur in small-scale enterprises; and if larger-scale enterprises are part of the solution, how can they be brought about? The low level of investment and capital intensity in small-scale enterprises is a reflection of the high capital costs they face. Such costs are intrinsic to Nigeria's present market structure. There is nothing immutable about such structures, but given the higher relative capital costs in small enterprises, investment is inevitably going to be limited. With such low investment, jobs paying higher incomes (which are going to be wage jobs) will also be very limited. In fact, with the present growth path, the number of wage jobs in Nigeria is falling.

The reason for this is that manufacturing occurs in larger-scale units with higher levels of capital than most forms of agriculture and services. Such forms of organization support the wage contract form of employment. As these larger-scale units have higher levels of labor productivity, their employees have higher wages.

There is another reason why rising wage employment is likely to be associated with sustained increases in incomes: it leads to a relative decrease in the supply of workers in the self-employment sector, resulting in an increase in incomes in that sector. The failure to create more wage jobs puts continual pressure on incomes in the self-employed sector, where those unable to find wage employment end up working. Thus, a policy focused on creating wage jobs not only benefits those who obtain those jobs, it also helps those who do not, leading to lower levels of competition in both sectors.

While wage jobs are a small part of employment, the expansion of this sector must be the focus of any policy that is to have a long-run impact on poverty reduction.

Policies for Growth in Wage Employment
In Africa, generally, policies to promote the growth of industry, and thus higher-paying wage employment, have not been successful. A common failing across the continent, with very few exceptions, is that the growth of the manufacturing sector has been below the world average and far below the growth rates of successful LICs. Africa's industrial policy has had three broad elements. The first has been the promotion of output for the domestic market, the earliest aspect of this being the policies of import substitution industrialization pursued in the 1960s and 1970s. The second has been the promotion of processing of domestically produced natural resources on the grounds that such processing creates jobs and value added. The third has been a focus on skills on the grounds that this will improve the efficiency of enterprises and thus their ability to grow. All these elements of policy have in common a focus on domestic markets, resources, and skills.

There are good reasons for such a focus. Domestic markets, resources, and skills are the dimensions of the economy that domestic policy can control. However, these policies have two fundamental weaknesses. The first is that if they are pursued in a manner that ensures domestic costs are higher than international ones, then market demand will be limited.

This is because the goods cannot be exported, and their high prices limit demand and encourage smuggling. The second, and more basic, problem is that output growth is limited to the growth in domestic demand. The key point about successful processes of structural transformation is that in expanding access to export markets, demand is divorced from domestic supply and from the limits of domestic demand. Such a divorce is a key to getting higher rates of growth for wage jobs.

It may well be thought unrealistic for Nigeria to rapidly enter the international market for labor-intensive goods. Indeed, since 1970, Nigeria has basically retreated from exporting any product other than oil. How, then, can policy overcome the limitations inherent in a domestic focus? That is, in part, the subject of the next chapter, which outlines options for industrial policy in Nigeria. The next sections of this chapter will set out some of the potential gains for wage employment if such policies can be successful. They will show how new policies need to go beyond the traditional ones—promotion of output for the domestic market, processing of domestically produced natural resources, and skills—to look at factors important for a higher-wage, unskilled, intensive growth pattern.

The previous section identified three broad types of manufacturing, all of which are pursued in Nigeria: (a) the natural resource processing industry (high skill, high capital); (b) skill-intensive services (high skill, low capital); and (c) unskilled labor-intensive manufactures (low skill, low capital). These three sectors are largely complementary; policy does not need to choose among them. However, their relative rates of growth have very different implications for the creation of jobs for the unskilled, and it is increasing the rate of wage job creation that needs to be at the core of the longer-run objectives for policymakers in Nigeria.

The following sections look at policies that can affect all three types of manufacturing and then look more narrowly at policies of particular importance for unskilled intensive growth. The analysis begins with the role of infrastructure.

Infrastructure and Firm Efficiency

Firms in any part of manufacturing can only produce efficiently if they have access to suitable transport infrastructure and their production is not hampered by unreliable supply of utilities, such as energy and water. Yeaple and Golub (2007) and Njikam et al. (2006) investigate the impact of infrastructure on productivity (total factor productivity growth) using panel data from a set of developing and developed countries, and from Sub-Saharan Africa, respectively. These studies find support for a close link between infrastructure and productivity improvements. Canning and Pedroni (2004) find considerable heterogeneity in the link between infrastructure and economic growth at the aggregate level, both across countries and in infrastructure measures. While the question of exactly how much infrastructure matters for growth is essentially an empirical one, the suggestion that infrastructure matters more for LICs is commonly accepted (Estache 2008).

As the World Bank Chief Economist for the Africa Region recently noted (Devarajan 2008):

> "In the past, policy advice on promoting trade in Africa may have overstressed the need for African countries to bring down their own trade barriers, such as import tariffs, and insufficiently emphasized the need to improve trade logistics, infrastructure, business competition, and regulation. . . . [P]oor infrastructure—such as road and communications networks—could be as much a barrier as trade tariffs. Furthermore, some of these infrastructure constraints may be due to excessive regulation and barriers to entry in the trucking industry. Finally, Africa's 'spaghetti bowl' of overlapping regional trading arrangements makes it difficult for firms to compete abroad."

According to the World Bank, the poorest countries need to spend around 9 percent of GDP on operation, maintenance, and expansion of their infrastructure if they are to achieve the Millennium Development Goals (Estache 2008). Actual investment in most LICs is typically around 2 to 3 percent (UNIDO 2009). Note that the returns required to start an infrastructure project in an average LIC are 2 to 3 percent higher than in richer developing countries and more than twice what is generally expected in developed economies (Sirtain et al. 2005). Private sector involvement in infrastructure provision is still limited, particularly in LICs. Having independent regulatory agencies—one of the main policy recommendations of the past ten years—does not by itself guarantee private participation in infrastructure investment. On the contrary, a country does not need an agency to attract the private sector. Prime risks to overcome in increasing the low participation rate of the private sector are exchange rate risks, commercial risks, and political instability (Estache 2008).

Eifert et al. (2005) suggest that LICs focus on reducing the most severe indirect costs faced by firms and argue that, in most countries, the availability and reliability of power emerges as a clear priority.

Malik and Teal (2008) conclude from their research on Nigeria that the "absence of a well-functioning infrastructure—electricity, water, roads, and telephones—acts as a severe handicap for Nigerian manufacturers."

They single out electricity provision as the most pressing aspect deserving immediate government attention. This view is echoed in a chapter on the Nigerian power sector by Tallapragada and Adebusuyi (2008) in the same publication (Collier et al. 2008). Attempting to remedy these issues for locally concentrated areas—export processing zones, free trade zones, industrial clusters—may be a more realistic target for LICs than trying to increase infrastructure provision in the country as a whole (UNIDO 2009).

Enterprise Size, Efficiency, and Exports

The role of infrastructure investment is particularly critical for the natural resource processing industry. This has been denoted a high-skill, high-capital-using sector, and as such, it will not generate the wage jobs for the unskilled that Nigeria needs. In light of the analysis in the previous section, there is no alternative in the longer term but to ensure that labor-intensive exports rise rapidly. Rapid growth in the demand for unskilled labor is the key to the job creation dilemma that Nigeria faces.

One option for increasing the demand for labor would be to target labor-intensive manufacturing exports. However, compared to 30 years ago, as Collier (2007) suggests, LICs now cannot compete with China and India in accessing developed country markets. Those two countries have such an abundant supply of cheap labor, efficient large firms specializing in labor-intensive goods, coastal province infrastructure, developed supply chains, and so on—in other words, such productive and export power—that African countries have difficulty competing with them. One policy option suggested by Collier (2007) is that there should be an expansion of existing schemes providing African exporters with preferential access to the North American and European markets. He argues that in the past, the European Everything But Arms scheme has not been as successful as the U.S. developed African Growth and Opportunities Act due to important differences in the design of the two policies.

Given the growth of China and its presence in the world economy, clearly the patterns of growth for exports from Africa are going to be different. Policy needs to focus not on what is being produced but on what is being produced for export (so that demand is unlimited) and on intensively using unskilled labor (so that wage jobs get created). That will be difficult but not impossible.

One important feature of the new economy is "trade in tasks." A global trade in tasks is emerging, whereby manufacturing production processes are split into a myriad of tasks, which are performed at various geographical locations by firms that are globally competitive in terms of location, flexibility, and cost structure. The emergence of trade in tasks is not limited to intermediate and high-technology goods, where, for instance, the automotive industry has been saving costs through global supply arrangements for decades. Trade in tasks also includes subsectors characterized by labor-intensive activities with relatively low skill requirements. A similar phenomenon is the specialization of locations in the production of certain products and their global marketing, identified through a process of experimentation and "self-discovery" (Rodrik 2004).

Where African countries have entered into successful production for regional or global markets (for instance, cut flowers in Kenya, garments in Lesotho, and to a limited extent, computer clones in Nigeria), the common features have been a geographically limited focus and the narrowly defined nature of the task or product in question. Kenya, Lesotho and Otigba were able to identify a task or product within global trade that represented their competitive niche. Any policies through which governments were able to foster these developments were specific to those tasks or products. In the Kenya case, there were efforts to reduce the cost of air freight to Europe, and in the Lesotho case, efforts to reduce infrastructure costs (including the time and cost of delivery to major harbors in South Africa). Due to this observed heterogeneity, any routine government intervention, for instance, the establishment of an industrial park with first-rate infrastructure and international trade links, will have different returns across industrial sectors. The failure or success of more specific policies is intimately linked to the sector of operation, and within this sector, to the product, task, or service provided by the firm.

None of this is to deny that sustainable capacity growth for manufacturing in outward-oriented production and export, if it could be brought about, would play a major role in generating jobs. Firm-level analysis in Africa has found two effects relating to exports and growth: on the one hand, more efficient manufacturing firms self-select into becoming exporters; and on the other hand, there is also evidence of firms developing expertise in a learning-by-doing process once they have started exporting (Söderbom and Teal 2000; Bigsten et al. 2004).

A study on Ghana and Mauritius (Teal 1999) found that having more than 100 employees is an important determinant of exporting in both of these countries (this result is also found in other empirical work; for example, Söderbom and Teal 2003). Among large firms, those in Mauritius have three times the wage bills of those in Ghana, while productivity is four times higher, making the former clearly more profitable (Teal 1999; Söderbom and Teal 2000). If wages exceed opportunity costs for African firms, "then the potential for a successful and profitable export sector exists, and its lack may be a crucial part of the explanation for the failure of African economies . . . to emulate the Newly Industrializing Countries" (Söderbom and Teal 2000). At present, it is found that "[f]or those firms able to export, wages are too high to enable [them] to compete given the efficiency at which [they] operate" (Teal 1999).

The studies on African firms show that in the labor-intensive sectors, they tend to be small (thus facing high fixed costs of exporting), whereas larger firms tend to have higher capital intensity, which renders them uncompetitive internationally. This interpretation of the literature concludes that a key to sustainable levels of labor-intensive exports for African manufacturing "is to enable larger firms to be relatively more labor-intensive than is the case at present" (Söderbom and Teal 2003).

The Job-Creating Sectors

The previous sections identified three broad manufacturing sectors that depend, respectively, on natural resources, high-tech skills, and low skills. Across these broad sectors, the level of capital required can differ substantially. There is a trade-off when it comes to creating jobs; activities with low capital intensity can generate a lot of jobs per unit of capital, but these jobs will generally be low paid. Broadly speaking, the evidence suggests that firms with more than 100 employees pay substantially more than microenterprises. This suggests that an industrial policy needs to provide a framework that allows firms to form and grow beyond the micro level. At the same time, this industrial policy should lean away from encouraging enterprises in sectors with relatively high capital intensity. The reason for this is simple: the number of jobs that such enterprises will create will be extremely small.

Sectors and Skills

The focus on jobs points toward three sectors that can grow and generate a range of jobs from the unskilled to the highly skilled. The first of these is the natural resources–based manufacturing sector (for example, forestry and food products). It is important to recognize why enterprises in these sectors provide the basis for employment growth in a manner that the more capital-intensive oil sector (which is not specific to Nigeria) does not. While the forestry and food product sectors are capital intensive relative to basic services and even to low- and intermediate-technology manufacturing, they are not readily replicated. However, the oil sector produces an internationally standardized product that can easily be shipped in bulk across great distances. Local wood and food-based industries are heterogeneous in terms of both the product and the market. Food tastes vary, even within West Africa, and forestry resources can also differ radically by geographical area. Thus, there are possible competitive advantages based on the specific local characteristics of the natural resources. In this context, natural resources would be the element of the production where a potential cost advantage would arise. However, evidence suggests the skill requirements would be medium to high, so natural resource endowment alone would not be sufficient.

A further limitation of the focus on the natural resources processing sector is that the number of jobs per unit of capital is very limited. It is through the creation of jobs that the most rapid route to sustained poverty reduction lies. Here it is argued that there are two entirely complementary routes to poverty reduction: first, the high-skill, low-capital manufacturing and related services sector; and second, the low-skill, low-capital sector. With regard to the former, the Otigba computer cluster has been mentioned as an example. Born out of the ingenuity of highly skilled but unemployed graduates with an entrepreneurial spirit, this experience demonstrates that Nigerian manufacturing already can have a regional dimension to its activities. Once set in motion, this sector has been able to compete with global multinationals at the regional level by providing viable low-cost alternatives tailored to the local markets in West Africa.

Other manufactured products with relatively high skills content could follow the lead taken by the computer (and related services) sector and build up a competitive edge at the regional level. This advantage would be based on the ingenuity of highly skilled people in the sector, their knowledge of the local operating environment, and their ability to provide low-cost alternatives. Although some evidence was found of value-chain upgrading among the Otigba entrepreneurs by shifting toward more labor-intensive assembly activities, the employment creation potential of this sector is limited to relatively high-skilled graduates for the foreseeable future.

Another sector that can deliver jobs at low capital requirements is the low-skill, labor-intensive manufacturing sector. So far, industries in this category have declined in the Nigerian context. Despite the apparent lack of profitability for Nigerian firms to compete within large-scale, labor-intensive manufacturing activities such as garments, footwear, leather products, and virtually any type of assembly production (from toys and low-tech electronics to more sophisticated computers), this sector could be effectively influenced by solid industrial policy.

One of the most serious challenges to manufacturing in Nigeria is reliable power supply. For any budding entrepreneur engaged in or planning to enter into low-skill, labor-intensive manufacturing, however, the profit margins at present cannot merit the use of generator power. This constraint prevents larger, more competitive firms from emerging and limits this sector to inefficient and uncompetitive microenterprises, or even no enterprises at all. Apart from unreliable power supply, other binding constraints (such as product time to market, cost of transport, import logistics, and administration) affect firm profitability and eventually, expansion and job creation. Firms in this sector would benefit particularly from the provision of reliable power supply, sound transport infrastructure and logistics, and related services.

Figure 3.5 provides a stylized representation of the nature of the policy choices that can be made across the identified manufacturing and service sectors.

In the graph, the vertical axis indicates the skills requirements of workers in the sectors, while the horizontal axis indicates the importance of

Figure 3.5   Sectoral Job Creation, Skill Requirements, and Export Importance

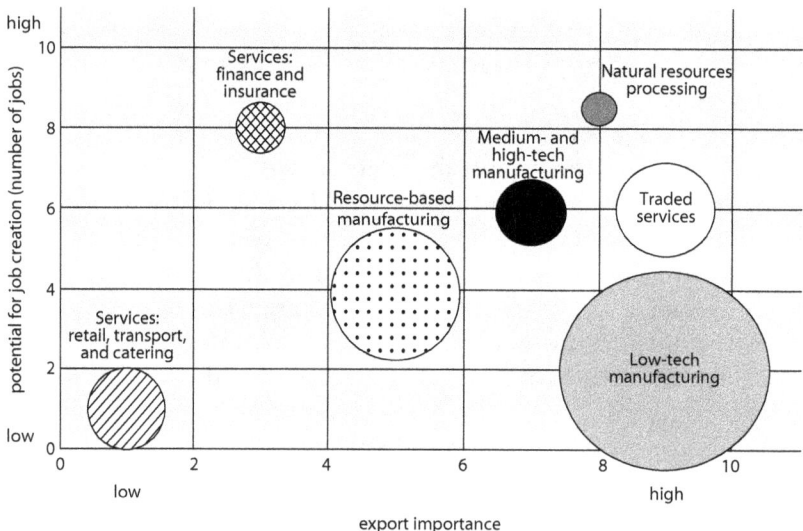

Source: Authors' calculations
Note: Size of circles indicates the number of better-paid jobs that can be created.

production for export. The bubble size indicates the number of better-paid jobs that can be created. A process can be envisaged by which the low-tech, low-skill sector expands in parallel with the high-tech, regionally focused market. The problem of job creation in Nigeria at present is that both of these markets are extremely limited. A key policy objective needs to be the relaxation of that constraint.

The Path to Jobs

The common factor across all aspects of development policy is the need to increase productivity, thus reducing costs and driving up demand. Increasing productivity is at the heart of any successful strategy for job creation. The key question that policy needs to address is which investments will achieve this goal most rapidly. It is in this context that policies towards agglomeration in general and clusters in particular may be central. Due to high infrastructure costs in Nigeria, it may be more efficient to concentrate resources geographically so that costs can be reduced in certain localities, rather than attempt a countrywide increase in productivity. How the Nigerian Government can improve the productivity and performance of local firms in a manner that will create the highest number of wage jobs is the focus of the next chapter.

Note

1. As a first, very rough way of identifying slow-growing and fast-growing countries, aggregate economy growth was used. The per capita gross domestic product growth rate (using constant U.S. dollar values) was computed for each year from 1970 to 2003 for the overall sample of countries to obtain the global median growth rate. Then the number of growth episodes for each country (a growth rate above the median) was counted; using a certain cut-off, a country with many growth episodes is referred to as fast-growing, and one with few such episodes is referred to as slow-growing. This was done for both the Low-Income and Middle-Income Country Groupings (where these two groupings follow the World Bank classification). According to this methodology, which is also used in the UNIDO *Industrial Development Report* (2009), Nigeria is in the slow-growing group within the LICs.

CHAPTER 4

Building the Enterprise Sector for Employment and Growth: Some Policy Options

Peter Mousley

Overview

In 2007, the Ministry of Commerce and Industry published "Nigeria's Industrial Development Strategy 2007–2011: A Cluster Concept." The prior policy statement had been in 2003, in a publication titled "Industrial Policy of Nigeria—Policies, Incentives, Guidelines and Institutional Framework." The two documents are distinct. The 2003 document identifies a range of initiatives and policies encompassing (a) tax and trade incentives (exporter grants, duty drawback and manufacture-in-bond schemes, pioneer tax status, and other tax incentives provided to industry[1]); (b) the Small and Medium Industries Equity Investment Scheme; and (c) free trade zones (FTZs).[2]

The 2007 document, by contrast, emphasizes clusters as part of a public infrastructure-led program targeting small and medium-size enterprises (SMEs). The cluster approach has four different variants covering: (a) FTZs (b) industrial parks, (c) enterprise zones, and (d) incubators. While the 2007 policy is still new and does not have an implementation or results track record, the 2003 policies have been in place longer, and their results can be assessed.

This chapter has four principal sections. In order to frame recommendations for policy actions to promote enterprise growth and employment creation, the first section provides some descriptive analysis and assessment of the government's different programs. The second section extends the analysis using data from the Investment Climate Assessment (Iarossi, Mousley, and Radwan 2009) to further investigate the characteristics of firms that operate in FTZs and utilize government tax and trade incentive programs. This section also includes some comparative country analysis. The third section details the preliminary conclusions to be drawn from the analysis and goes on to identify other characteristics of more successful enterprise growth in Nigeria. The fourth section suggests some elements of a forward-looking policy and program framework that could serve to extend enterprise growth more broadly across the country. The latter two sections draw extensively on recent work on competitiveness, value chains, and the knowledge economy conducted over the past year as part of a joint World Bank–U.K. Department for International Development (DFID) initiative in support of growth and employment in key economic corridors across the country.

The Current Enterprise Policy and Program Environment

This section will focus on specific policies and programs drawn from the 2003 policy statement. In particular:

- *Tax and trade incentives*, including exporter grants, duty drawback and manufacture-in-bond schemes (MIBSs), pioneer tax status, and other tax incentives provided to industry (excluding oil and gas exploration, development, and production);
- *FTZ services*, including the current status of 16 of the 17 existing FTZs in Nigeria,[3] with more detailed assessments of selected FTZs based on field visits;
- *The Bank of Industry*, including a review of its portfolio, which focuses on SMEs.

Tax and Trade Incentives

The Export Expansion Grant (EEG) scheme provides grant incentives to stimulate export-oriented activities. The program provides for grants of 15 to 30 percent of export value depending on eligibility scores, which are based on weighted eligibility criteria (WEC). This eligibility assessment is conducted annually and the resultant WEC applied for the year. Companies awarded the EEG are excluded from seeking other trade incentive benefits, such as the manufacture-in-bond program.

The weighted eligibility criteria have four bands—30 percent, 20 percent, 10 percent, and 5 percent. The eligibility framework shown in table 4.1 is used to assess the incentive rate for every EEG applicant. The maximum EEG allocation, amounting to 30 percent of export proceeds, is allocated to applicants that have an assessed eligibility score in excess of 70 percent.

A number of other requirements also need to be met for an EEG award[4]:

- Exporter must be registered with the Nigeria Export Promotion Council (NEPC).
- Exporter must be a manufacturer, producer, or merchant of Nigerian products, with a minimum annual export turnover of ₦5 million and evidence of repatriation of proceeds of exports.
- Exporter must submit baseline data, including audited financial statements and information on operational capacity, to NEPC.
- Qualifying export transaction must have 100 percent of the proceeds fully repatriated within 180 days, calculated from the date of export.

In addition, the exporter must meet a number of administrative conditions summarized in box 4.1. This includes a highly discretionary requirement of "other documents" by NEPC.

The EEG scheme is managed by NEPC in conjunction with an implementation committee comprising seven agencies of government. Once NEPC has processed the application, it is the implementation committee, in a scheduled monthly meeting, that recommends to the Ministry of Finance the allocation of the EEG.

Table 4.1   Export Expansion Grant Eligibility Framework

Criteria	Weighting (%)	Threshold
Local value-added	25	20%
Local content	20	35%
Employment (Nigerians)	20	500
Priority sector	10	Manufacturing only
Export growth	20	20%
Capital investment growth	5	10%
Total	100	

Source: Babalola 2008.

Box 4.1

Export Expansion Grant Implementing Arrangements

All EEG applications must be completed in three copies for transmission to the NEPC, the Central Bank of Nigeria (CBN), and the Nigerian Customs Service (NCS). The application includes the following documents:

- NEPC export certificate
- Clean certificate of inspection, including quality certification
- A Nigeria Export Proceeds form (form NXP) duly certified by processing bank, NCS, and preshipment inspection agents
- Single goods declaration forms, duly endorsed by NCS on both front and back
- Final commercial invoice
- Bill of lading
- Evidence of full repatriation of export proceeds (CBN confirmation of repatriation of proceeds by exporter)
- Certificate of manufacturer
- Other documents that may be required by NEPC

Source: Babalola 2008.

In addition to the retention of 100 percent of export proceeds by exporters under the EEG, a duty drawback and suspension scheme is in operation. This allows for exporters and producers to import raw materials and intermediate products for use in the manufacture of export products, free of import duty and other indirect taxes and charges. The scheme includes a rebate of duties already paid on imported inputs, and the suspension or exemption from the payment of such duties by exporters. For qualification of duty drawback payments, the export of the product that was produced with imported inputs must be completed within 18 months from the importation of the inputs. Duty suspension becomes a permanent waiver of duty payment only when inputs imported under the suspension scheme are used to produce export products that are exported within 12 months of the importation.

The MIB involves the importation of duty-free raw materials for the production of exportable goods on the basis of a bond issued by a commercial bank guaranteeing that all the end products will be exported. The performance bond is discharged after evidence of exportation and repatriation of foreign exchange has been produced. Any raw materials under import prohibition (the list varies over time and has included bagged cement, timber, and a range of agricultural commodities such as rice and edible oils) can be imported under this scheme, which is designed to encourage manufacturers to import duty-free material inputs and other intermediate products, whether prohibited or not, for the production of goods for export. The imports must be backed by a bond issued by any recognized commercial bank, merchant bank, insurance company, or the Nigerian Export-Import Bank. The bond is discharged after evidence of exportation and repatriation of foreign proceeds has been produced. The following eligibility requirements apply:

- MIBS is applicable to export manufacturers only.
- Interested manufacturers apply to the Ministry of Finance using prescribed forms.
- Factory premises must be approved for specified purposes by the Nigerian Customs Service.
- Approval includes the import requirement certificate, which is transmitted to the Nigerian Customs Service for implementation.
- The Nigerian Customs Service determines the acceptable guarantee bond, covering not less than 110 percent customs duty payable on each consignment.
- MIBS operates on a calendar year importation basis. For prohibited items, however, the scheme operates on an import-by-import basis.
- The bond will be effective from the date of its issuance and discharged when the stipulated conditions have been fulfilled.
- The Nigerian Customs Service will periodically monitor the utilization of raw materials imported under this scheme until the bond is fully executed.
- In the event of a manufacturer's inability to fulfill the conditions stipulated in the bond, the manufacturer should apply to the Nigerian Customs Service through the approved guarantor for an extension of the bond, particularly when the life of the bond has expired. The extension of the bond shall not exceed three months.
- Repatriation of foreign exchange realized from transactions will be confirmed by the Central Bank of Nigeria before the bond is discharged.
- A single good declaration form C.2010, marked "manufacture-in-bond scheme," must be used for the clearance of goods under the scheme.

Administration of the MIBS involves a committee comprising representatives of the Ministry of Finance, Nigerian Customs Service, Nigerian Export Promotion Council, the Standards Organization of Nigeria, and the Central Bank of Nigeria. A quarterly report of the MIBS is provided for committee monitoring and review. Other significant administrative features of the program are as follows:

- In the event of default by the manufacturer, the Nigerian Customs Service will redeem the bond by calling on the guarantor to pay the appropriate customs duties and associated charges.
- In the case of liquidation, the company may be allowed to sell the goods in the local market with the approval of the Minister of Finance on the condition that appropriate customs duties and other associated charges will be paid.
- A manufacturer participating in the MIBS is expected to designate a warehouse or storage area in the factory premises for the storage of inputs and finished goods.
- Clean report of inspection Form M and other relevant documents for this scheme will be clearly marked "MIBS."

The Pioneer Tax Program provides tax holidays on corporate income to manufacturing exporters that export at least 50 percent of their turnover. The scheme is designed to encourage the establishment of export-oriented industries in Nigeria. It extends over a period of up to five years, and the benefits can be drawn down in consecutive years or up to five times over a longer time frame depending on the annual evaluation of the company by the Nigerian Export Promotion Commission and the Nigerian Investment Promotion Commission (NIPC). Pioneer status is granted by NIPC and administered by the tax authority, the Federal Inland Revenue Service (FIRS). Although the administering authority states that it recognizes NIPC's decisions on a company's pioneer status, it appears that an NIPC declaration is not always sufficient for an investor to receive a pioneer firm tax holiday. Additionally, a pioneer status award can require the involvement of the Ministry of Finance, the Ministry of Commerce, and the Joint Tax Board located in FIRS.

Eligibility criteria and terms and conditions for the application to the Pioneer Tax Program include the following:

- Applicant must be a manufacturing company that exports at least 50 percent of its turnover.

- Applications must be submitted to the NEPC, along with information on the total volumes/values of production and exports over a period of three years.
- Applicant must submit annual statements of accounts and copies of form NXP.

In addition to these eligibility criteria, the pioneer status award also has discretionary features that can discourage investors. For instance, the five-year tax holiday is available not only to industries that produce products declared to be "pioneer products" (a long list),[5] but also to such "other deserving enterprises, as may be approved by NIPC." Moreover, it seems that incentives are awarded only after an investor has made a major commitment to a project. For instance, the investor is required to prove acquisition of land and importation of capital goods before confirmation of pioneer status. This could significantly limit the extent to which the program provides an incentive to invest. To have an incentive effect, pioneer status should be awarded prior to investment with suitable caveats confirming the investment before the benefits can be drawn down.

Current Information on Extent and Impact of Export and Trade Incentive Programs

What is the current evidence on the impact of these different programs? Unfortunately, data are incomplete and difficult to obtain, reflecting capacity and systems constraints that hinder the efforts of Ministry of Commerce and Industry staff to collect and collate key indicator data. This is particularly true with respect to the EEG, the duty drawback scheme, and MIBS. In the case of EEG, it is clear that the program was viewed as a key revenue source for the survival of the remaining textile firms assessed during a World Bank Value Chain exercise in 2005 (Consilium International 2005), and its suspension that year hit those remaining textile firms hard. This being said, there were other international market fundamentals moving against a Nigerian textile industry. Poor infrastructure and financing, skills and labor practice constraints, and competition from China arguably made the deployment of the EEG purely a short-term palliative in support of the industry. It offered no longer-term access to greater competitiveness.

In the case of the Pioneer Tax Program, there is some modest information available on its scope and impact to date. This information is set out below in table 4.2 and figure 4.1. A total of 94 firms were awarded pioneer status between 2004 and mid-2008. On the basis of

Table 4.2   Pioneer Status Awards and Employment Numbers Involved

Year	No pioneer awards	Employment level
2004	24	7,243
2005	13	5,587
2006	15	5,917
2007	24	11,576
2008	18	2,355
Total	94	32,688

Source: Babalola 2008, based on Nigerian Investment Promotion Commission data.

Figure 4.1   Pioneer Program, Recipient Company Employment Levels by Year

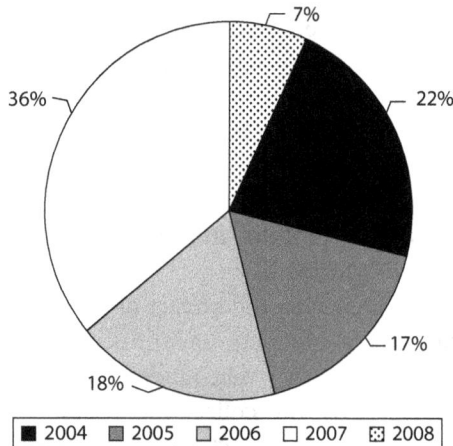

Source: Babalola 2008, based on Nigerian Investment Promotion Commission data.
Note: Percentages represent number of employees attributable to Pioneer Program.

the information provided by the firms, the program generated a total of 32,688 jobs. The high point years to date—in terms of both the number of awards and the employment levels involved—were 2006 and 2007, which were also the two fastest growing years on recent record for the non-oil economy in Nigeria. However, there is no information available to complete any sort of cost-benefit analysis. Efforts to collect key data on staffing levels and on the level of effort required by government and enterprises to prepare and process, and thereafter to implement and monitor the program, were unsuccessful. Moreover, it is unclear—given that the pioneer status is only awarded ex post, based on proof that the investor has made certain business decisions—whether the Pioneer Program can, in fact, lay claim to any resultant investment or employment outcomes.

More generally, with regard to the tax structure for business, the World Bank Group, through its Foreign Investment Advisory Service, has prepared two reports looking at tax and other industry incentives in Nigeria. The first report was entitled "Nigeria—Joining the Race for Non-Oil Investment" (FIAS 2000). The second report, "Sector Study of Effective Tax Burden" (FIAS 2008a) looked at the overall marginal effective rate of taxation across different sectors of the economy (a summary of the findings and recommendations of that report are included in Appendix D). Both reports highlight the generally complex and inefficient structure of the taxation and incentives, which militates against the overall policy objective of providing a supportive tax environment for business. While the net burden of taxation is internationally competitive, this benefit dissipates as a result of the limited implementation capacity and myriad of exceptions and special incentives designed to favor particular groups or industries.[6] The net effect is a government that struggles to provide an overall enabling environment and finds it difficult to successfully target benefits or incentives.

Free Trade Zones

Under the Nigeria Export Processing Zones (NEPZA) Authority Decree of 1992, Nigeria established 17 special zones, the first of which was Calabar and the most recent is Tinapa (see Ndibe 2007). These special zones are a combination of FTZs and export processing zones—some with industry specialization, such as the Onne Oil and Gas Free Trade Zone and the Lagos Deep Offshore Logistics Support Services. Export processing zones are purpose-built facilities, geographically delineated, locally administered, and geographically eligible for benefits. FTZs are small areas designed to support trade, typically with restricted entry of the quantity of goods allowed into the domestic market. These separate customs areas are typically duty-free and low-tax areas, with simplified customs procedures conducted by the Nigerian Customs Service at the perimeter of the zone (box 4.2).

In 2005, following an internal review undertaken by NEPZA, a presidential committee made recommendations for reform, including conditions under which banned goods could be imported from an export processing zone (EPZ) into the customs area, better minimum infrastructure platforms, and improved administrative arrangements

Box 4.2

Administrative Process for Entering an Export Processing Zone

Step 1.   An application form is obtained online from the administration of the free zone where investors wish to locate or from the NEPZA office in Abuja. The nonrefundable application fee is ₦50,000, or about US$380.

Step 2.   The application is submitted to the zone administration or the NEPZA office in Abuja along with required feasibility study. Applications are reviewed and either approved or returned with observations within five working days.

Step 3.   If the application is approved, the required operating license can be obtained from the free zone administration. As soon as the operating license is obtained, the firm is officially incorporated and no additional paperwork is required. At this point, the zone administration will assign an onsite location to the firm.

Step 4.   Investors are to remit investment capital through banks located in the zone, which will, in turn, provide them with a certificate of capital importation.

Step 5.   Investors are to prepare the building or warehouse space. Those constructing their own buildings must submit four copies of full architectural drawings, compliant with established building codes, for approval by the free zone administration. Built-up area should not exceed 70 percent of the leased land, and construction should start within three months after execution of the agreement.

Step 6.   Some companies/investors may be required to follow additional procedures, such as obtaining permission to hire foreign nationals, which can be done at immigration offices within the zone.

Source: Babalola 2008.

across principal government agencies (one-stop shop facilities). Additional legislation to loosen EPZ restrictions has been prepared in line with the recommendations, but to date, this legislation has not been enacted. The new legislation would allow for the sale of 100 percent of production into the customs zone compared to the 25 percent permissible under current legislation (section 18.1 of the Customs Act of 1992).

A preliminary agreement has reportedly been reached among the Ministry of Finance, the Ministry of Commerce, and the National Customs Service to allow goods up to a total value of US$10,000 per quarter to be sold at retail shops in Tinapa and Calabar (contrary to section 14.1 of the current Act), free of duty for non-commercial use in the Federation of Nigeria by individual customers. This agreement could represent an innovative approach to modernizing and broadening of the local economic impact of these free zone facilities. However, controls would need to be in place to ensure compliance with this exceptional arrangement. Such controls may be difficult to implement over the short term in view of capacity constraints in the administration.

To better understand the current state of these different EPZs, site visit assessments were undertaken to the EPZs in Lagos and Osun states (all under construction) and Cross River (operational). Additional EPZs planned for Kano and Abuja, which are also under construction, were not visited. The findings are summarized below.

Lagos free zones. There are six FTZs in Lagos State (table 4.3). The Lekki FTZ, covering a total area of approximately 16,500 hectares, commenced construction and site preparation in 2002. It is a public-private partnership (PPP) initiative of the Lagos State Government; Lekki Worldwide Investment Ltd., a private company incorporated March 2006 to promote and manage the development of the Lekki FTZ; and CCECC-Beyond International (a consortium of Chinese investors and Nanjing FTZ). There are currently 35 investors in the LFZTZ that have signed an investment agreement. The signatories include furniture and shoe manufacturers, a motorcycle assembly plant, a plastic products and packaging plant, palm oil processors, an independent power producer (IPP), and a number of companies that will be providing petroleum product services, including storage. Current development in and around the zone includes road construction, an integrated electronic security and traffic control system, alternative power supply (gas, solar, and wind turbine), and a refuse management system. An information and communication technology

Table 4.3   Lagos Free Trade Zones

Name	Description/sector	Status	Ownership (%)
Airline Services EPZ		Operational	Private (100)
Ladol Logistics	Oil and gas	Operational	Private (100)
Lagos FTZ	Oil and non-oil	Under construction	Private (100)
Lekki FTZ	Oil and non-oil	Under construction	State (40) FDI[a] (60)
OILSS Logistics	Oil and gas	Declaration	Private (100)
Snake Island Integrated	Oil and gas	Operational	Private (100)

Source: Babalola 2008.
a. Consortium of five state-owned Chinese companies.

(ICT) project is also under design. While there are not yet any structures in place, the plan is for the Lagos Free Trade Zone (LFTZ) to be split into zones ranging from an oil and gas logistics park to a light and heavy industrial and manufacturing zone, a media center, and an urban/residential zone.

Information on the entirely private sector–owned Lagos FTZ is not readily available. The facility is expected to span approximately 200 hectares, and currently there are three investors on site (Insignia Packaging Company, a vehicle assembly factory, and a body-building company).

Both the Lekki and Lagos FTZs are located within the corridors of Lekki, which is one of the fastest growing areas of Lagos, comprising middle–class residential living, the Chevron headquarters, the Enterprise Development Centre of the Lagos Business School, and growing retail facilities. Beyond what is already in place in terms of businesses locating to these zones, targeted sectors include manufacturing (home and electronic appliances), textiles, light industries, agriculture and by-product processing, oil and gas, automobile components, transportation and logistics, and research and development for science and technology.

Cross River: Calabar Free Trade Zone. This is the first and most functional FTZ. It was established in 1992 in Calabar, the capital of Cross River State, in the southeast of the country. It has the capacity to accommodate between 80 and 100 industrial firms. About 80 investors have received licenses to operate in the zone, comprising 26 manufacturing, 17 oil and gas, 10 service provider, and 6 trading companies. Thirty-four have commenced production and exportation of goods and services. In order to cope with potential growth of investor demand to be part of the zone, the Cross River State government has granted an additional 63 hectares of land for further development and expansion. Facilities available in this zone include a free port, which has an estimated annual capacity of 1.5 million metric tons of cargo; serviced plots; and one-stop business procedures covering licenses and customs services.

Osun State—Oshogbo Living Spring Free Trade Zone. One of the new Special Economic Zone (SEZ) initiatives currently under development through a PPP is in Osun State, where the state government has, for the past three years, been working with a Chinese firm and a local Nigerian company on the development of the Oshogbo Living Spring Free Trade Zone (OLFTZ) and Industrial Park Project. The state government and the Industrial Development Group—a company with offices in Miami and Lagos—set up Riverbanks Trade and Investment Ltd. (a PPP/special purpose vehicle) to develop the project in Oshogbo, the state capital.

Osun State is rich in agriculture, and the SEZ is intended to provide basic infrastructure and production services to foster agroprocessing and other activities, including processing of (a) local cassava, used to produce commercial quantities of industrial-grade starch, baking flour, pellets, animal feed, and cassava-plantain chips; and (b) tropical fruits, used to produce a wide variety of juice concentrates and pulp, fresh fruit juice, and tomato pastes. The state is also looking at other manufacturing sectors that can attract private investment. Key benefits of the initiative are expected to include 6,000 direct and indirect jobs.

The OLFTZ is currently in its first phase of development, involving the construction of ten hectares principally for manufacturing activities, including the production of licensed generic pharmaceutical medications, intravenous solutions and oral rehydration products, and aluminum roofing sheets for construction. This phase of the OLFTZ, at an estimated cost of US$63.7 million, is currently being completed. There are two subsequent phases planned. On completion, the facility is expected to span about 1,200 hectares of land.

It is too early in the development of this initiative to assess its economic benefits. However, the upstream public-private sector collaboration it entails, and the targeted character of the industrial development that it seeks to support, do capture some of the key elements of successful government-supported, market-based industrial development. For this initiative to be successful in practice, the challenge will be to ensure that the public investment does not end up underwriting all the commercial risks and undermining the private sector's incentive to properly assess commercial feasibility and deliver market-determined outcomes. It is in attempting to achieve this balance that public sector support to industrial development so often fails, leading to unsustainable initiatives that drain the public purse.

Current Information on Extent and Impact of the Free Export Zones Policy

Free zones can boost national and subnational economic performance through job creation, foreign direct investment, exports, technology transfer, and regional development. Notwithstanding this promise, a recent report by the World Bank's Foreign Investment Advisory Service (World Bank 2008b) finds that the experience of free zones in Africa has been mixed. This can be attributed to a range of factors including uncompetitive policies, rigid regulations for investors, poor labor policies and labor relations, lack of incentives for private zone development, poor maintenance of zone infrastructure, low net exports due to low local value-added, and limited forward and backward links.

These findings hold true anecdotally for Nigeria, although there has not been a systematic review of performance and results. In the case of the Calabar Zone,[7] the principal benefit was to have been employment, but customs restrictions have inhibited the growth of industries in the zone. Interviews suggest that this problem has been experienced in many of the EPZs in Nigeria, where coordination between NEPZA and the Customs Authority has considerable room for improvement.

Any analysis of this problem is constrained by the absence of a core information set on EPZ economic performance in Nigeria,[8] as well as by lack of data from the individual EPZs. In the case of the yet-to-commence FTZ operations in Lagos, there is no track record. In the case of Calabar, information on firm turnover, investment, and export levels is unavailable. The operating firms reported employment figures (table 4.4).

The available information provided by the zone management suggests that, after being in operation for more than 17 years, the total labor force in the zone amounts to approximately 1,200 across 36 firms. This is equivalent to an average of 40 employees per firm—essentially a small enterprise operation, although most of the firms operating in the zone have a labor complement well below this average figure. In addition to this apparent inability of firms to grow to any significant scale since the inception of the EPZ, there is also a dearth of other potential benefits from being located in the EPZ. The local Calabar Chamber of Commerce expressed its frustration at the lack of links with zone-based firms.

Table 4.4   Employment Level of Operating Enterprises in Calabar FTZ

Sector (number of firms)	Employment level (number of staff)
Manufacturing (11)	742
Stone processing (1)	72
Assembling (2)	55
Wood processing (2)	49
Trading (6)	10
Oil and gas (4)	88
Service providers (10)	140
Total (36)	1156

Source: Babalola 2008.

Rather than providing potential business, the ability of EPZ firms to sell into the domestic market was resulting in additional competition with local businesses in terms of both labor and product markets. This suggests that if economic benefits are to be more effectively captured from EPZ arrangements, much greater attention will need to be paid—in addition to EPZ management performance—to the need to augment domestic supply-chain links and the local economic development impact of the industries operating in the zones.

The Bank of Industry

The Bank of Industry (BOI) was established in October 2001 out of the reconstruction of the Nigerian Industrial Development Bank, the Nigerian Bank for Commerce and Industry, and the National Economic Reconstruction Fund. Its authorized capital share is US$400 million and shareholders include the Ministry of Finance (59.4 percent), the Central Bank (40.36 percent), and 42 private shareholders. The Bank's current share capital stands at naira 6.6 billion (approximately US$57.5 million). The BOI provides a range of financial and nonfinancial services, including short-, medium-, and long-term lending, equity and lease financing and cofinancing, and syndication. The following sectors are accorded priority: (a) agro-industries, textiles, and leather; (b) polymer-based industries; (c) solid minerals; (d) local content initiatives in tele-com, oil, and gas; and (e) ICT services. Important targeted criteria for support include: (a) high local content; (b) SMEs and projects with strong backward or forward links or both; (c) high job creation potential; and (d) projects and businesses promoted by women.

In the period from January to June 2007, BOI made 73 investments amounting to   7.4 billion (approximately US$63 million); this repre-sented a 96.8 percent increase in value over 2006. Fifty-nine percent of the investment value went to SMEs and the balance to larger firms. The cumulative loan portfolio stands at   29.02 billion (approximately US$250 million), with an employment generation target of 403,000 direct and indirect jobs. Portfolio at risk was assessed at 12.5 percent, represent-ing further improvement on progress made in 2006. Profit before taxes increased by 55.7 percent over 2006, to   794.6 million. In 2006, BOI supported some 181 firms and 50 cooperatives with term finance. A more detailed portfolio breakdown is in Appendix E.

There has been significant progress in reforming this institution since its restructuring in the earlier part of the decade. Despite the interest cap of 10 percent and a nonperforming loan rate of 12 percent, BOI has a relatively modest overhead (120 permanent staff) and achieved a profit of   1.3 billion in 2006.

Review of Investment Climate Assessment Data on Economic Zones and Industrial Policy

The 2008 Investment Climate Enterprise Survey (World Bank 2008a) involved a firm sample of 2,300. Of these firms, only five self-identified as using fiscal and other government incentives.[9] More than 900 simply skipped the question. Data on firms in special export zones are more extensive. Differentiating the firm data according to whether firms used industrial policy benefits (an industrial policy "taker" or "receiver") versus those that did not (industrial policy "decliner"), and whether they operated inside a SEZ ("in-zone") or not ("out-of-zone"), provides for the following story of capital intensity and productivity performance, as detailed in figures 4.2 and 4.3.

Figure 4.2 shows that in-zone firms have overall higher capital/labor (K/L) ratios, as portrayed in the capital intensity bar chart measures (refer to the yellow and light blue bars in the table) and value-added per worker. Wage levels are more varied across the different categories of firms, with out-of-zone receivers of policy incentives and in-zone decliners enjoying

Figure 4.2   Productivity Measures for In-Zone and Out-of-Zone Enterprises

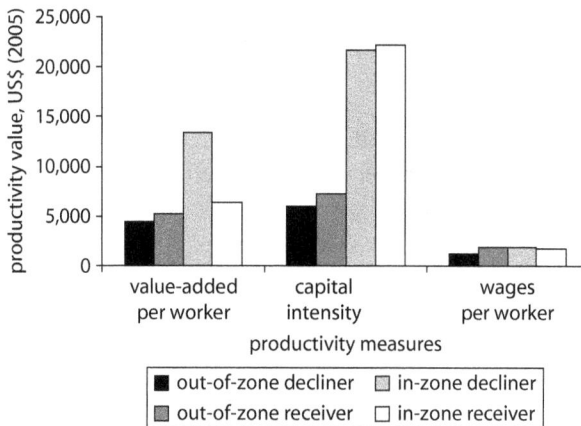

Source: World Bank 2008a.
Note: Capital intensity = capital/labor (K/L) ratio.

Figure 4.3   Enterprise Wages to Value-Added, Locational, and Policy Variants

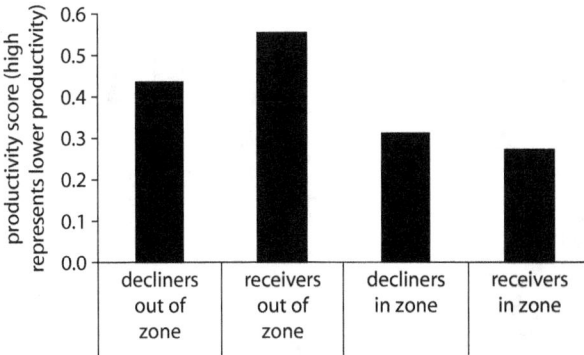

Source: World Bank 2008a.
Note: Wages to value-added are unit labor costs.

higher wages per worker. In terms of the value-added/wage level ratio, how-ever, as shown in figure 4.3, the highest productivity score is for in-zone receivers and decliners. The worst productivity score is for out-of-zone receivers, and the best performance is for in-zone receivers of policy incentives. This suggests that firms operating within zones tend to be more productive overall.

Figures 4.4. and 4.5 look in more detail at productivity performance. The scatter diagrams of firms' technical efficiency show that those firms that are accessing government incentives (takers) have no particular clustering of characteristics. The technical efficiency measure captures a range of key economic variables that influence firm performance, including value-added, capital, labor, size, locality, and industry dummies weighted by the sample weights. In figure 4.4, enterprises that are incentive takers are clustered around the median in the region where the majority of firms can be found, although four out of the five observations fall below the median technical-efficiency line. This suggests that the firms drawing down these incentive options are not particularly dynamic, although it is not possible to determine from these data the extent to which the incentives may have improved their firm's technical efficiency beyond what they would have achieved in the absence of the incentives.

Information on firms operating within different zones is more comprehensive. Figure 4.5 suggests that a significant number of the more productive firms are operating from within a SEZ. In fact, of the 34 firms operating in the top right-hand quadrant, 19 are based in zones.

Figure 4.4   Firm Technical Efficiency: Incentive Takers and Incentive Decliners

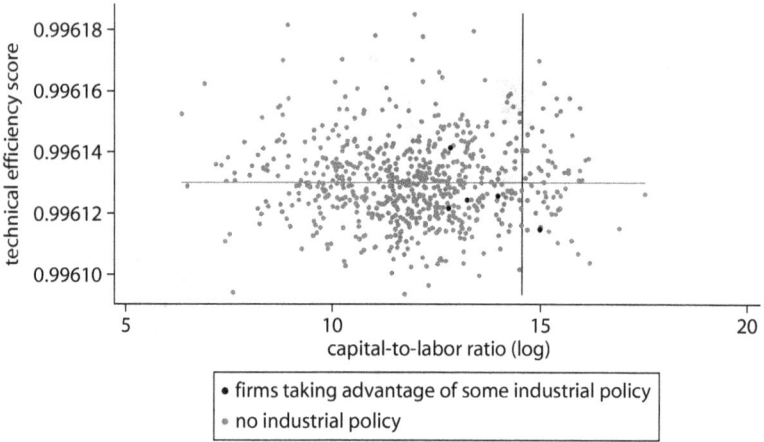

Source: World Bank 2008a.
Note: The technical efficiency score is a rating calculated from the estimation of total factor productivity (TFP). The TFP comes from a frontier regression on capital, labor, and several firm characteristic controls (size, locality, and several interactions). The scatter-plot chart captures the notion that a small firm may be very efficient even if its capital holdings and labor force are small. The converse is also true: big companies may be technically ineffi-cient. The chart has four quadrants formed by the median capital intensity and median technical inefficiency.

Figure 4.5   Firm Technical Efficiency, Inside and Outside Special Economic Zone

Source: World Bank 2008a.
Note: See note for figure 4.4.

Further evidence of this can be found in table 4.5, which shows that across all sectors, firms within zones have stronger productivity performance and wage levels than firms outside the zones. The most striking case is that of the electronics industry, where the survey sam-ple revealed a ten-fold difference between the wage/value-added ratios

Table 4.5   Productivity Measures Within and Outside of Zones, by Industry

Industry	Zone	VA per worker	Capital intensity	Wages per worker	Wages to VA
Agro	In-zone	9,855.77	25,407.38	1,825.18	0.32
Agro	Out-of-zone	4,653.43	9,058.02	1,214.39	0.42
Chem	In-zone	12,327.43	25,143.73	1,920.15	0.28
Chem	Out-of-zone	5,007.16	10,944.61	1,596.17	0.44
Electronics	In-zone	71,429.42	58,226.85	2,498.12	0.05
Electronics	Out-of-zone	6,323.02	4,727.44	1,705.18	0.53
Garments	In-zone	4,276.88	5,712.47	1,313.53	0.36
Garments	Out-of-zone	3,007.42	4,108.12	1,101.85	0.46
Machines	In-zone	17,540.90	31,327.21	6,020.49	0.62
Machines	Out-of-one	14,254.28	6,032.41	3,502.63	0.34
Minerals	In-zone	19,491.96	58,631.52	2,881.74	0.19
Minerals	Out-of-zone	8,648.34	4,803.56	2,052.27	0.34
Other manuf	In-zone	10,380.59	24,869.79	2,058.06	0.27
Other manuf	Out-of-zone	5,004.50	5,030.46	1,192.86	0.46
Textiles	In-zone	5,211.74	9,490.65	2,716.85	0.62
Textiles	Out-of-zone	4,938.99	4,294.83	1,514.89	0.58

Source: World Bank 2008a.
Note: VA = value-added.

for firms operating in and outside the zones. On the other hand, firms that self-identified as receiving industrial or fiscal policy benefits from the federal government—albeit a very minimal number—had average ratios of wage to value-added marginally below those that opted not to take up industrial policy benefits (0.417 versus 0.441).

Looking beyond Nigeria at the productivity differentials in other countries between in-zone and out-of-zone firms and those that are policy takers and decliners, the story is quite variable. In South Africa, firms outside zones were generally more productive than those inside zones. In Thailand, firms accessing industry policy products had better wage/value-added ratios than those that did not use these policy products. Some of the key explanations behind these differential results are detailed in the following paragraphs.

Turning from productivity measures to investment climate, to what extent does a firm's status in or outside a zone impact its perceptions of investment climate constraints? In the case of Nigeria, the same priority constraints affecting the firm in the domestic market also rank highest for those in a zone. This is quite consistent across all the industrial sectors, as shown in figure 4.6. The following table ranks the 16 key constraints identified in the enterprise survey (World Bank 2008a),

Figure 4.6   Nigeria In-Zone Perceptions of Key Investment Climate Constraints

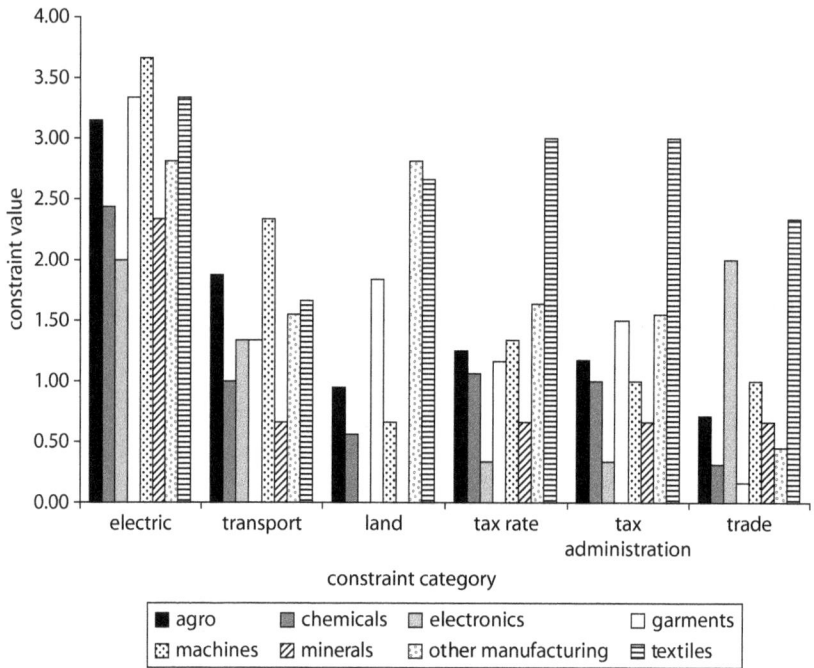

Source: World Bank 2008a.
Note: Constraint value: Zero (no obstacle), 1 (minor obstacle), 2 (moderate obstacle), 3 (major obstacle), 4 (very severe obstacle).

including corruption, credit, crime, electricity, interest, labor, legal, land, macro-economy, monopoly, regulation, tax administration, tax rate, ICT, trade, and transport.

Figure 4.6 shows that power is the main concern for in-zone firms, particularly for those in the machinery, garments and textiles, and agro-business sectors. This is as expected, since these production processes are highly dependent on sustained and predictable power sources. Conversely, the electronics industry is most concerned with trade obstacles, which are ranked equally with power supply. What this suggests is that, despite the efforts of the Nigerian government to provide islands of greater infrastructure efficiencies within zones, the same investment climate constraints persist in inhibiting industries both inside and outside of zones. Across comparator countries, a different picture emerges. For instance, in South Africa—which, across the board, attributes lower weights to investment constraints—crime is one of the top concerns, although this constraint is consistently ranked lower by firms operating within a zone.

Looking more generally at the comparative stories revealed by the data for firms inside and outside zones across the 16 key investment climate constraints in Nigeria, Kenya, South Africa, and Thailand, firms inside a zone in Kenya and Thailand consistently ranked constraints higher than those outside a zone. The converse was true for South Africa and Nigeria. There is no clear explanation for these different results across countries, although they do tend to suggest that locating operations within a zone is, at best, a partial panacea for investment climate obstacles. These results may also reflect an adverse selection problem; that is, that firms in zones tend to be those that are better run, have better-educated managers and employees, and have higher expectations of a good investment climate, and so are more vocal when these services are not sufficiently forthcoming.

Breaking down the data further by firm size, the larger in-zone firms in Kenya rank investment constraints the highest, but it is the small firms that are most impacted by these constraints in Nigeria. What this suggests—consistent with the broader analysis of the investment climate in Nigeria—is that the larger firms in Nigeria relative to both Kenya and South Africa have tended to greater internalization of investment climate costs. As a result, these larger firms do not place such a high priority on these constraints, viewing them as fixed costs of doing business.

Industrial Policy—Current Challenges and Successes

What can be said, in summary, about the current industrial policy framework in Nigeria? The analysis provided above, while not definitive due to data limitations, highlights the following:

- *Uptake.* There is a lack of uptake of these services by the private sector. The outreach to firms from the different policies and programs is overall quite limited, as evidenced by the fact that only a total of 94 firms accessed the Pioneer Program over the past four years; and only about 180 sought BOI loans in 2006. In the case of the export zones, after some 15 years, very few outside of the oil and gas sector are active. The exception is Calabar, which nevertheless has only 36 firms in operation.

- *Economic impact.* There is very little evidence that these policies and programs have had significant economic outcomes, whether measured in terms of employment, revenues, foreign exchange, or technology transfer.

- *Adverse selection.* The extent to which a positive impact of these policies and programs can be ascertained must be balanced by a consideration of the extent to which the firms that access the services, particularly the EPZ opportunities, tend to be those with better management performance, higher capital-labor ratios, and modestly better productivity. In other words, these firms are likely to have been successful and pursued their investment and business strategies irrespective of the existence of the policies and programs provided.

- *Administrative and institutional capacity constraints.* Firms need to satisfy an extensive set of administrative requirements in order to access the incentive programs. Some of these requirements are susceptible to highly arbitrary decisions by officials. Additionally, in the case of some tax and trade benefits, there is, after submission of the relevant application, a hierarchy of decisionmaking, including interdepartmental committee reviews that add complexity, time, and uncertainty to the process. If lack of administrative capacity is the source of the problem, then improved administrative efficiencies, greater simplicity, predictability, and transparency in processes could make a significant difference.

- *Policy efficiency and relevance.* Conversely, if the priority issues highlighted in the investment climate survey (World Bank 2008a)—including infrastructure, access to finance, and the Doing Business issues, particularly land usage, transfer and registration, and overall tax simplification—are given more emphasis, then a different set of policy and program actions needs to be considered. These actions need to be based on what is most relevant, feasible, and cost effective, and what will have the greatest near- and medium-term benefits. More recent economic zone initiatives, such as the Lekki Free Trade Zone, have sought to address these infrastructure and business constraints rather than trying to provide fiscal and other tax incentives.

Some Industrial Success Stories

Whereas the picture drawn of special economic and enterprise incentive policies and programs does not suggest that they promote better performance, there are some significant success stories elsewhere in Nigeria and internationally. This section seeks to draw out the factors underlying good performance, with a view to framing more effective enterprise development options for the future. Consider first some stories of cluster development in Nigeria, particularly the automobile component industry at Onitsha in Anambra and the computer village in Otigba in Lagos.[10]

The Nnewi automotive cluster, based in Anambra in Southeastern Nigeria, is one of the most longstanding and durable in Nigeria. Building on core entrepreneurial capacities, and reinforced with a substantial apprenticeship program and technology transfer networks with Taiwan, China, the Nnewi cluster has managed to survive over a period reaching back to the 1980s, spanning some of the most difficult political and economic times that Nigeria has faced. The companies from the Nnewi cluster—many of which have been in operation for 10 to 20 years—have not relied on government programs and support.[11] Instead, the cluster has relied predominately on its own financial, technical, and entrepreneurial capacities. This includes investments made to develop key infrastructure services within the zone, as well as to extend the supply chains of companies in the cluster to Taiwan, China, particularly for spare parts and know-how.

Despite the common industry focus of the Nnewi firms (in contrast to the sector diversity of firms operating in government-sponsored SEZs)— which could provide the enabling conditions for agglomeration economies and cluster spillovers—there are relatively modest levels of inter-firm cooperation within the cluster, including outsourcing. The areas of greatest cooperation are in the sharing of skilled personnel and equipment, and in their defense against predatory government practices. This has arguably been one of the most important functions of the different business membership organizations operating in the cluster.

The Otigba Computer Village is a more recent development, dating back to 1995. It covers an area of some 325 square kilometers in Ikeja, Lagos, and provides, as Zhihua Zeng (2008) notes, for the "sale, service, and repair of IT products and components, particularly to the Lagos industrial base, led by the oil and financial sectors. Increasingly the Otigba cluster is meeting regional West African market demand with some 392 SMEs employing more than 3,000 workers." The cluster development has been characterized by significant inter-firm cooperation and joint action. As with the Nnewi cluster, this cooperation has been particularly noticeable in dealing with (municipal) government's treatment of the cluster; the Computer and Allied Products Association of Nigeria (CAPDAN) has been very active in this regard. This has resulted in a supportive municipal government that has, for instance, facilitated property access, rental, and licensing and refrained from heavy-handed inspection and licensing practices. Other areas of significant cooperation relate to technology and market support, security, and infrastructure maintenance.

A key factor at play in this cluster appears to be the relatively high educational level of the workforce and the fact that many of the skilled workers have ties with one another going back to their school or college. This has contributed to a high level of commercial trust among the firms, as reflected, inter alia, in the appetite for the provision of supplier credits among firms in the cluster, as well as know-how exchange and joint warehousing. Given the cluster's dependence on imported inputs (63.5 percent), the quality of trade facilitation services is an important determinant of cluster competitiveness. Government policy in support of the industry includes the standard package of duty rebate and tax holidays. There is also a preferential public procurement policy in place that directs government ministries, departments, and agencies to source ICT products domestically.

The experiences of the Nnewi and Otigba clusters conform with a worldwide picture of well-performing clusters, the success of which is based on their capacity to exploit opportunities for market and intermediate input access, labor market pooling, technological spillovers, and joint actions. Additionally, the clusters have been enterprise led rather than government led, and "not part of a systemic plan or policy" (Zhihua Zeng 2008). This certainly characterizes the Nigeria success stories summarized above. Invariably, there are some core competences that lie at the heart of a successful cluster. In the two Nigeria examples, these competencies include access to key inputs (computer parts for Otigba and automotive parts for Nnewi), labor supply advantages (skilled IT cadre in Otigba and the apprenticeship program in Nnewi), and inter-firm cooperation covering a range of supply chain issues from access to finance and technology transfer to public-private dialogue around policy and program initiatives.

What is also striking is the extent to which the Nigerian SEZs have fallen short in some of these critical performance areas. For instance, the Calabar FTZ—the most successful of the government facilities— comprises a heterogeneous group of firms from different sectors. This pulls against the type of agglomeration and cooperation externalities that have proved so essential to the Otigba and Nnewi experiences. Public sector, supply-led initiatives are the least successful, but this does not mean there is not a significant role for the public sector. However, the extent to which this role can be taken up depends critically on government capacity—and not just in policy and program design and implementation, but also its capacity to contain the transaction costs that come with inter-departmental cooperation and to effectively collaborate with the private sector. What is equally important is the extent to which the successful cluster stories are dependent on private sector capacity for entrepreneur-ship, and this entrepreneurship finds ways to overcome the different product and factor market failures highlighted in the investment climate survey (World Bank 2008a). The durability of enterprises in the face of these constraints (and related policy errors and implementation ineffi-ciencies), and their ability to sustain effective business-to-business coop-eration within value chains and clusters, are hallmarks of the Nigerian private sector. Some of the basic rules and best practices for channeling government support in line with its capacities, and promoting private sec-tor firms in line with theirs, are set out in box 4.3.

Existing Nigeria industry policy falls short against many of the guide-lines set out in box 4.3. In the first place, effective coordination across gov-ernment agencies is weak. A significant number of public institutions are

---

Box 4.3

Some Policy Principles for Effective Enterprise and Industry Development

I. Targeting Sectors: Crowding In, Not Picking Winners

- Industrial policy has tried to pick winners; disappointing results usually attribut-able to *information asymmetries* and *perverse incentives*, given the rent-seeking potential made possible by the role of the government.

- There has been a range of market failures due to incompleteness of information, coordination failures, negative externalities (for example, information spillovers and pollution). But it is sometimes difficult to effectively isolate or understand these failures, which inhibits solution design. The two most recurrent problems are *coordination failures and information spillovers:*

  a. *Coordination failure* occurs where markets are incomplete, so return on one investment depends on whether another investment is made (guarantees are often the instrument of choice in this instance). Often the dependencies of one market (for example, real estate) on others are very specific (insurance, titling, legal advice, and so forth), and the institutional requirements are both highly specialized and very different from those in other markets.

(continued)

Box 4.3 *(continued)*

  b. *Spillover effects* include the self-discovery process of finding out the cost structure of an economy for the production of new goods. The incentive for the entrepreneur is weak because if the initiative is profitable, others enter the market and squeeze the profit. If not, then the entrepreneur bears the full cost. Another spillover issue is investment in training, where the social rate of return is greater than the return to the enterprise.

II. Building on Industry Know-How: Demand Rather than Supply Driven

- The policy challenge is to effectively enter into a *discovery process* wherein high-potential firms and governments learn about underlying costs and engage in strategic coordination.
- To the extent possible, build on or exploit existing capabilities. *The market on its own will only jump short distances*. The best first option for short- or medium-term outcomes is to build and innovate within existing firm concentrations and business or industry clusters, where there are similar and requisite services or capabilities and exploitable scale and agglomeration economies.
- If activities are already in place or can be built upon rather than created, it is much easier to work out coordination failures and accumulate the specific capabilities required.
- A key constraint to productivity growth is not a particular *supply-side phenomenon* (for example, technology), but rather *lack of demand* caused by entrepreneurs' perception that activities are low profit or that profit is not "appropriable" (World Bank 2007a).

III. Structuring Public-Private Partnerships for Enterprise Growth

- *Open architecture:* Government should not predetermine sectors and activities for partnership; partnership building is endogenous and develops out of the process.
- *Self-organization:* Encourage groups to organize themselves according to some predetermined criteria and therefore according to some common needs that are not narrowly self-interested (for example, infrastructure rather than tax holidays).
- *Transparency:* Perform independent evaluations of requests made of government by the private sector.
- *Accountability:*
  a. Clear benchmarks for success and failure
  b. Built-in sunset clauses linked to ex ante definition of success or failure
  c. Subsidized activities with clear potential for providing spillover and demonstration effects

Sources: Hausmann and Rodrik 2006; Rodrik 2004.

currently active in the delivery of industrial policy. Key ministries include the Federal Ministry of Finance and the Federal Ministry of Commerce, Industry, and Trade. The key agencies involved include the FIRS, NIPC, the Corporate Affairs Commission (CAC), NEPZA and the separate EPZs themselves, NEPC, and NCS. While there has been recent progress in cooperation among NIPC, CAC, and FIRS,[12] such cooperation needs to be broadened to cover the wider array of incentive programs involving NCS, NEPZ, and NEPC if overall government effectiveness in supporting enterprise growth is to be improved. Further, these government agencies would need to commit to simplifying administrative procedures and programs. There is also a potentially significant e-government program opportunity, but for this to be successful, the interdepartmental commitment to cooperate closely would need to be clearly and resolutely in place.

In the case of spillover effects, the available evidence from the current generation of EPZs suggests that such effects are very limited across resident firms—thus reducing the likelihood that they will result in important economic agglomeration and cross-industry learning benefits. This is not surprising, given the supply-side approach underlying this policy and the fact that there are limited incentives for cooperation, since most of the firms are driven to locate solely to access government incentives and other benefits. Most significantly, self-discovery processes are all too often undermined by this incentive environment, with firms looking to have commercial risk transferred to the public sector rather than seeing the government policies as a means to improve their capacity to manage risk—thereby diminishing the prospects for productivity improvements.

Turning next to the public-private dimension of coordination, the current weak government institutions, combined with a public sector–driver approach and insufficient transparency regarding the costs and outcomes of industrial policy, further weaken public sector accountability for performance. Successful coordination, which lies at the heart of effective PPP, requires responsiveness to private sector drivers, complemented by market information exchange with the private sector and robust monitoring and performance assessment. Without these features at the forefront, it is not possible for policy makers to consult effectively with the private sector or to arrive at informed assessments of performance and priority areas for policy and program reforms.

Establishing the enabling conditions for robust enterprise cost discovery remains a primary role of government. The *Nigeria Competitiveness and Growth—Country Economic Memorandum* (World Bank 2007a) identified a wide range of key government actions to be taken at the macro and sectoral levels that would foster self-discovery. Sound macroeconomic management must provide the interest and exchange rate climate conducive to private sector investment. This does not need to involve, for example, an exchange rate strategy targeting export growth (which would be particularly difficult in an oil-exporting country such as Nigeria), but these economy-wide prices need to be managed with a view to their impact on key costs within priority value chains. Infrastructure is another major determinant for the sustainability of vibrant cost discovery processes. Special export zones clearly have a role in providing lower cost and stable infrastructure services to targeted sectors or spatial areas, but cannot correct for high-cost distortions deriving from fundamental structural failures in the sector. Additionally, trade policy must facilitate access to international markets and to the key inputs, technology transfer, and cost competitiveness opportunities that key industry sectors require for growth. These broader macroeconomic and trade policy issues are the focus of other chapters of this report.

Enterprise and Industry Diagnostics and Policy Selection

Industry Diagnostics

Beyond this, and in keeping with the industry-specific orientation of the present chapter, the next section will focus on more targeted approaches to fostering these enabling conditions at a subsector or value chain level, drawing on a three-staged approach to policy and program development that has been designed over the past two years.

Recent work undertaken to identify industry and enterprise development opportunities within Nigeria has followed a three-step process. The first step was a market and industry structure assessment of performance and potential in key subsectors. The second stage involved an in-depth breakdown of sources of value addition and causes of value subtraction in selected high-potential value chains that make up those subsectors. The final stage, which is currently being applied in selected value chains, is an assessment of the policy and reform strategy that may be considered to improve value chain performance.

The first stage (see Emerging Market Economics 2008) involved a broad assessment of 15 sectors that, based on consultations with key stakeholders, were considered to be principal economic sector drivers in four states representing the northern (Kano and Kaduna), Lagos, and eastern (Cross River) corridors of the country. The screening process for establishing this initial list of prospective sectors entailed an assessment of their contribution to non-oil growth over the past few years, combined with local stakeholder perceptions of industry potential. The first stage analysis was undertaken through detailed interviews with key actors within each of the 15 subsectors, complemented by additional analysis of state-level investment climates and GDP data provided through the work being done under the World Bank Group and DFID–Funded Investment Climate Program.[13] This exercise provided some key insights into areas for value chain improvement, as summarized in table 4.6, which also breaks down value chain weaknesses across the public and private sector domains for remedial interventions.

The next step in this process was to further rank these value chains, not in terms of current performance and constraints, but in terms of their development potential as determined against the following criteria: (a) capacity of the value chain to grow in terms of value-added, (b) potential employment creation capacity, (c) industry spillovers and then three feasibility criteria: (d) competitiveness, (e) prospective responsiveness to policy reform actions, and (f) private sector capacity to lead the value chain. This exercise culminated in the following prioritization of value chains, as depicted in figure 4.7.

Specifically, the following value chains, drawn from the upper two quadrants of figure 4.7, were identified as having particularly strong upside economic opportunities and greater feasibility for further progress over the short to medium term. Summarizing the analysis in terms of the aforementioned criteria:

- *Wholesale and retail.* The final prices of products that dominate the consumption basket of most Nigerians are significantly influenced by the performance of the wholesale and retail marketing chains in the country, with high food costs pushing Nigeria's cost of living well beyond that of comparator countries. Evidence indicates that this is the largest service sector in the country, accounting for some 20 percent of non-oil GDP and, at 15 percent, the largest source of employment for the population outside of agriculture. The sector is currently going through a transformation as modern-format retailing increasingly develops alongside traditional wholesale and retail modes. The full competitive and price advantages available through modern-format retailing are not yet available, since key aspects of its supply chain are either embryonic or not operational in Nigeria. The further development of these retail market structures offers significant upside potential for business growth and employment creation throughout the supply chain. Moreover, some key drivers—for example, market leaders such as

Table 4.6 Value Chains—Reform and Instrument Interventions Matrix

Value chains

Interventions	Light manufacturing	Construction	ICT	Tourism	Solid minerals	Wholesale and retail	Food processing	Leather	Dairy	Rice	Cocoa	Oil palm	Meat and poultry	Aquaculture	Calabar Port and EPZ
Public															
Policy reform/ regulation	●	●	●	●	●	●	●	●		●	●	●	●		●
Institutions	●	●	●	●		●	●	●	●	●	●	●	●	●	●
Infrastructure	●	●	●	●	●	●	●	●	●	●	●	●	●	●	●
Other public goods[a]	●	●	●	●					●	●	●		●	●	
Public/private															
Training	●	●	●	●		●	●	●	●	●	●		●	●	
Planning/coordination	●	●	●	●	●				●	●	●		●		
Business development/ support services	●	●	●	●	●										
Information systems	●	●	●	●		●	●	●	●	●	●		●	●	
Technology transfer	●	●				●	●	●	●	●	●		●	●	●
Private															
Supply chain logistics				●		●	●	●	●	●	●			●	
Market governance		●				●		●					●		
Access to finance	●	●	●	●	●	●	●	●	●	●	●	●	●	●	
Additionality[b]	3	3	2	4	1	3	4	1	4	3	3	3	3	3	2

Source: Emerging Market Economics 2008.
a. e.g., research. b. poor = 1, good = 4. EPZ = export processing zone.

Figure 4.7   Prioritization of Value Chains for Further Investigation

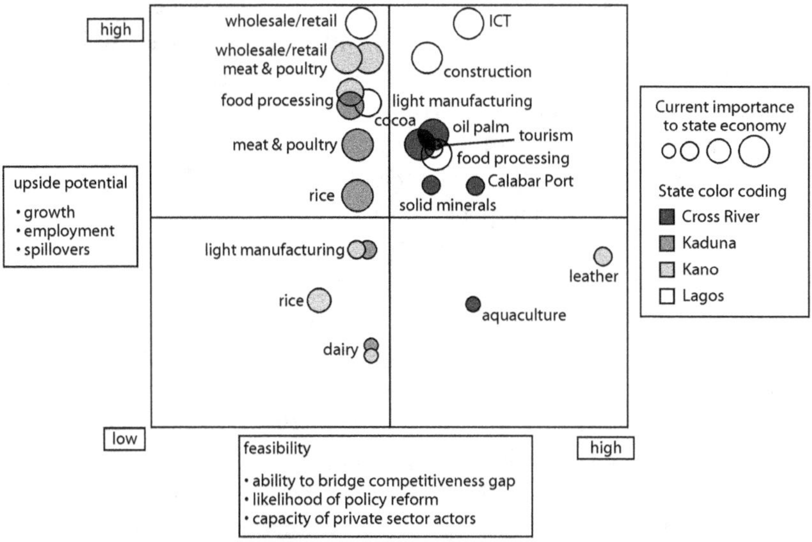

Source: Emerging Market Economics 2008.

Shoprite—are now investing in Nigeria and remain poised to extend their engagement as the enabling environment improves.

- *Information and communication technology.* The ICT sector contributed an estimated 2.4 percent of non-oil growth in 2006. It is, however, the fastest growing sector of the economy, with estimates of close to 35 percent growth per annum. Official 2005 data show employment in the sector at approximately 500,000, although this underestimates upstream and downstream employment opportunities created by the sector. Recent figures from the Nigerian Communications Commission estimate indirect job creation from the telecommunications revolution at one million. A further major change in the industry will occur once plans to connect the country to the international SAT-3 submarine cable system are completed. Other significant constraints that can feasibly be addressed include the quality supervision problems that remain throughout the value chain, particularly with cellular services. Additionally, there are major skills shortages and associated inflated salaries for qualified workers. These factors, in turn, inhibit efficient new technology absorption, adaption, and application. The potential spillovers up and down the value chain are substantial and also extend across value chains to those industries for which the ITC sector provides integral inputs. Government initiatives have real potential to boost the sector. In addition to improving service standards, programs such as Wire Nigeria and the State Accelerated Broadband Initiative are further contributing to industry expansion and fostering new business opportunities within a value chain that is increasingly competitive (90 internet service providers in 2006, up from 18 in 1999, and 10 mobile telephony operators in a market that is still only at 35 percent penetration).

• **Construction.** This sector has experienced rapid recent growth, and is a significant source of employment. Demand is strong, particularly for residential and commercial building. It is also a value chain with significant spillover opportunities in skills development, financing, outsourcing, and business development, despite the fact that the sector's competitiveness is significantly limited by the high cost of construction materials—due, inter alia, to quantitative restrictions, high duties, and bans on the import of key inputs (for example, rebars and structural timber); to the overall lack of competition in the industry; and to the generally high unskilled labor costs in the country. These constraints, in turn, offer opportunities for reform.

Once the key prospective growth sectors have been prioritized, the second stage of the diagnostic work comes into effect (Consilium International 2008). At this point, the task involves further unbundling of the value chains to identify and quantify the value-adding and value-subtracting aspects and the factors that need to be addressed in order to improve value chain efficiencies and returns to the key stakeholders (entrepreneurs, labor force) operating in them. This stage provides not only guidance on specific remedial or development actions to be taken but also a baseline against which to monitor and measure impact. Tables 4.7 and 4.8 detail estimated transformation rates of value-added at the different stages within the construction and food (meat) retail value chain, from the origin of the value chain through the processing phase to final delivery to the end market. In the case of the construction industry, the data indicate that a commercial construction transaction offers the greatest value-added, at 1,045 percent versus 915 percent for residential and 467 percent for industrial. This, in turn, suggests where the greatest potential and orders of magnitude for growth can occur. Even more striking is the relative value-added potential of modern retailing of meat products versus the traditional supply chain. The analysis suggests that in the case of Lagos, the modern-format retailing

Table 4.7   Transformation Rates in the Construction Industry
(₦ millions)

Construction	Land acquisition	Project preparation and financing	Construction	Real estate	Total value transformation (%)
Residential	215	460	2,099	2,183	915
Commercial	45	114	517	—	1,045
Industrial	75	138	424	—	467

Source: Consilium International 2008.
.Note: — = not available.

Table 4.8   Transformation Rates in the Retail Meat Industry
(₦ thousands)

Meat markets	Animal farming	Wholesaling in rural markets	Animal processing	Meat wholesaling	Meat retailing	Total value transformation (%)
Kaduna and Kano traditional	50	62	77	80	84	68
Kaduna and Kano modern	50	62	89		135	170
Lagos traditional	50	62	88	93	98	96
Lagos modern	50	62	101[a]		149	198

Source: Consilium International 2008.
a. The numbers for Kaduna and Kano and for Lagos modern format retailing are aggregates covering both animal processing and meat wholesaling.

generates more than twice as much value addition as the traditional retailing approach. In the case of Kano, it generates more than two and a half times the value addition of the traditional chain.

Aside from any potential to increase the value addition in these different industries, there is also the issue of value allocation. This pertains to the distribution of value-added within the chain among the different stakeholders. Assuming that the estimates of these values internalize all costs involved in getting from one stage of the supply chain to the other, this implies that the distribution of value is among not just the private sector suppliers and purchasers, but also the public sector actors in the form of both official and unofficial costs. For instance, how much of the transformation that takes place in the construction chain is attributable to government charges and costs? The analysis suggests that this is significant. Transaction costs associated with land purchases include government consent and title certificate fees, registration charges, and ad valorem stamp duties, to name a few. These can amount to between 19 and 25 percent of the total land acquisition cost. Additionally, there are time delays caused by inefficient bureaucratic procedures; while they may not have an immediate monetary cost, they can delay completion, push back revenue streams, and reduce the profitability of the project.

In addition to value losses due to government inefficiencies, there are also market conditions that impact value distribution. Current import policies provide protected status to local cement producers and push up local prices, leading to a situation where domestic supply cannot meet demand. In response, the government has been issuing import licenses, in large part to domestic producers, further increasing their market control. Trade policy-induced distortions are also at play with regard to timber and finished steel inputs to construction. The upshot is value capture based not on productivity, but on policy and administrative factors that are not fostering efficient cost-discovery behavior on the part of key firms in the industry.

In conclusion, sector opportunities have been identified based on the key criteria of growth, employment creation, and spillover effects. Value chains within these sectors have then been inventoried in terms of value addition, and the results then broken down to determine the allocative efficiency of this value addition. The analysis reveals considerable value subtraction and diversion. This being the case, what can be done given what is known about government and firm capacities and performance in Nigeria? A review of policy and program choices and implementation options is the third stage in this industry diagnostic methodology.

Policy and Program Choices

Good policy choice is a function of a number of factors. As detailed in table 4.9, these include relevance, feasibility, sustainability, and synergies and impact. The table also suggests some of the principal considerations behind these different policy factors. First and foremost, a policy choice must respond to a priority. It must be relevant. If that priority is growth and employment creation, then the conclusions of the sector choice and value chain analysis directs policy focus toward service industries— notably construction, retail markets, and ICT. But is it feasible to focus on these sectors? Do the political commitment, institutional capacity, and reform champions at the technical and implementation levels exist? Are there sequencing constraints that would undermine the likely success

Table 4.9   Assessing Policy Options

Criteria	Variable	Description of variable
Relevance	Policy priority	Do the actions focus on improvements that can have a measurable impact in support of a key policy or strategic objective?
Feasibility	Political will and institutional capacity	Does political commitment for the policy exist? Beyond the reform champions, is there sufficient institutional capability to implement the policy?
	Sequencing	Are there sequencing considerations? Do certain measures better suit shorter or longer timeframes?
Sustainability and cost	Budget and other resource implications	Are there significant upfront or recurrent cost or revenue gain/loss considerations? Is the reform financially sustainable? Can gaps in institutional capacities essential for success be addressed in parallel with implementing the reform program?
Synergies and impact	Demonstration Links Measurement	Do the planned initiatives have the potential to catalyze a broader alliance for reform that will follow through or scale up? Three elements by which to assess this potential are • *Demonstration effects:* Does the initiative offer quick wins and tangible impacts to lock in commitment and maintain momentum? • *Links:* Are there links to other stakeholders, capacity to scale up reforms, or positive spillovers to other areas (for example, can institutions created for one reform then apply the know-how gained to champion related or other reforms)? Are there knock-on effects where a reform initiative raises awareness and appetite to deal with related reform areas? • *Measurement:* Can the policy impact be credibly measured? Do objective and broadly accepted benchmarks exist?

Source: World Bank 2008a.

of the policy over the targeted timeframe? Is the reform affordable for government? Does the policy have built-in momentum—for instance, "low-hanging fruit," demonstration effects, or links—and can these results be measured and marketed to key stakeholder groups and thereby sustain support?

Beyond a consideration of policy focus, there is the question of policy instruments and actions. These can be classified either as policy tinkering—selecting options from the existing policy regime, or as institutional reform—selecting from a different or new policy regime (Iyigun and Rodrik 2004), such that:

In the policy tinkering category, where a current policy regime is assumed, there can be

- Operational rule changes (such as regulatory and procedural changes)
- Behavioral or situational changes (such as civil service practices, physical supply, and access to services)

In the institutional reform category, where new policy options are developed, there can be

- First-order governance (including political and constitutional change, such as land use and budget and taxation authorities)
- Second-order governance (legislative changes such as the Customs Act or the NEPZA Act)

Some of the key sources of value subtraction or diversion—which constitute key areas for policy action—are summarized in table 4.10. The analysis includes not just government policies and practices, where improvements could allow value to be channeled in more allocatively efficient directions, but also areas where investments and reforms are needed in factor markets (infrastructure, labor, finance) and business production processes (logistics, standards). While many of these constraints are common across industries, the specifics and extent of impact can vary significantly. Notably, many of the required government responses amount to no more than policy tinkering. That being said, these responses require thoroughness in design, adroitness and discipline in implementation, and, at all times, responsiveness to market signals and private sector leadership.

Table 4.10   Key Constraints in Selected Value Chains

Constraint	Construction	Wholesale and retail marketing
Poor quality and high-cost infrastructure, financial services, and labor inputs Inadequate financial services	- unreliable and high-cost finance and infrastructure services - poor labor productivity and skill shortages - Inadequate vocational training and skills development - lack of access to affordable and industry-tailored term finance	
Distortionary trade policy	- import bans and tariffs and duties affect factor inputs, reducing quality and increasing cost of final products - porous borders undermine trade policy and foster rent seeking and misallocation	
Onerous administrative procedures	- land registration - planning approvals and building permits	- land registration
Poor logistics and handling	- underdeveloped freight transport services system	- poor smallholder farm linkages to wholesale/retail - poor handling practices - underdeveloped freight transport services system
Lack of regulatory enforcement on product standards	- lack of SON regulatory standards enforcement - inadequate disposal of construction materials	- inadequate veterinary services - inadequate disposal of animal waste at abattoirs

Source: Consilium International 2008.
Note: SON = Standards Organization of Nigeria.

Looking in more detail at the scope for policy tinkering versus institutional reforms to address the key constraints to cluster and value chain development, the following conclusions and actions can be proposed:

Factor markets. Factor market constraints have a significant impact at both the feasibility and sustainability levels. Infrastructure remains the key overriding constraint, but solutions are mostly realizable only in the medium to long term and require both tinkering and institutional reform types of policy actions. Some of these actions are now being taken with the promulgation of the federal government's Public-Private Partnership Framework, which looks to mobilize greater private sector finance and expertise in support of ongoing government efforts to improve infrastructure services. One element of this effort, which is of particular interest to the Lagos State government, is the provision of dedicated infrastructure services to targeted industrial and economic zones, such as the aforementioned Lekki initiative. It is here—in targeted clusters—where the potential exists to realize competitive improvements in infrastructure and related trade facilitation services. These types of initiatives will require legislative change of a second-order character, cutting across a number of infrastructure subsectors and complemented by institutional and behavioral changes—both within government agencies and in terms of PPPs. So policy and program reform is in process, and the prospective demonstration effects or low-hanging fruits available over the short term will largely lie with targeted cluster initiatives that provide support to sectors with higher growth potential.

Where indirect costs such as infrastructure and trade facilitation services can be reduced, and service quality can be stabilized, firms will have better enabling conditions to access both debt and equity financing, the lack of which is another key constraint. Allied to reforms on the demand side of the financial sector—such as collateral registries, independent credit bureaus, and secured transactions legislation—it will be possible to significantly reduce some of the information asymmetry risks that are a key factor in the undersupply of credit and capital funds. These measures will also foster the development or deepening of new financial product markets, including leasing, factoring, and the use of credit guarantees.

Building the supply side and financial architecture is necessary, but often not sufficient, to realize significant improvement in growth and employment opportunities in targeted value chains. Another aspect of this evolving value chain approach to industry development is the potential to work with key private sector value chain actors that are leading cost discovery efforts and supporting innovations across a wide range of value chain subsectors (maize, cocoa, palm oil) based on commercial business models.[15] The role of these anchor companies encompasses technology transfer, market links, and know-how. Additionally, they bring financial market access as they can deploy their deeper financing pockets to promote new financial instruments, building on the policy and legislative efforts of government to create a better enabling environment for financial services. The two interrelated areas of outgrower association development and input credit mobilization provide a good example of how, in the context of a relatively stable macroeconomic environment, cost discovery can be enabled and then, through targeted market-based interventions, scaled up and made sustainable.

More specifically, anchor private sector firms, drawing on their business and market acumen and resources, are able to coordinate smallholders into outgrower schemes in which, through technical and market guidance, they aggregate the smallholders' yields and facilitate cost effectiveness and standards compliance. They often provide financing as well—essentially factoring—including the development of warehousing receipt programs. Another variation comes in the form of a guarantee or collateral coverage, against which farmers—in a contract with the anchor firm, which often includes a fixed purchase price for the harvested crop—are then able to obtain credit for input purchases through existing financial institutions. Moreover, the anchor firm's involvement in the downstream marketing of the harvested crop further mitigates risks that can discourage lenders. Most often this value chain development also entails the establishment of outgrower associations, which, over time—as the association establishes a reputation and a credit history—are then able to obtain credit in their own name and without anchor firm guarantees. This is a key contributing factor to their ability to scale up and eventually achieve long-term sustainability.

In addition to these policy and legislative actions, the public sector can further assist the development of associations with the most basic type of policy tinkering, namely, the smart (market-based) use of matching grants. Such grants could be used to help strengthen the financial, credit, and loan portfolio management capacities of the associations. These associations would, in effect, be correcting for a key market failure—the information asymmetries that curtail smallholder access to credit. The deployment of matching grants, in this instance, would be an ideal government response that would not have been nearly as effective in the absence of the value chain leader to first develop the business side of the industry and support the initial cost discovery efforts.

As suggested by the outgrower example, results will be highly sensitive to correct design and attention to implementation capacities. Thus, a high level of coordination will be needed across different ministries, departments, and agencies; between governments (particularly federal and state); and between the public and private sectors. Program design and delivery should, prima facie, be private sector–led. This would involve a level of collaboration among policymakers, industry leaders, and business associations that represents a significantly different approach to the mostly supply-driven and control models of government intervention detailed in the earlier assessment of existing industry policy performance.

Trade policy. Another area where policy tinkering could have an immediate effect is trade policy. For the most part, this does not require new legislation, but rather a reversal of exceptions granted and ad hoc protections imposed, often by executive order. What is critical for this effort is successful marketing of the wider benefits that can result from lifting import bans and reducing tariffs that are negatively affecting the overall development of key value chains. This is not a straightforward task given the vested interests at play, but it has a lower budget cost than the current efforts to administer a system involving import controls, even with adjustment funding provided to currently protected producers.

Administrative procedures and quality standards. A tremendous amount of policy tinkering can be undertaken to streamline administrative procedures and enhance the efficient application of quality standards. In terms of feasibility, sustainability, and synergy, a strong case can be made for comprehensive policy tinkering on these fronts. While there are aspects to land transfer that require first-order institutional reform (governor consent, for instance, is embedded in Nigeria's constitution), a wide range of administrative actions can be taken to streamline the land transfer aspect of both construction and retail marketing. With respect to quality standard improvements, weak government capacity and rent seeking pose the usual challenges to making reforms effective. It is to these aspects of policy feasibility that most attention needs to be paid. Additionally, policy and program design should be informed by past experiences of public sector–led solutions (for example, the track record with special enterprise zones) and should build on best practices of public-private collaboration. Close attention should be paid to enforcing transparency and accountability in administrative practices in order to augment performance and contain rent-seeking.

Logistics and handling. This is an area for private sector action. Aside from rural infrastructure services to better link farmers and producers to the value chain, the government should focus on coordinating efforts to improve the enabling environment with the private and financial sectors—including support to key business development and financial services through, inter alia, market-based matching grant schemes.

Conclusions

A thorough sector and value chain diagnostic can help to identify coordination failures and information spillovers. It can also serve to quantify and make transparent where value-added in different sectors gets directed, and this can provide valuable information for targeted policymaking. Identifying and building on industry leadership, rather than reverting to the disappointing government supply-led initiatives of the past, is also an important lesson that needs to be transferred to design and implementation. Government policy should seek to build markets, not firms, respecting the open architecture principle set out in box 4.3. The impact that can be realized through objective diagnostic and subsequent transparent and accountable measurement of results is arguably the most powerful constituent of effective policymaking. Where this is in place, policy misfires could be more clearly and immediately identified and corrected. This approach would represent a paradigm shift for government officials administering the existing body of industrial policy.

This chapter has focused largely on the service sectors. Infrastructure constraints will require a more complex set of multisector policy and institutional reforms, on which the government has already embarked. There are relatively limited near-term growth and employment creation opportunities to be realized from the manufacturing and agro-processing sectors before results from the infrastructure reforms become apparent. Nevertheless, the service industries have contributed more than 30 percent of the country's recent growth performance. Improving the environment for further cost discovery by these industries depends very little on the infrastructure sectors and, therefore, offers significant short- and medium-term economic opportunities. If the government can successfully make the relatively short jumps to improving policymaking and implementation in these areas, and implement some of the principles outlined above, the economic outcomes available from these service sectors could be further strengthened.

Laying the foundation for dynamic cost discovery in the service sectors over the shorter term will also constitute a demonstration effect for more modest policy tinkering and second-order institutional reforms. The momentum of effective industry development made possible through these efforts will better position both the public and private sectors to efficiently capture the additional cost advantages and market opportunities that will arise as infrastructure reforms take root. More effective public-private cooperation will be key to the sustainable development of the infrastructure sectors. This cooperation will need to embrace sector policy development and implementation, PPPs in infrastructure investment, and skills training. This is the platform of collaboration that will be needed to reawaken the country's manufacturing, downstream natural resource, and non-traditional export sectors.

Notes

1. Tax incentives exclude oil and gas exploration, development, and production.

2. There are 17 existing and planned FTZs in Nigeria, administered by NEPZA: Calabar, Kano, Onne Oil and Gas, Maigatari Border, Banki Border, Lekki, Lekki Export Processing Zone, Oil Integrated Logistics Support Services, Olokola, Snake Island, Lagos Deep Offshore Logistics Support Services, Ibom Science and Technology, Living Spring, Oshogbo, Lagos Airline Services, Abuja Technology Village FTZ, Brass LNG, and the Tinapa Business Resort.

3. Excluding Tinapa, the currently listed licensed FTZs include Calabar FTZ, Kano FTZ, Onne Oil and Gas FTZ, Maigatari Border FTZ, Banki Border FTZ, Lekki FTZ, Lekki EPZ, Oil Integrated Logistics Support Services FTZ, Olokola FTZ, Snake Island FTZ, LADOL FTZ, Ibom Science and Technology FTZ, Living Spring FTZ, Oshogbo FTZ, Lagos Airline Services FTZ, Abuja Technology Village FTZ, and Brass LNG FTZ.

4. See http://www.nigerianexporter.org/download/EEGGuidelinesRevisedApr 2006.pdf.

5. See the Industrial Development (Income Tax Relief) Act No. 22 of 1971, as amended in 1988.

6. Another area needing clarification is the extent to which tax and other incentives are provided for investment funds to operate in Nigeria. The one known case is the Small and Medium Industries Equity Investment Scheme, which provides tax rebates for commercial banks and microfinance operations against the 10 percent of pretax profits they are providing to the scheme. Banks are doing this, for the most part, either through affiliate entities or—as has been the case for other schemes— through private placements with fund managers. This tax incentive for micro, small, and medium (MSME) investment is not available to other types of investment funds (for example, infrastructure or natural resource development funds) operating in Nigeria.

7. Based on discussions with Acting General Manager, May 24, 2008.

8. Unfortunately, key offices at the NEPZA headquarters in Abuja were burned down during the course of this study, and many files were destroyed. NEPZA staff indicated that detailed economic performance data were not recorded by the organization. Available data collected by the management of individual EPZs are reported in this chapter.

9. While this sample is insufficient to undertake any statistically significant infer-ential analysis, the following descriptive analysis, based on this limited sample, is provided as the best available information to date. During the upcoming next round of Investment Climate Enterprise Survey work which com-menced in 2009, the data sample will be adjusted to increase the available information on firms using government incentives, in order to further investi-gate and validate the initial insights provided in the current exercise.

10. The summaries provided here are drawn from case studies found in Zhihua Zeng (2008).

11. A recent survey of Nnewi businesses, as referenced in Zhihua Zeng (2008), indicates that between 77 and 95.7 percent of them had looked at govern-ment support for a range of activities, including innovation, available skilled manpower, research and development, intellectual property protection, ICT support, and venture capital; and had assessed that support as weak.

12. In 2007, NIPC, CAC, and FIRS signed a Memorandum of Understanding on cooperation as part of the Business Registration Reforms program being sup-ported under the World Bank's Micro, Small and Medium-Size Enterprise project.

13. The World Bank Group/DFID-funded Investment Climate Program is a trust-funded program executed by the World Bank Group, with a US$11.5 million contribution from DFID. The program supports diagnostic analysis of the investment climate, allied to capacity building in public private dialogue and policy reform development, decision making, and implementation. It has financed the enterprise survey work used in this report. The program com-menced in 2007 and concludes in 2011.

14. A table summarizing the principal constraints in agriculture value chains, as identified in Consilium International (2005), is included in Appendix C.

15. Two leading value chain actors are Yara (http://www.yara.com); and Olam (http://www.olamonline.com), both of which operate all over Nigeria.

CHAPTER 5

Labor Market Trends and Skills Development

Jorgen Billetoft

Overview

The relatively slow growth of employment opportunities in the formal sector, combined with rising population levels, means that the informal sector will become one of the central vehicles for employment generation.[1] The government of Nigeria recognizes this but has given limited attention to the skills needed to support productivity and structural change in the informal sector. In many sectors of the economy, there are strong vertical and horizontal links between formal and informal business activities. In addition, the knowledge and skills required to perform tasks in the formal sector have a certain impact on those required in the informal sector. Therefore, policymakers must become more strategic and anticipate what skills should be developed for the informal sector, as opposed to providing skills when there is a need or in response to a crisis.

Based on a review of the available data about the skills structure, labor demand, and landscape of technical and vocational education in Nigeria, this chapter examines how policies could become more effective at promoting employment generation within the informal sector, with special attention to the three basic avenues of skills acquisition: formal technical and vocational education and training (TVET), traditional apprenticeship (the predominant avenue), and non-formal training.

This chapter concludes that there are mismatches between skills being developed by present public policies and those required to support structural change and employment in the labor market. In order to reduce this mismatch and ensure that skills development is tackled in a more strategic manner, there is a need to support greater coordination across government departments and ensure that interventions target areas that are linked to growing market demand, both within Nigeria and overseas.

The chapter begins with an outline of the methodologies and approaches used in the analysis. This is followed by an overview of the Nigerian technical and vocational education (TVE) landscape and a discussion of the performance of secondary and tertiary TVE in relation to the employment situation. The next section outlines the basic features of the informal sector and the various modes of relevant skills acquisition. It also investigates what skills are in highest demand in the informal sector and the factors driving the demand for skills; and it discusses where support for skills development should occur and where employment absorption is likely to be greatest. Finally, the chapter turns to the ways forward in public policies, looking at how institutions can become more effective at producing skills that are responsive to structural changes and can improve peoples' earning potential in the informal sector.

Methodology

An eclectic approach was used to conduct this study, drawing on qualitative data, a series of interviews with planners and stakeholders, and reference to a number of empirical research studies. The study is underpinned by the proposition that the constraints facing productivity in the informal sector include low educational level, lack of appropriate technical skills, and shortage of adequate production equipment (Resman Associates 2007; NISER 2007). In order to understand the nature of the mismatch between skills needed and those provided by institutions at present, it is necessary to tackle three inter-related issues:

First, the chapter analyzes the trends of post-primary education in order to understand the relative weight of different types of education in light of the increasing importance of the informal sector as the primary source of employment for new entrants to the labor market. Information for this analysis was obtained from various government statistics, combined with data provided by the National Board of Technical Education (NBTE), the National Directorate for Employment (NDE), and the Ministry of Labor and Productivity (data on trade testing).

Second, the chapter discusses the different streams of skills development, particularly with regard to the content of existing programs, the number of people they benefit, and how well they prepare people for work in the informal sector. Emphasis is given to programs supported by NDE and the provision of education by different institutions operating at the federal and state levels, especially those under the purview of NBTE. Special attention is given to skills acquisition in the informal sector. In this way, the study develops a picture of which skills are being developed and the extent to which supply is responding to demand.

The chapter also discusses the institutions involved in supporting the implementation of labor market policy.

Reflecting the mode of delivery and its official status, TVET[2] is divided into three broad streams:

- *Formal training programs* refer to officially accredited and recognized TVE programs. TVE is offered at the postbasic level by technical colleges and at the tertiary level by polytechnics and monotechnics (specialized colleges).
- *Non-formal vocational training* is short-term vocational training provided by government and nongovernment institutions.
- *Apprenticeship programs* are predominantly of an informal nature. While NDE operates the Open Apprenticeship Scheme, the informal sector organizes apprenticeship training to a significant extent by itself.

With particular attention to the rising importance of the informal sector, the three streams of TVET are analyzed in relation to five dimensions considered important for its future direction:

- *Relevance.* The relevance of the TVET system refers to the skills workers acquire through the three streams and to the skills required by the labor market.
- *Quality.* The quality of the system concerns the actual knowledge and competencies acquired by new labor market entrants.
- *Efficiency.* Nonformal training is generally conducted in an uncoordinated and disjointed manner, leading to resource suboptimization. There also seems to be scope for improvement of the internal efficiency of the formal TVET system, as demonstrated by the high dropout rates.

- *Sustainability.* Quality improvements and increased access to TVET cannot be meaningfully discussed without addressing the issue of mobilization of resources to finance them.
- *Institutional framework.* At present, there is no articulation of a coordinated institutional framework for non-formal, informal, and formal TVE. It is vital for the upward mobility of the labor force that skills acquired outside the formal system, for example, through traditional apprenticeship, are formally recognized.

The conclusions focus on how to improve existing labor market institutions and ensure that government policies are more responsive to the labor market with reference to international best practice and what lessons Nigeria can gain from the experiences of countries that have followed a similar development trajectory.

The Nigerian Skills Development and Training Landscape

This section provides an overview of the three types of training streams.

Postbasic Education Trends

Nigeria's education system comprises six years of primary, three years of junior secondary, three years of senior secondary, and four to six years of tertiary education. Basic education is referred to as the six years of primary together with the three years of junior secondary education. Tertiary education is provided by universities, mono- and polytechnics, and technical colleges.

Primary school enrollment made impressive gains from 2000 to 2005. According to national sources, the total gross primary school enrollment rate increased from 98 percent in 2000 to 120 percent in 2005, while the total secondary school enrollment rate rose only marginally, from 34 to 36 percent, during the same period. Although the intended official minimum number of years of schooling is nine, the transition rate from primary to junior secondary school is only 80 percent (National Bureau of Statistics 2005). An estimated 76 percent complete primary school, and 25 percent of the relevant age group (6–11 years) do not enroll in primary education at all (table 5.1). Hence, in spite of the remarkable progress, almost half of the youth still enter the labor market with six or fewer years of schooling. Many studies have found a marked correlation between income and education. It is therefore realistic to assume that those

Table 5.1   Enrollment and Output in Basic Education
(Primary and Junior Secondary)

Level of education	Enrollment and completion rate	Data year	Data source
Primary school output after grade 6	2,774,292	2005	Universal Basic Education Commission
Primary school completion rate (%)	76	2005	UNESCO
Transition rate from primary to junior secondary school (%)	80.5	2003	Nigeria 2003 Demographic and Health Survey (National Bureau of Statistics)
Enrollment in junior secondary education	3,624,163	2005	Federal Ministry of Education

Sources: National Bureau of Statistics 2005; NBTE, Federal Ministry of Education and Universal Basic Education Commission (unpublished data) 2008; UNESCO, http://www.unesco.org.
Note: UNESCO = United Nations Educational, Scientific, and Cultural Organization. Sources do not indicate how nonformal education is defined. Hence, the term may not refer to exactly the same kind of nonformal training discussed in this paper.

who enter the labor market without completing primary education join the group of working poor.

Technical and vocational education is provided at the secondary level by technical colleges and colleges of science and technology. Technical colleges are the only alternative to senior secondary schools as a route to further formal education and training after junior secondary education. At the tertiary level, technical education is available from polytechnics, monotechnics, and some universities.

Merely 14.7 percent of those completing junior secondary school advance to senior secondary education (table 5.2). Approximately 3 percent of those who do not progress to general senior secondary school continue their education at technical colleges. In 2005, gross senior secondary school enrollment stood at 2,773,418, according to the Federal Ministry of Education (2008), while enrollment in technical colleges, according to NBTE (2008), was 72,978, reflecting the poor reputation of technical education, due in part to underfunding of technical colleges and in part to poor employment prospects for their graduates. As a result, a substantial number of young people entering the labor market after grade 9 choose other ways to acquire work-related skills, such as in the informal sector, or they simply enter the labor market without any additional education and training.

A similar picture can be observed at the tertiary level. There are approximately four times as many students enrolled at universities as at polytechnics and monotechnics (725,000 against 160,000; National Bureau of

Table 5.2   Enrollment in Senior Secondary Education

Type of education	Enrollment	Data year	Data sources
Enrollment, senior secondary education	2,773,418	2005	Federal Ministry of Education
Total enrollment, technical colleges	72,978	2004–05	NBTE
Total annual output, technical colleges	15,144	2004–05	NBTE
Total enrollment polytechnics	139,070	2004–05	NBTE
Total enrollment monotechnics	20,853	2004–05	NBTE
Total enrollment at universities	724,856	2005	National Universities Commission

Sources: Federal Ministry of Education; National Board of Technical Education; National Universities Commission.

Statistics 2005). This is further confirmation of the strong preference for academic education and the low esteem in which Nigerian youth hold blue collar occupations—resulting in the mismatch between the output of the education system and the employment opportunities of the labor market.

Formal Technical Education and Training
This section reviews key institutions involved in formal technical education and training.

National Board of Technical Education. The NBTE is the principal organ of the Federal Ministry of Education, mandated to address all aspects of TVE that fall outside of university education. There are presently 110 approved tertiary polytechnics and monotechnics and 159 technical colleges under the purview of the NBTE. In addition, there are more than 10 technical universities outside the purview of NBTE (table 5.3). While technical colleges produce craftsmen and master craftsmen, polytechnics and monotechnics produce technicians and technologists, professionals, and engineers.

The NBTE has recently embarked on a new initiative—the creation of private Vocational Enterprise Institutions (VEIs) and Innovative Enterprise Institutions (IEIs).[3] These institutions are described in box 5.1. There is also a considerable, and increasing, number of accredited privately owned polytechnics.

For public technical and vocational education, NBTE has the mission of promoting the production of technical (skilled and semi-skilled) and

Table 5.3   Polytechnics, Monotechnics, and Technical Colleges, by Ownership

Type of institution	Federal	State	Private	Total
		Ownership		
Polytechnics	21	30	7	58
Monotechnics:				
Colleges of agriculture	17	13	—	30
Colleges of health technology	4	1	1	6
Other specialized institutions	13	—	3	16
Subtotal monotechnics	34	14	4	52
Total	55	44	11	110
Technical colleges	19	137	3	159

Source: NBTE 2008.
Note: — = not available.

Box 5.1

Vocational Enterprise Institutions and Innovation Enterprise Institutions

VEIs and IEIs—an outcome of a 2007 reform initiative of the Federal Ministry of Education—provide an alternative route to higher education. They are private institutions that offer vocational, technical, technological, or professional education and training at post-basic and tertiary levels. They are designed to equip secondary school leavers and working adults with vocational skills and knowledge to meet the increasing demand for technical manpower by various economic sectors. Being driven and owned by the private sector, they seek to address the shortcomings of existing vocational training programs. The government's role in VEIs and IEIs is limited to ensuring compliance with standards that have been established by the private sector.

VEIs and IEIs offer part-time and full-time education, leading to the award of certificates and national diplomas. VEIs admit candidates with a minimum of a basic education certificate and cover multidisciplinary areas that prepare learners for jobs in most industries. IEIs admit students with a minimum of five credits beyond a senior secondary school certificate. Hence, the VEIs present a senior secondary alternative to the technical colleges, while IEIs are alternatives to monotechnics and polytechnics.

VEIs run three-year modular programs, with each year of study having a cogent and flexible structure and content that equips the trainee with a practicable working skill if he or she exits at that level. VEIs give National Vocational Certificates

(continued)

Box 5.1 *(continued)*

(NVCs) Part 1, Part 2, and Final. IEIs, on the other hand, run full-time (2-year) and part time (3–4 year) diploma programs, with the curricula in modules of employable skills. IEIs give National Innovation Diplomas (NIDs).

While the experience with VEIs, which have a somewhat lower standard than IEIs, has been mixed, demand for IEIs has exceeded expectations. Potential target groups include school leavers, persons who want to upgrade their skills, university graduates seeking employable skills, and adults seeking an opportunity to re-skill themselves.

By late 2008, a total of 138 programs in 2 VEIs and 22 IEIs had been awarded accreditation. Of these, 124 are technology based and 14 are non-technology based; 106 are at NID level and 32 are at the NVC level. The projected annual enrollment in these programs is about 4,280 students. The first group of graduates will complete their studies at the end of 2010. However, some interim certificates may be awarded in 2009.

Source: NBTE 2008.

professional manpower. It provides standardized minimum curricula guides, and, through an accreditation process, supervises and regulates the programs offered by technical institutions at senior secondary and post-secondary levels. NBTE also defines course specifications for all national diploma, higher national diploma, and professional diploma programs offered by polytechnics and similar institutions; awards the corresponding certificates and diplomas, presently covering 190 programs; and coordinates government allocation of resources to federal polytechnics funded by the Federal Ministry of Education. NBTE also consults with the National Manpower Board on the use of the Industrial Training Fund (see below). The relevant federal and state ministries are responsible for financing the programs; for example, the Federal Ministry of Health is responsible for training nurses, midwives, and medical technicians; and the Federal Ministry of Agriculture operates 17 colleges of agriculture. At the state level, Lagos State has been financing Centers of Excellence that provide vocational education programs in key growth sectors.

Technical colleges and science technical colleges. Technical colleges are primarily operated by state governments with little federal participation. The Federal Ministry of Education operates 19 science technical colleges, which are intended as role models for the state governments, and plans to establish such colleges in all 36 states. These colleges tend to be better resourced than those operated by state governments. The federal colleges are of various sizes, with an average student enrollment of around 700 and teacher-student ratios of up to 1 to 40. The technical and vocational education they offer is seen as an alternative to traditional academic post-basic education; it prepares students for entry into the labor market by providing job-specific skills in the applied sciences appropriate to technical, agricultural, commercial, and economic development. The curricula emphasize self-reliance and preparation for self-employment; however, the relative youth of the graduates (most of them are under 20), combined with the poor quality of the practical training, undermines achievement of this objective. Furthermore, the curricula of most of these institutions do not include entrepreneurship training.

Technical colleges primarily serve youth from low-income households who are unable to enter general senior secondary education. According to data provided by NBTE (2008), the programs with the highest number of graduates are conventional blue collar courses, for example, electrical installation, vehicle mechanics, and bricklaying (table 5.4). Female participation in technical colleges is less than 20 percent. The majority of girls are enrolled in programs that lead to professions traditionally held by women (for example, bookkeeping, business studies, catering, home economics).

Table 5.4   Technical College Graduate Output by Program and Gender, 2004–05

Trade or course	Male	Female	Total
Electrical installation and practice	3,255	162	3,417
Auto mechanics	1,912	42	1,954
Bricklaying, blockmaking, concrete work	1,420	58	1,478
Carpentry and joinery	1,038	69	1,107
Welding and fabrication	998	4	1,002
Mechanical engineering craft practice	862	20	882
Radio, TV, electronics	781	69	850
Bookkeeping	284	443	727
Furniture making	600	1	601
Business studies	235	304	539
Catering craft practice	28	485	513
Plumbing and pipe fitting	223	5	228
Other programs	1,354	492	1,846
Total	12,990	2,154	15,144

Source: NBTE 2008.

A diagnostic study of Nigeria's technical colleges by the African Development Fund (2005) concluded that the colleges encounter a number of serious challenges: "The vocational and technical education subsector [the technical colleges] is unable to respond to the changing labor market requirements because of its present supply-driven orientation. Its curricula, instructional equipment, teaching methods, and evaluation techniques are outdated, leading to inappropriate low internal and external efficiencies" (p. viii). In cases where curricula have been updated, the equipment and teaching aids required to teach the curricula are often missing. A lack of adequate labor market information and monitoring of leavers, combined with limited involvement of potential employers in the planning and design of the programs, adds to the problem.

No system exists for monitoring the labor market performance of graduates from technical colleges. Given the constraints discussed above, it is difficult to imagine that more than a small fraction of graduates find employment in the formal sector. Considering the fact that skilled craftsmen are in short supply, it is surprising that this stream of senior secondary education has received relatively little attention by the federal and state authorities. If adequately resourced and with the right institutional framework, technical colleges have the potential to provide the economy with skilled workers who possess a functional combination of practical and theoretical knowledge of the vocations covered by their programs.

Polytechnics and monotechnics. The number of tertiary education institutions, including polytechnics and specialized monotechnics, is increasing steadily. In 2005, approximately 110 accredited polytechnics and monotechnics existed to serve a total of 237,700 students. There is a preponderance of non-technical and technological programs at polytechnics, although the government recommends a 70 to 30 student ratio in favor of technical courses. Of the 15 most popular programs, only four or five provide students with competencies needed for self-employment, such as business administration and estate management (table 5.5). Courses related to administration, marketing, banking, estate management, and so forth, are all clearly directed at salaried employment in the formal sector.

Polytechnic and monotechnic enrollment together is less than one-third that of university enrollment (table 5.2), while the output (number of graduates) from polytechnics and monotechnics is almost five times higher than from technical colleges (table 5.6). Most parents send their children to polytechnics and monotechnics as a second choice if they are not admitted to a university.

Table 5.5   Polytechnic Graduate Output by Program and Gender, 2004–05

| Program | National diploma (ND) | | | Higher national diploma (HND) | | | Total |
	Male	Female	Total ND	Male	Female	Total HND	
Accountancy	4,644	2,805	7,449	2,855	1,894	4,749	12,198
Business administration and management	3,413	2,044	5,457	2,315	1,347	3,662	9,119
Business studies	2,686	1,410	4,096	263	280	543	4,639
Electronics and electronics engineering	2,990	338	3,328	1,130	104	1,234	4,562
Marketing	1,280	1,156	2,436	1,008	662	1,670	4,106
Banking and finance	1,895	1,272	3,167	588	329	917	4,084
Secretarial studies	710	1,801	2,511	248	988	1,236	3,747
Mechanical engineering	2,058	128	2,186	988	74	1,062	3,248
Science laboratory technician	1,386	1,238	2,624	275	278	553	3,177
Computer studies	990	725	1,715	372	262	634	2,349
Estate management	1,018	526	1,544	435	241	676	2,220
Statistics	1,122	452	1,574	414	204	618	2,192
Civil engineering technician	1,176	214	1,390	499	129	628	2,018
Public administration	892	569	1,461	406	150	556	2,017
Mass communication	643	727	1,370	154	279	433	1,803
Other programs	6,265	2,314	8,577	3,187	1,298	4,476	13,089
Total	33,168	17,719	50,885	15,137	8,519	23,647	74,568

Source: NBTE 2008.

The low societal status of polytechnics affects their performance. For instance, they have difficulties attracting competent staff and complain that they constantly lose qualified staff to the universities, which pay better, are considered more prestigious, and offer better career opportunities. In an attempt to confront this problem and enhance the reputation of technical education, a number of polytechnics have recently been granted the right to introduce degree programs at the bachelor's level. Further, as noted above, the Federal Ministry of Education has recently introduced

Table 5.6   Graduate Output, Tertiary Education

Type of education	Number of graduates	Year	Data source
Graduate output, polytechnics	74,568	2004–05	NBTE
ND output, polytechnics	50,885	2004–05	NBTE
HND output, polytechnics	23,683	2004–05	NBTE
Graduate output, monotechnics	4,898	2004/05	NBTE
ND output, monotechnics	3,463	2004–05	NBTE
HND output, monotechnics	1,486	2004–05	NBTE
Graduate output, by bachelor's degree	26,042	2004–05	National Universities Commission
Graduate output by master's degree	8,385	2004–05	National Universities Commission
Graduate output by postgraduate diploma	4,651	2004–05	National Universities Commission

Source: NBTE 2008, National Universities Commission 2008.
Note: ND = national diploma; HND = higher national diploma.

VEIs and IEIs as a means to enhance public-private partnership in the field of technical education.

Contrary to the global tendency toward outcome-driven and modularized education, the polytechnics still use a content-driven approach, with most examinations giving little attention to practical application of the acquired knowledge. With few exceptions, they have no tradition of partnerships with private companies. This results in a deep gap between the competencies of the graduates and the needs and opportunities of the labor market. Furthermore, the lack of active learning opportunities that characterizes polytechnic education produces graduates who are ill prepared to master new skills and adapt to new situations. NBTE's ongoing curriculum review,[4] which aims at improving the balance between subject content and development of technical and intellectual skills required by the labor market, is hampered by lack of facilities and equipment, including ICT. Lack of resources and weak management also constrain the maintenance of existing equipment and the replacement of consumables. The shortage of facilities is more pronounced at newer institutions.

No reliable data exist on unemployment among graduates, but all sources agree that it is high. The World Bank's review of post-basic science and technology education (World Bank 2006) estimated that 50 to 60 percent of the graduates from tertiary institutions could not find an adequate job. The review concluded that the demand is not for more graduates, but for more highly skilled graduates. NBTE management (NBTE 2008) estimates that, at most, 30 percent of the graduates from polytechnics are able to secure paid jobs within their area of competence after completing their education. Those with a technical or science background are reported to experience the fewest difficulties, while graduates with an education directed toward a white collar job are having the toughest time.

The relative size of the output of polytechnics and monotechnics vis-à-vis technical colleges is indicative of Nigeria's passion for higher education, with its promise of higher salaries. However, in light of the graduates' difficulties finding relevant employment, and the lack of qualified skilled craftsmen, it is difficult to justify the heavy investments in tertiary technical education at the expense of secondary technical education such as that offered by technical colleges.

According to NBTE management (NBTE 2008), the programs in highest demand are those related to science and technology and to engineering. However, as noted, there is no hard evidence available to underpin this assertion. In response to changing demands and the ongoing curriculum review, NBTE anticipates introducing new programs in the polytechnics in areas such as interior design, optometry, occupational therapy, physiotherapy, and radiography.

Industrial Training Fund. The Industrial Training Fund (ITF) is a parastatal under the purview of the Ministry of Commerce and Industry, funded by a 1 percent training levy payable by private enterprises. ITF has two principal mandates:

- *The provision of short-term skills programs and apprenticeship programs for industry.* ITF offers a broad range of courses for skills upgrading, typically three to five days in length, throughout Nigeria (see table 5.7 for details of attendance). Companies paying the mandatory training levy can be reimbursed for up to 60 percent of the amount paid for these courses; and
- *The provision of practical training for students and graduates of tertiary institutions* through the Student Industrial Work Experience Scheme (SIWES). The scheme introduces students to industry-based skills, thereby easing the transition to the world of work. Participation in SIWES has become a necessary precondition for the award of a diploma and degree certificates in specific disciplines in most tertiary institutions (table 5.8).

Table 5.7   Industrial Training Fund, Number of Participants in the Manpower and Development Program, by Main Category of Course, 2006–07

	Number of participants	
Type of course	2006	2007
Machining	1,500	1,500
Electrical and electronics	3,000	3,000
Automotive/mechatronics	3,000	3,000
ICT	1,500	1,500
Welding and fabrication	1,500	1,500
Agriculture mechanization	1,500	1,500
Plumbing and pipe fitting	1,500	1,500
Carpentry and joinery	1,500	1,500
Refrigeration and air conditioning	1,500	1,500

Source: Industrial Training Fund 2008.
Note: ICT = information and communications technology.

Table 5.8   Industrial Training Fund, Student Industrial Work Experience Scheme, Number of Interns, 2006–07

	Universities		Polytechnics		Colleges of education		Total
SIWES Year	Institutions	Interns	Institutions	Interns	Institutions	Interns	interns
2006	48	60,317	71	65,191	67	36,860	162,368
2007	56	69,487	81	78,742	70	46,661	194,890

Source: ITF 2008.

ITF also provides human resource information and advice to industrial and commercial companies. It operates two skills centers and a Center for Industrial Training Excellence. With assistance from the government of Singapore, ITF is planning to establish a hospitality and catering training center that will offer two-year diploma courses.

Financing of technical and vocational education. Financing of TVE is predominantly the responsibility of the federal and state governments.[5] (As noted above, the 1 percent training levy that private enterprises contribute to the ITF is largely used for funding short-term, nonformal skills courses.)

As a proportion of GDP, Nigeria's education expenditure is high by both regional and global standards. Federal education expenditure has increased in absolute terms and on a per student basis, growing by as much as a third since 1999. In 2005, the 17 federal polytechnics were allotted 9 percent of the budget for the Federal Ministry of Education (US$406 million). The unit costs of different levels and types of institutions cannot be estimated because of the lack of data on overall actual spending. Polytechnics and monotechnics do not report on financial support from the government, which in some cases seems to be rather significant. Some polytechnics generate an income from fee-based training activities and sale of other services. Technical colleges receive very little extra-budgetary support, but some may engage in small income-generating activities.

Conclusion

A striking feature of Nigeria's public technical and vocational education system is the disproportionate enrollment in tertiary technical education compared to enrollment in secondary vocational education. The preponderance of tertiary graduates means that the responsibility for training skilled craftsmen is largely left to the informal sector and private training institutions. The government's initiative to establish VEIs and IEIs in partnership with private operators is an important effort to address this problem. It is too early to assess whether this effort will help to level out the imbalance between secondary-level vocational training and tertiary-level technical education.

The most serious challenge confronting formal TVE is the gap between acquired competencies and available employment opportunities. This, in turn, is the result of quality constraints and institutional deficiencies. The problems are most pronounced in the case of technical colleges, but polytechnics and monotechnics face many of the same shortcomings. Although the government has increased its allocation to the education sector, underqualified staff, a shortage of equipment and materials, inadequate facilities for practical training, and outdated courses are still the order of the day for most public institutions.

These problems are compounded by a shortage of data for monitoring and planning purposes at both the institutional and the system levels. There is no systematic assessment of the labor market relevance of the education offered at the secondary level by the technical colleges and at the tertiary level by monotechnics and polytechnics. Neither NBTE nor the individual institutions have mechanisms for tracing the whereabouts of graduates. These shortcomings impede adequate assessment of performance and quality. Most institutions lack a mechanism for self-evaluation, and NBTE lacks a system for assessing the external efficiency of the TVET programs.

Two prerequisites for improving the efficiency and flexibility of the institutions are (a) a greater degree of professional and administrative autonomy, including autonomy on key financial matters; and (b) the establishment of mechanisms for dialogue with prospective employers, including consultative fora, public-private joint initiatives, and the use of teaching staff from private companies.

Skills Acquisition in the Informal Sector

In the informal sector, skills are acquired through two principal avenues—non-formal training and traditional apprenticeship.

The Informal Sector—Some Features

Two recent studies of Nigeria's informal sector offer useful insight into the dynamics of the sector and its skills tendencies (NISER 2007; Resman Associates 2007). Both studies emphasize the heterogeneity of the sector, and one suggests that the informal sector is best viewed as a continuum including a wide range of activities—from mobile phone recharge card hawkers and newspaper vendors to the neighborhood retail shop, market hawkers, makeshift mechanic, unlicensed taxis, small-scale manufacturers, and informal education and health services. Needless to say, the competencies required for these different types of activities, and thus the way in which skills are acquired, vary considerably.

The key findings of the two studies were the following:

- *Level of education.* Approximately one-third of the interviewed business operators had completed senior secondary education. Those who had completed primary school education accounted for approximately 20 percent, while slightly more than 20 percent had a postsecondary school educational qualification (including 8 percent with a higher national diploma or bachelor's degree). In all, more than 60 percent had completed junior secondary education. In both samples, operators without any formal education or schooling made up less than 10 percent. The relatively high level of education among business operators is an indication of the widespread expansion of educational opportunities in Nigeria and the difficulties of securing employment in the formal sector. Just 10 percent of the operators interviewed for NISER (2007) had a formal vocational education, likely reflecting the relatively small number of youths who attend this type of institution. The picture was not markedly different for the sampled employees, although in general their level of education tended to be lower. However, employees who were university graduates accounted for a significant share (6 percent). These findings show that the informal sector is not universally characterized by low education levels. Indeed, many young people who have completed senior secondary education and beyond seem to attend some sort of informal, structured learning process before setting up their own business.

- *Source of skills acquisition.* NISER (2007) found that more than half of the operators had acquired their skills in the informal sector from master craftsmen or master trainers, male or female. Business operators who had received training in firms, either publicly or privately owned, represented 16 percent of the sample. Approximately 12 percent of respondents had acquired their skills through apprenticeships arranged by NDE. Finally, 8 percent were trained in specialized government-owned training organizations or institutions. There was no dramatic difference between the number of male and female informal business operators. NISER (2007) also looked into constraints to skills acquisition in the informal sector. Illiteracy and poverty were rated the most serious barrier by 57 percent of all respondents. Approximately 53 percent found that changes in government policies are a major constraint; 42 percent cited the non-availability of equipment and tools; 28 percent cited "crude technology"; and nearly the same share said that a major barrier was the disconnect between theory and practice.

The studies also found increasing female participation in the informal sector. As expected, female participation is overwhelmingly concentrated at the lower end of the sector. Women are primarily engaged in retail trade and service-related activities such as catering.

With employment opportunities in the formal sector worsening significantly over the past few years and the number of tertiary institution graduates increasing, it is fair to assume that a growing number of people with higher education are becoming engaged in the informal sector. In the long run, this will affect the productivity and quality of products and services deriving from the sector, and thus the sector's potential to forge stronger links with the formal economy. However, this situation also suggests that the ease of entry often associated with the informal sector may not hold true. Indeed, activities that generate attractive returns to their owners are characterized by quite high entry barriers in terms of both skills and investments. There are also signs of increasing income disparity between informal occupations associated with low investment and limited education, such as petty trade and ad hoc personal services, on the one hand, and those that require technical expertise and certain facilities (for example, furniture makers, auto mechanics, and welders) on the other.[6]

Skills Demand

A study undertaken by the National Universities Commission (2005) provides further insight into skills demand in the informal sector. The objective of the study was to identify what knowledge and skills graduates require to successfully enter the labor market. The study asked employers and stakeholders about their perceptions of graduates' skills from the following disciplines: administration; agriculture and veterinary medicine; arts and social science; engineering; environmental sciences, medicine, dentistry, and pharmacy; education; law; and science. The study concluded that recently qualified graduates exhibited a number of skill deficiencies, including lack of analytical and ICT skills. From interviews with employers in the formal sector, the study also found that graduates had underdeveloped entrepreneurial and problem solving skills, as well as poor communication and literacy skills. These results indicate priority areas for investment in skills development (see table 5.9).

In 2007, the ITF, in cooperation with the Nigerian Employers' Consultative Association, conducted a survey of manpower requirements that looked into the question of skills required by the labor force. Approximately 26 percent of the interviewed organizations indicated that their employees do not possess the requisite competencies to perform their jobs. Lack of practical hands-on experience, ICT knowledge, and communication skills were the most cited shortcomings (ITF/Nigeria Employers' Consultative Association 2007).

Finally, the Federal Public Service Program recently conducted an assessment of the demand for vocational and technical skills in the Federal Capital Territory (Federal Public Service Program 2008). The study identified the top ten skills in demand as auto/vehicle mechanics, electrical installation, fish farming, poultry farming, catering and confectionery, weaving works and embroidery, aluminum works, painting/decoration/sign writing, agricultural equipment mechanics, and computer/secretarial work. The findings correspond to those of the ITF/Nigeria Employers' Consultative Association (2007) study. This result is surprising since many training institutions offer courses in these occupations. It may indicate that

Table 5.9   Priority Areas for Skills Development

Growth areas	Broad occupations in demand	Specific occupations	Generic skills
Agricultural	Livestock rearing	Poultry farming	Communication
	Crop rotation	Dairy farming	skills
	Animal husbandry	Aquaculture	Supervisory skills
Manufacturing	Food processing	Food preparation	Numeracy skills
	Light manufacturing	Metal fabrication	Work-related skills
		Carpentry	Literacy skills
		Furniture making	ICT skills
		Structural timber	Entrepreneurship
		Boat making	
Services	Wholesale and retail	Garments and tailoring	
	ICT	Computer programming	
	Vehicle repair	Motor vehicle mechanic	
		Hairdressing	
Hotel	Catering	Cook	
and restaurant	Hotel management	Supervisor	
	Tourism	Pottery making	
Construction	Masonry	Electrician	
	Carpentry	Electrical installation	
		Brickmaking	
		Scaffolding	
		Arch welding	
		Bricklayer	
		Carpenter	

Source: National Universities Commission 2005.

the graduates do not possess the competencies considered relevant by the companies. The data are not sufficient for further discussion of this issue.

Nonformal Skills Acquisition

Nonformal training refers to training provided outside the mainstream education system. It is offered by many different types of organizations, public and private, and caters to a diverse audience including youth who have never attended a formal school, those who once attended but withdrew, and people of all ages who want additional knowledge and proficiency in their area of qualification. Nonformal skills acquisition does not, at present, lead to a recognized qualification.

In terms of attendance, the volume of nonformal training exceeds that of formal TVE. Nonformal skills acquisition is provided by public as well as private institutions, for profit and not for profit. At the federal level, the Ministry of Labor and Productivity (through the NDE), the Ministry of Commerce and Industry (through the ITF), the Ministry of Agriculture, and the Ministry of Youth Development are the leading providers of non-formal skills development. Most state governments also operate such schemes. In addition, an unknown number of nongovernmental organizations and private commercial training providers offer short-term vocational courses in a variety of subjects, from beekeeping and dressmaking to information technology applications and entrepreneurship development. Most of these courses are short term, from a few days to several months. The demand seems to be high, but the quality of training is often problematic. There is no information available on the labor impact of non-formal training.

This section discusses some of the more important non-formal schemes in relation to their labor market relevance. It also discusses the country's trade testing system, which—if carried out correctly—could be an important way for people who have acquired their skills outside the formal education system to get official recognition of their competencies.

National Directorate of Employment. The NDE is the principal government institution dealing with nonformal training and skills development for the informal sector. Its mandate is to design and implement programs to combat mass unemployment and to articulate policies aimed at developing work programs with labor-intensive potential. The principal target groups are unemployed school leavers and other persons who lack productive and marketable skills. Skills are imparted through four main types of programs (table 5.10): Rural Employment Promotion (including the Rural Agriculture Development Training Scheme); Special Public Works (including the Graduate Attachment Scheme); Small-Scale Enterprise Development (including the Start-Your-Business Scheme); and Vocational Skills Development (including the Open Apprenticeship Scheme and School on Wheels).

All four NDE programs described in table 5.10 emphasize the development of work-related skills, but there are significant constraints facing each of the programs. Perhaps the most important crosscutting problem is the large volume of applicants and the limited resources to meet this demand. For the Graduate Attachment Scheme, for example, only a small number of industrial attachments are available, so the majority of applicants have to be turned away. An important question is why people are attracted to this program. Is it due to the economic returns of acquiring skills, or because they will receive a stipend for participating in the scheme?

Table 5.10 Employment Program Supported by the National Directorate of Employment

	Objective of program and activities	Outputs
Rural Employment Promotion		
Rural Agriculture Development Training Scheme	Training takes place over four months and occurs twice a year at one of the 14 agricultural training centers across Nigeria. The curriculum is based on traditional techniques, but incorporates modern technology and processes. The training covers all aspects of agriculture, crop rotation, poultry, fish processing, and marketing. Participants can specialize in a specific area. All participants are given a daily stipend, and they form cooperatives at the end of their training. They can subsequently apply for funding.	Around 300 youths per state participate in this program.
Integrated Farming and Training Scheme	Training equips young people with the skills to support crop production but in the rainy season focuses on poultry farming. This ensures that the student can be productive for the entire year.	This has been piloted with 20 graduates; after 3 years, they will be in a position to start their own business.
Rural Handicraft Scheme	This ensures that farmers acquire handicraft skills so that they can earn a living during the non-farming season. Youth are attached to master trainers but are not paid. Crafts include basket, mat, and craft weaving; pestle and mortar making; furniture making; etc.	About 14,775 young people participate in this scheme.
Special Public Works		
Graduate Attachment Program	This program targets graduates and provides them with work experience. After three months of experience, if they do not get a job they will be given another opportunity. Subsequently, they will attend a start-up business program in order to establish their own business.	There is a total of 1,536 beneficiaries.
Environmental Beautification Scheme	This is a collaborative venture with local communities that focuses on construction. NDE provides the labor (either unemployed adults or youth), and the communities provide the resources and materials.	Around 2,220 have participated in this scheme.

(continued)

Table 5.10   Employment Program Supported by the National Directorate of Employment *(continued)*

	Objective of program and activities	Outputs
Small-Scale Enterprise Development		
Entrepreneurial Development Program	This program attempts to sensitize the unemployed and young people to the possibilities of working for themselves in the formal and informal economies. This is normally a precursor to the other programs that involve starting a business.	More than 900,000 have benefited from this program.
Start-Your-Business	This program provides skills training for those who want to establish a business for the first time. It covers starting up a business, management techniques, sources of credit, and bookkeeping. Participates receive help in developing a business plan, which then is submitted to the microcredit bank for assistance.	The training program has had 6,975 participants; the loan program has had 109 participants.
Vocational Skills Development		
National Open Apprenticeship Scheme	These schemes are targeted at young people and those unable to find work, primarily in urban areas. They are attached to a master craftsman to learn a trade. The length of the apprenticeship varies according to trade.	
School on Wheels	This involves master craftsmen going to a rural area with fully equipped mobile facilities and providing intensive training for three to six months.	More than 8,000 youths have been trained by the program. The employment effect has never been evaluated.
Resettlement Scheme	The purpose of the resettlement scheme is to support those who have participated in schemes to establish their own businesses in more prosperous regions of the country. Part of the resettlement scheme involves a campaign to persuade families to support their relatives. In addition, a considerable number are recommended to microcredit institutions for start-up funding.	

Source: National Directorate of Employment 2008.
Note: Output figures from 2005.

There are also serious quality issues related to the programs. There is no systematic monitoring of the quality of the training and no assessment of the trainees' skills at completion. In addition, there are issues of homogeneity and comparability of skills taught in different parts of Nigeria and of the lack of resources to support resettlement and help people establish their own enterprises. The fact that the vast majority do not receive tools when they finish the training acts as a disincentive to others to complete the programs.

Ministry of Youth Development. As part of its mandate, the Ministry of Youth Development offers short-term skills training for unemployed youth 18 to 25 years of age. In 2007, the Ministry trained 3,700 young people in agriculture and agro-processing. Most courses last for two weeks. At the completion of the training, participants are given some startup materials, provided they form cooperatives.

Trade Test Office of the Ministry of Labor and Productivity. The Employment and Wages Department of the Ministry of Labor and Productivity is in charge of national trade testing services. Trade testing is the official system for assessing, classifying, and certifying artisans and craftsmen in 47 approved trades. The tests take place at designated trade testing stations. The Ministry also operates two skills upgrading centers; six more such centers are planned.

There are three grades of trade test, grade 3 being the lowest. To be eligible to take the grade 3 test, a candidate must have served as an apprentice for at least three years, have at least three years of experience in his trade, and be able to read metric rule. This means that only apprentices trained by a master trainer or at a vocational training institution meet the eligibility criteria.

In 2006, a total of 24,283 people acquired a trade test certificate (see table 5.11). In 2007, that number increased to 30,676. Approximately 15 percent of the candidates aim for grade 1 certificates. The most popular trades, according to the number of certificates issued, are driver and mechanic, electrician, carpentry, motor mechanic, and construction-related trades. However, the popularity of these trades may not be a proxy for the trades in demand by the labor market, since there is unequal access to different categories of trade tests. As demonstrated by the popularity of white collar education, there is not always a logical correspondence between demand for a particular trade and its popularity among workers.[7]

Table 5.11   Number of Trade Certificates Issued by Grade
and Year, 2006 and 2007

	2006	2007
Grade 1	3,557	3,963
Grade 2	7,284	11,422
Grade 3	13,442	15,291
Total	24,283	30,676

Source: Federal Ministry of Labor and Productivity 2008b.

The trade testing system suffers from a range of constraints. These include lack of workshop facilities for testing candidates' practical skills; insufficient funds to pay qualified testers and to upgrade the skills of existing testers; the unavailability of trade test certificates; and the counterfeiting of certificates, which allows for abuse of the whole process. Another concern is that the curricula used as a basis for trade testing are updated only every five years, raising questions about whether they reflect the changing demand for skills.

Private initiatives. All over Nigeria, private organizations offer nonformal training programs. In many cases, the quality of this training compares favorably with that of government institutions. Some examples are as follows:

* *Nigerian Institute of Welding, Delta State.* The institution was established by the Nigerian Welders Association. In collaboration with a South African partner and support from the Niger Delta Development Authority, it offers accredited welding courses for young people with a science background. The training is modularized, with the basic courses lasting six weeks. The program is targeted at the oil and gas industry.
* *Shell Youth Development Scheme* was established in the 1980s.[8] It uses an institutionalized training model in conformity with the National Policy on Vocational Education. In 2006, 206 youths were trained in welding and fabrication, electrical, electronics, carpentry, auto mechanics, fashion design, and hairdressing. The trainees are also exposed to enterprise management, peace education, and leadership training. Graduates are offered tools and a take-off grant. The training is provided by the Nigeria Opportunities Industrialization Center and the Imo State Technological Skills Acquisition Center in Orlu. Other programs funded by Shell Oil are the Shell Intensive Training Program under the Youth Oil and Gas Training Scheme, which trains secondary school leavers as technicians for the oil industry (handled by the Government

Craft Development Center); the Citizen Education Scheme for school districts; and the Peace Education Program for youth leaders.

- *The Nigerian Association of Small-Scale Industries* is an umbrella organization advocating for the interests of small-scale industries. It provides courses in management skills as well as technical subjects. The Ministry of Commerce and Industry uses NASSI as a vehicle for dissemination of information and skills upgrading.

- *The Nigerian Association of Small and Medium Enterprises.* To address the skills shortage among small and medium-enterprises, the association carries out a number of programs in the fields of management, administration, and accounting, in collaboration with various government agencies.

- *Julius Berger,* the leading civil engineering and construction company in Nigeria, has a staff of more than 15,000, including about 600 expatriates who provide technical training through the company's comprehensive training program.

It is notable that most of these skills development initiatives are conducted in collaboration with government institutions, at either the federal or state level. Several of these initiatives also benefit from access to the expertise and resources of international partners.

Apprenticeship Schemes
The most pronounced structured apprenticeship scheme is NDE's Open Apprenticeship Scheme, but apprenticeships are also practiced by retail traders, roadside mechanics, makeshift tailors, and other artisans who require special skills. Traditional informal apprenticeship is the predominant source of skills acquisition in Nigeria; it is estimated that more than 50 percent of young people entering the labor market acquire their skills through some sort of apprenticeship arrangement.

Open Apprenticeship Scheme. The Open Apprenticeship Scheme operated by NDE provides vocational skills to unemployed school leavers and dropouts in approximately 80 trades. The school leavers are attached to master craftsmen and women for 3 to 24 months, depending on the trade. At the completion of the training, the apprentice is provided with a certificate of attendance. NDE does not encourage the apprentices to sit for a trade test, and no information is available on how many actually do so. The main reason is that the majority of NDE apprentices do not meet the educational requirements of the trade testing system.

The NDE budget provides for 1,000 new trainees to be approved for each state and the Federal Capital Territory every year, meaning the intake under the scheme is approximately 37,000 per year. In 2006, the total number attending vocational training under the scheme was 49,800, including the spillover from the previous year. About 17,215 trainees reportedly completed the apprenticeship scheme that year. A small number of apprentices are provided with basic tools and equipment at the completion of the training, so they can start their own business. The limited credit scheme, operated by NDE, is not available to the apprentices, however; instead, they are referred to existing microfinance institutions. Approximately 3,000 master trainers are authorized by NDE to conduct training under this scheme, each working with an average of 15 trainees per year, according to NDE. Given the lack of tools and equipment in many informal workshops, master trainers will be hard pressed to provide a high quality of training to that number of trainees.

Though only a small percentage of unemployed youth and apprentices benefit from the scheme, which suffers from underfunding, the NISER (2007) study nevertheless found the Open Apprenticeship Scheme to be the principal source of practical skills acquisition for 12 percent of the interviewed informal sector operators.

The National Directorate of Employment frankly admits that the apprenticeship scheme does not adequately correspond to the realities of the labor market. There are several reasons for this: (a) course content is rarely adjusted to reflect changes in the labor market and emerging technologies, (b) the quality of the training provided by the master trainers is not monitored, and (c) some master trainers lack the necessary competencies. Further, many workshops do not have the facilities required to meet the requirements of the curricula developed by NDE. In order to address this problem, NDE has launched a Trainer Capacity Upgrading initiative, from which 27 master trainers benefited in 2007. The effect of this initiative has been minimal so far. NDE is soliciting funds to establish its own training facilities, which can serve as a site for developing training standards for the informal sector.

A tracer study conducted in 1999 found that about 70 percent of the Open Apprenticeship Scheme graduates were gainfully employed, either through direct or wage employment, self-employment, or other activities, including retention by master craftsmen for further training. Out of those, 38 percent were self-employed. Given the deterioration of the labor market, NDE believes that this figure has diminished considerably since then.

Traditional apprenticeship. The distinguishing characteristic of an apprenticeship is that it is essentially a contractual (written or verbal) arrangement between a master craftsperson and, typically, the parent of the apprentice, in which the trainer is obligated in accordance with the provisions of the agreement. Traditional apprenticeships are usually self-financing (the apprentices pay for the training) and provide practical experience with good chances for employment after the training. In practice, however, most artisans have to sustain themselves after completion of the training through odd jobs with different employers. The duration of and payment for the training varies according to the trade and the circumstances of the apprenticeship. In some instances, apprentices do not pay for the training. In the case of blue-collar occupations such as carpentry, vehicle repair, and welding, the duration is typically three years, while it is shorter for less skill-intensive trades.

As noted above, there is no officially recognized certification for those who acquire their skills through apprenticeship. The individual master craftsman determines when the apprentice has acquired the necessary skills and is qualified to start working on his or her own (in Nigeria, this is known as "getting one's freedom"). The master usually issues a certificate asserting the artisan's qualifications. In rare cases, the apprentice may sit for an officially recognized trade test, but as the numbers illustrate, this is far from common. In Nigeria, unlike other countries, trade associations seem to play a very limited role in the regulation of apprenticeships and issuance of certificates.[9]

There is no information available on the number of traditional apprentices in Nigeria, but information from Ghana suggests that the number may be three to four times as high as that of youth enrolled in public and private formal TVE institutions (Adams 2008). Although traditional apprenticeships primarily target youth with weak educational backgrounds, there seems to be, as discussed above, an increasing number of youth with post-basic education who perceive this mode of learning as useful for acquiring a practical skill that enables them to earn a decent living.

Associations of micro- and small enterprise operators exist within several trades, including furniture making, welding, vehicle repair, and leather work. Their strength varies considerably, but most are organized at the federal and state level. The majority also have local chapters. Resman Associates (2007) found that approximately half of informal sector operators belong to, and pay fees to, their respective trade associations. "The associations need to be assisted to organize themselves as effective instruments for promoting the types of intra-sector interactions and collaboration that can stimulate business development in their groups" (Resman Associates 2007). Furthermore, trade associations have a potentially important role to play in terms of skills acquisition by, for instance, facilitating course upgrading, overseeing apprenticeship training, and issuing certificates. The associations may also take part in trade testing as a means of enhancing the credibility of the tests.

Conclusion

The most important finding is that non-formal training is conducted in a disjointed manner with no uniform certification system, and its quality varies widely. The diversity of the training is both a strength and weakness. On the one hand, it allows the programs to serve different target audiences in a flexible, demand-responsive way. But at the same time, the lack of minimum training requirements means that the credibility of the training depends on the reputation of the individual training organizations. Furthermore, much of the training seems to be conducted without proper assessment of the demand for the skills in question.

With regard to labor market relevance and acceptance of various types of training, there is little information available, which makes it difficult to assess the strengths and weaknesses of different TVET sub-systems and thus to optimize resource utilization. As no government agency has responsibility for coordinating and monitoring of non-formal training, no systematic assessment of its relevance and quality takes place. However, on the basis of experience from other countries, there is reason to assume that much of this training, especially in traditional vocations such as tie and dye, beekeeping, and dressmaking, has limited effect unless conducted in an integrated and innovative manner.

The advantage of traditional apprenticeships is their flexibility, the fact that they combine work and learning, their affordability and self-financing, their connection with future employment, and their low entrance standards, all of which makes them attractive as a source of learning to youth from disadvantaged families. The drawback is the limited theoretical knowledge of most master craftsmen, their lack of pedagogical expertise, and the poor equipment in many workshops, which means that more often than not, the master craftsmen teach outdated technologies and methods. The challenge is to enhance the way in which skills are acquired through traditional apprenticeship, while acknowledging its importance for future skills development in Nigeria. At the same time, the issue of how to ensure more standardized certification procedures needs to be addressed.

Concluding Remarks and Ways Forward

The main challenge facing the Nigerian education sector is the profound mismatch between the employment opportunities offered by the labor market and the types of qualifications provided by the education system. Every year, thousands of young people graduate from tertiary institutions with very bleak prospects for finding a job in the formal sector. Many eventually start their own business or find a job unrelated to their education. While this development is likely to have a long-term positive effect on the dynamic of the informal sector, the absence of adequate practical training that characterizes most tertiary education means the graduates are poorly prepared for a future either as self-employed or as employees in companies.

At the same time, the formal education system does not pay sufficient attention to senior secondary vocational education (the technical colleges), which represents a practically oriented alternative route to the labor market. Instead, the sector gives priority to general secondary education and various kinds of tertiary education geared toward employment in the formal sector. This situation calls for a reprioritization of the government's resource allocation to the technical and vocational education stream of the education system and a reconsideration of the importance assigned to the tertiary education system.

In addition, existing policies for skills development must be geared toward anticipated growth areas. At present, this occurs only to a limited extent, and strategies for skills development tend to be created in response to a crisis or as a temporary social measure to tackle unemployment as opposed to facilitating structural change in growing sectors of the economy. Moreover, the existing programs are adversely impacted by a lack of appropriate funding, outdated curricula, and a shortage of qualified teaching staff.

At the macro level, the government of Nigeria has a policy to support employment growth through its Vision 2020 strategy.[10] The objective of this strategy is to transform Nigeria into one of the leading world economies. Employment generation through the creation of small and medium-size enterprises is one of its four key pillars. Strengthening of the skill base, by providing courses that build vocational and entrepreneurial skills, is a basic tenet of this pillar. However, the link between NEEDS and the implementation strategies of different ministries responsible for TVET appears rather weak. There also seems to be limited coordination, both horizontally across different ministries and vertically between federal and state structures. In addition, implementation strategies are not based on timely or accurate labor market information. As a consequence, government ministries often fail to develop a shared vision about which economic sectors are most likely to result in productive employment, and which skills are most likely to improve the income earning potential of those working in the informal sector—both of which are vital for achieving the goals of Vision 2020.

A number of policy documents, including the National Policy on Education (Federal Republic of Nigeria 1977), state that the objective of Nigeria's education system is "to equip every individual with the skills and job competencies for gainful employment." In 2000, the Federal Ministry of Education formulated a Masterplan for TVE Development in the 21st Century, spelling out specific actions for the decade 2001–10 (Federal Ministry of Education 2000). The key message of the document was that TVE must be more responsive to the demands of the labor market and produce a skilled and technical workforce capable of handling state-of-the-art technology in their various vocations. The means to achieve this include significant improvement in the quality of existing TVE, better articulation of formal and non-formal technical TVE through a national vocational qualification system, and increased access to quality TVE at the post-basic level.

As discussed above, NDE has taken a number of steps to enhance the labor market relevance of its skills development programs for the informal sector by encouraging more apprentices to move into areas of high demand such as computer training and by providing pedagogic training for selected appointed master craftsmen. These are moves in the right direction, but more needs to be done to help ensure that skills formation reflects changing economic demands.

Many of the problems of the TVET system are rooted as much in structural deficiencies as in immediate resource constraints. For example, the system for planning and implementation of training does not include labor representatives or sustainable mechanisms to monitor and align the training with changing labor market demands. Other challenges concern the absence of transparent quality assurance mechanisms; the fragmentation and lack of articulation of training offers, especially the absence of a mechanism for the recognition of skills acquired in the informal sector; and structural resource constraints as a result of an undiversified funding system that is largely dependent on government allocations.

The following are key recommendations to improve the responsiveness of the vocational education system to the demands of the labor market.

National Vocational Qualifications Framework—Linking Growth to Skills Development

An appropriate regulatory and institutional framework is a precondition for the long-term development of a demand-oriented, efficient, and relevant TVET system. The Masterplan for TVET of 2000 (Federal Ministry of Education 2000) has already emphasized the importance of establishing a National Vocational Qualifications Framework (NVQF), including mechanisms for recognition of prior learning. The existence of an NVQF would facilitate the development and certification of new short-term programs that address emerging and short-term needs such as skills upgrading for the informal sector. An NVQF would also, if appropriately managed, open the national certification procedures to private and community-based training institutions. Hence, the establishment of an NVQF would provide opportunities for the large group of young people who have acquired their skills in the informal sector to get recognition for their competencies.

While NBTE has taken the first steps to initiate the preparation of an NVQF, the process needs to be accelerated and made more inclusive, with a view to ensuring the broadest possible ownership of the emerging new structure for regulation of TVET. To this end, NBTE could become a national authority for technical and vocational training. The authority should have a mandate to regulate and monitor TVET—formal, nonformal, and informal—but not be responsible for actually providing education and training. In order for NBTE to assume this function, its mandate must be redefined and the tasks related to allocation of funds to federal polytechnics handed over to another body, preferably the Federal Ministry of Education.

An NVQF, coordinated by NBTE, could also enable the systematic link of value chains through specific skills development programs in a strategic concept that takes into account geographical differences. The well-functioning trade associations that exist within major parts of the informal sector should be empowered to take part in the skills upgrading and certification of their members. The associations are also well positioned to participate in the design and management of the planned industrial zones and clusters. A facility to support trade associations in their role as advocates for and service providers to their constituencies should also be established. In addition, more Centers for Excellence might be encouraged to provide training for key value chains, including through a special window for targeted investment by enterprises needing to address critical skill constraints.

Private Sector Leadership and Government Support in the Context of Public-Private Partnerships

Nigeria's private sector has been highly responsive to the improved policy environment and has successfully created pockets of excellence. Vocational training would ideally be led by training institutions run by the private sector, which would offer programs that are responsive to its specific needs and administer relevant exams. Government could support such institutions through standardization of curricula and accreditation of programs.

An effective way to strengthen links between employers and training programs would be through tripartite governance frameworks, involving training institutions, public sector agencies, and the private sector. These agencies could review and coordinate public expenditure on training and help monitor quality control mechanisms. The recent establishment of VEIs and IEIs, as discussed above, is a potentially promising route to facilitate this approach.

Providing Financial Incentives for Vocational Training

The TVET system offers few financial incentives to schools that produce graduates who find employment with the private sector. Providing financial rewards to such institutions requires effective monitoring and evaluation of their existing programs.

Planning and Demand Assessment

The TVET system suffers from inadequate capacity for planning and policy analysis, and from a lack of information, including enrollment data, internal efficiency, financial data, and demand trends. These deficiencies hamper initiatives to improve performance. Similarly, there is no framework, at either the federal or state level, to link the few existing attempts to produce labor market statistics and assess the needs for skilled manpower.

Formal vocational and technical education institutions show little concern for the labor market relevance of the programs they offer and even less for the skills needs of those employed in the informal sector. As proposed by Adams (2008), this could change if public financing for these institutions were based on rewarding outcomes—such as their success in serving target populations, including the informal sector—rather than simply financing inputs. Performance-based budgeting for public institutions could provide incentives to upgrade technical skills for master craftspersons and improve their teaching methods. More attention should also be given to forming partnerships with private business, including associations representing small and medium enterprises. At the level of individual institutions, the dialogue with the private sector could be intensified through private sector participation in the governing bodies of colleges and polytechnics, and the individual institutions should be given more leeway to prioritize the use of funds.

For government policies on skills development and employment to become more strategic, a mechanism is needed to monitor the labor market and aid in the understanding of where employment absorption is highest, including what skills are required. The system should be able to produce information on broad employment trends, skills needs, and what skills are in demand in different states. It would also be useful to understand the returns from particular types of skills in terms of the relationship between acquisition of skills and earning levels. Whatever approach is used, it will be important to anticipate future requirements. There are several cost-efficient, user-friendly mechanisms available for assessing skills needs. It is essential that the models selected for gathering labor market data meet the specific information needs of key TVET stakeholders within and outside the public sector. Experience from other countries suggests that often simple, localized labor market information systems provide better results than ambitious, all-embracing systems, which are costly to maintain and often produce data that exceed the needs of those dealing with skills development. Panels of informants knowledgeable about local skills trends have proven useful for this purpose.

Skill Formation in the Informal Sector

While the traditional apprenticeship system has a number of evident advantages, especially strong practical skills training and exposure to the world of business, many master craftspersons and master trainers need help in upgrading their technical and didactic skills.

Skills upgrading initiatives yield the best results by focusing on selected, particularly dynamic informal sector operators and new entrants with high learning potential. Well-equipped TVET institutions should be encouraged to provide organized training programs and schedules for those engaged in the informal economy, both master craftspersons and other relevant business operators. Programs should be modularized, flexible, and located as close to trainees' homes as possible. They may take the form of part-time programs, long vacation courses, or weekend programs. To ensure proper recognition of the acquired skills, the programs should be geared to the requirements of the trade testing system. At the same time, the trade testing system should be refocused to reflect the circumstances of the informal sector. Finally, in line with the practice of other countries, monotechnics, polytechnics, and technical colleges should be used as outreach centers for the informal economy. Potential service areas include business advice, technical support, and product development.

It is well recognized that the level of technical and managerial competence is a critical determinant of incomes in the informal sector; therefore, the government should investigate ways to finance skills programs for informal workers. International experience suggests that a government-funded voucher system may be a feasible option. The ITF could spearhead such a voucher system. However, management of such a system is challenging and requires robust monitoring and auditing mechanisms; so the relevance of this modality for Nigeria depends on the prospects of identifying adequate, sufficiently robust implementation structures.

Further, the trade associations that represent major parts of the informal sector could be empowered to take part in the skills upgrading and certification of their members, as described in box 5.2. The associations are also well positioned to participate in the design and management of planned industrial zones and clusters. A facility should be established to support trade associations in their role as advocates for and service providers to their constituencies.

Box 5.2

Role of Trade Associations in Skills Development

West and Central Africa offer interesting examples of the role that (informal) trade associations can play in apprenticeship training. In Ghana, associations of dressmakers, carpenters, and others are actively involved in the supervision of skills training. Member master craftspersons monitor the training providers and award their own certificates upon completion of the training. In various countries, especially in donor projects, trade associations are used to identify the training needs of their members and to prepare the training curricula.

However, the use of trade associations is no guarantee of success. In the Ghana Vocational Skills Project, the associations were not helpful with distributing intake vouchers to members. Incentives were missing. Small, grassroots associations, although weaker, tend to be easier to work with than large, national, more bureaucratic associations.

The Ministry of Commerce and Industry is planning to establish industrial clusters and enterprise zones in selected growth centers of Nigeria. If well planned and managed, such clusters open up the synergy potential of different categories of formal and informal sector enterprises. The clusters and zones could be equipped with facilities that can be used for training and counseling of small-scale informal business operators. The facilities could be leased out to relevant private training providers.

Notes

1. The informal economy of Nigeria comprises all forms of informal employment: self-employment in informal enterprises (registered or unregistered), including informal financial marketers; own account operators; unpaid family workers; wage employment without secure contracts, worker benefits, or social protection (both inside and outside the informal economy); and workers with constantly changing employers, such as domestic workers, casual and day laborers, temporary and part-time workers, industrial workers, home-based workers, and unregistered and undeclared workers. The present study agrees with this definition, but emphasizes the relationship between informal and formal sector employment as a continuum as opposed to a dichotomy. That is to say, at one end of the spectrum are standard forms of employment, followed by nonstandard forms of employment and, finally, informal sector employment. Such an approach can explain the close links between formal and informal sector employment.

2. Much of the literature employs the terms "skills development" and "TVET" interchangeably. However, skills development tends to be slightly broader, referring to all sorts of mechanisms for acquisition of skills, whereas TVET refers primarily to structured learning processes.

3. For detailed information, see National Board of Technical Education, http://www.nbte.gov.ng.

4. In collaboration with United Nations Educational, Scientific, and Cultural Organization and the Japan International Cooperation Agency, NBTE has embarked on a comprehensive review and updating of existing curricula. So far, more than 75 course and training curricula have been reviewed.

5. There is also a considerable number of private TVE institutions, not all of which are accredited.

6. This development raises important issues: How will wages evolve as people crowd into this sector? What returns to education exist? What returns to apprenticeship exist? Do the returns vary by gender? What kind of industrial distribution exists in the informal sector? Is apprenticeship a substitute for, or a complement to, formal education? How do the means of skills acquisition

vary across income quintiles? Existing data do not provide answers to these and other questions.

7. It would be useful to know more about the background and labor market performance of those who sit for the trade tests.

8. Shell Oil is sponsoring a number of skills development initiatives in Nigeria.

9. The role and internal organization of trade associations deserves more investigation as part of the follow-up to this study.

10. http://www.nv2020.org.

CHAPTER 6

Nigeria's Trade Policy Facilitates Unofficial Trade but Not Manufacturing

Gaël Raballand and Edmond Mjekiqi

Overview

One barrier to expanding (legal) trade in West Africa is the current restrictive trade regime in Nigeria, which includes import bans and numerous levies. Although Nigeria adopted the Economic Community of West African States (ECOWAS) common external tariff (CET) in October 2005 and lowered average tariff duties, the scheduled phasing out of import bans and levies on imports remains to be implemented. Linchpins of Nigerian trade policy have for many years consisted of (a) numerous import bans,[1] with trade protection justifications and (b) numerous tariff peaks, with the theoretical aim of boosting local production.

In an oil economy, trade policy is often used as an instrument to protect local industry, especially for agricultural goods. Moreover, at early stages of industrialization, governments have often considered restrictive trade policy to be helpful in developing a country's industrial capacity. In Nigeria, manufacturers—especially the Manufacturers Association of Nigeria—advocate the maintenance of a restrictive trade policy, whereas traders and most customs officials support reduced tariff protection.[2] Although Nigeria's National Economic Empowerment and Development

Strategy highlights an increasing need for the Nigerian government to expand its non-oil export performance by reducing tariff protections, many Nigerian officials and manufacturers still advocate a restrictive tariff policy.

Domestic supply, however, has failed to respond to the restrictive trade policy and tariff differentials with neighboring countries. Instead, these measures have created strong incentives for traders and importers to smuggle goods[3] from neighboring countries such as Benin to meet demand, inducing a noncompliant and nontransparent culture among traders,[4] which is aggravated by corrupt behavior on the part of many customs officials. Moreover, import bans have given the Customs Service a pretext to delay some important process and procedural reforms.

A review of customs and excise duties in the period 1995 to 2001, carried out by the Fiscal Policy Department of the Federal Ministry of Finance (Federal Ministry of Finance 2003), revealed endemic corruption within the Customs Service, with the collection of import duties limited to only 38 percent of potential duties.

Protective trade regimes usually hinder customs modernization and reform. Peru had accrued 539 import bans by 1990; and its customs administration was characterized by disorganization, inefficiency, endemic corruption, and bureaucratic and cumbersome procedures. In 2002, Peru removed import bans and reduced the peak tariff to 25 percent. This trade policy liberalization not only benefited customs administration reform but also contributed to the removal of administrative obstacles to trade (Goorman 2003).

The government of Nigeria and the Customs Service are pursuing an ambitious and far-reaching effort to facilitate legal trade between Nigeria and neighboring countries, including by reducing clearance time to 48 hours at all border points. However, this objective is unlikely to be met under Nigeria's existing trade policy.

Nigeria has also relaxed its policy on import bans; in October 2008, almost half of all banned import products were legalized (see appendixes F and G for details).[5] However, the impact of this action could be rather limited, because some of the main items subject to unofficial trade (garments, oil, and secondhand cars) are still prohibited.

Without further reform of the trade policy regime, the benefits of these trade facilitation measures could be limited. This chapter focuses on import bans, since they provide the strongest incentives for fraud and corruption, which in turn justify long and overly complex control procedures (Hors 2001). Any donor support in this environment, therefore, would not achieve the intended impact under the current regime. Up to 15 percent of Nigeria's total imports enter the country through unofficial channels. There is evidence that an additional US$200 million—more than one-tenth of the current revenue collected by the Customs Service—could be realized if trade restrictions on a limited number of products were adjusted to current practices in the subregion. The current system also exacerbates port traffic diversion and delays in port clearance, which explains why Nigeria, despite a good port reform, is a poor performer as far as trade facilitation is concerned (table 6.1).

Before any trade liberalization, which may be politically difficult, the government first needs to remove most import prohibitions—and change them into tariff peaks—to significantly reduce incentives for smuggling and trade re-export from Benin. Changing prohibited imports into tariff peaks would bring additional revenue for the Treasury and the Customs Service, and could give Customs a stronger incentive to curb unofficial trade. It could also make it easier for the Ministry of Finance to monitor customs efficiency and could contribute to enhanced transparency, since import prohibitions currently distort the revenues-per-staff ratio. Local customs officials can always give the pretext of import bans as a reason for being able to collect limited revenues. If such bans are removed, this justification would disappear. For the senior management of the Customs Service, it would also remove the excuse for not accelerating implementation of

Table 6.1   Comparative Rankings for Trading Across Borders

Economy	Rank	Documents for export (number)	Time for export (days)	Cost to export (US$ per container)	Documents for import (number)	Time for import (days)	Cost to import (US$ per container)
Singapore	1	4	5	456	4	3	439
Hong Kong, China	2	4	6	625	4	5	633
Denmark	3	4	5	681	3	5	681
Finland	4	4	8	495	5	8	575
Estonia	5	3	5	730	4	5	740
Ghana	76	6	19	1,003	7	29	1,130
Nigeria	144	10	25	1,179	9	42	1,306
South Africa	147	8	30	1,445	9	35	1,721
Kenya	148	9	29	2,055	8	26	2,190
Niger	169	8	59	3,545	10	64	3,545

Source: Doing Business Indicators, 2009 data time series.
Note: Rankings based on 181 economies.

reforms and would give them some incentive to collect more revenue given the expanded tax base. Therefore, even though it may be difficult for the government to stand up to strong vested interests in this area, removing major import prohibitions on textiles, vegetable oils, or secondhand cars, for instance, would help to significantly increase transparency. It would also lead to increased tariff revenues and give the government more power to monitor functioning of the Customs Service on a daily basis.

The next section presents Nigeria's current trade policy. The following section then provides data on the impact of trade policy on manufacturing in Nigeria. Next, mirror statistics are used to highlight the magnitude of smuggling activities to Nigeria. The subsequent sections describe the channels of unofficial trade to Nigeria, demonstrate the impact of trade policy on customs efficiency, assess the spillover effect of import bans on port productivity, and estimate the magnitude of the economic impact of current import bans on the Nigerian economy. The final section draws some conclusions for trade policy.

Nigeria's Current Trade Policy

Nigeria's trade policy has been based on tariff protection in order to stimulate production diversification and encourage increased value-added in the non-oil economy. The government has continuously pursued restrictive trade policies, especially for manufacturing and agricultural goods. Linchpins of the Nigerian trade policy are numerous tariffs peaks and import bans, with the theoretical aim of supporting local production.

A report by the World Trade Organization (WTO) highlights Nigeria's high average tariffs and import bans and demonstrates that trade restrictions have been on the rise since 2001 (World Trade Organization 2005). Import bans are highest in the textile sector: more than 70 percent of tariff lines in this product group are subject to import bans (World Bank 2007; International Monetary Fund 2005).

The ECOWAS CET requires tariff duty rates to be set between 0 and 20 percent. While the adoption of the ECOWAS CET lowered average import duties rate to 11.6 percent, high tariff duty rates still apply to numerous imports (table 6.2). Moreover, the government insisted on the introduction of a fifth band at 35 percent.

Nigeria also continues to apply a variety of import levies, such as a port development levy (7 percent of duty payable), a comprehensive import supervision scheme charge (1 percent of customs value), the ECOWAS levy (0.5 percent of customs value), and miscellaneous product-specific levies and excise duties, such as for rice and cement.

Table 6.2   Most Favored Nation Tariffs in Nigeria

	1997–98	1999–2000	2001	2002	2003	Average import duty	
						2005–06	2008
Simple average tariff rate	24.4	26.0	26.0	29.0	28.6	12.1	11.6
Agriculture (ISIC Div 1)	26.7	26.3	26.7	41.5	41.4	12.8	12.6
Mining and quarrying (ISIC Div 2)	18.3	18.4	18.4	18.4	17.9	5.2	5.2
Manufacturing (ISIC Div 3)	24.4	26.1	26.2	28.5	28.0	12.2	11.6
Domestic tariff spikes (% of lines)	0.5	0.5	0.5	5.2	5.0	1.9	—
International tariff spikes (% of lines)	51.6	57.9	57.9	57.4	56.5	41.3	41.3
Overall standard deviation	18.0	14.6	14.5	22.0	22.3	9.1	7.5

Source: World Development Indicators.
Note: ISIC = International Standard Industrial Classification. Domestic tariff spikes are defined as exceeding three times the overall simple average applied rate. International tariff peaks are defined as exceeding 15 percent of the overall simple average applied rate. — = Not available.

Additionally, nontariff barriers reinforce the protection of domestic industries and trade restrictiveness. In January 2004, the list of prohibited goods (appendixes F and G) was expanded and bans were introduced for most manufacturing goods, including textiles, footwear, and plastic and leather articles (table 6.3). In February 2008, 968 tariff lines were subject to import bans (up from 944 lines in November 2005). Partial bans (76 tariff lines) and restrictions on import quantities are also applied to imported consumer goods.

As noted above, Nigeria relaxed its policy on import bans in October 2008. However, the possible impact of these measures on trade flows and trade facilitation could be seriously limited because the vast majority of items subject to unofficial trade—rice, garments, oil, and second-hand cars—remain prohibited for import.

Impact of Trade Policy on Nigerian Manufacturing: Limited Results

There is little evidence that import restrictions and high tariffs on product-specific imports have helped local industries or the economy as a whole. Instead, the bans have proven difficult to enforce and have encouraged smuggling through Nigeria's porous borders.

Table 6.3   Import Bans and Tariffs by Sector

Sector (ISIC Rev. 2)	Share of tariff lines with import ban	2005/06 (simple tariff)		2008 (simple tariff)	
		Average in sector	Average, banned items	Average in sector	Average, banned items
Agriculture	23.3	13.5	18.8	13.3	18.8
Forestry	0.0	5.0		5.0	
Fishing	0.0	13.5		13.5	
Coal mining	0.0	5.0		5.0	
Crude petroleum and natural gas	0.0	5.0		5.0	
Metal ore mining	0.0	5.0		5.0	
Other mining	1.4	5.3	5.0	5.3	5.0
Food, beverages, and tobacco	17.3	17.8	22.4	16.0	18.1
Textiles, apparel, and leather	71.6	17.1	18.0	17.1	18.0
Wood and furniture	29.6	19.0	19.6	19.0	19.6
Paper, printing, and publishing	11.5	11.5	18.9	11.5	18.9
Chemicals, rubber, and plastic	3.9	8.2	13.5	8.0	13.5
Nonmetallic minerals	1.9	16.2	13.3	16.2	13.3
Basic metals	0.0	12.6		9.5	
Fabricated metals and machinery	1.4	8.9	14.5	5.4	14.5
Other manufacturing	5.6	17.4	20.0	17.4	20.0

Source: World Bank 2007.
Note: Rev 2 = Revision 2 (1968).

Nigeria's trade policy following independence was largely based on an import substituting strategy, which did not significantly improve Nigeria's industry. Such measures have only generated a marginal increase of value-added in the non-oil manufacturing sector (Akinlo 1996).

As noted in the Country Economic Memorandum (World Bank 2007), Nigeria's budget depends heavily on the level of international oil prices. Due largely to the high international price of oil, the country's overall fiscal balance improved from a surplus of 6 percent of gross domestic product (GDP) in 2004 to almost 8 percent of GDP in 2006. However, the non-oil primary deficit (as a share of non-oil GDP) deteriorated from 23.9 percent in 2004 to 30.8 percent in 2008. Oil revenue accounts for about 80 percent of fiscal revenue, while non-oil exports are negligible and have declined over the past three decades. In 1970, the non-oil sector contributed 42.4 percent of total export earnings, while the oil exports share was 57.6 percent of total export earnings. Since then, the share of non-oil exports has fallen dramatically, reaching less than 5 percent in 2002.

Trend analysis demonstrates a positive relationship between tariffs and agricultural production in many countries. In Nigeria, however, agriculture's share of total output decreased by 6 percent between 1981 and 2001 (Ogunkola 2005), and import prohibition policy has negatively affected the expansion of some sectors and increased consumer prices of some basic commodities. As an example, the import ban on cooking oil, which was intended to protect domestic oil producers, has failed to expand production, since oilseed crops are expensive to produce due to the high cost of inputs and yields are low due to obsolete production techniques. The resulting high prices of oilseeds, combined with high utility costs, means that cooking oil producers have remained uncompetitive in local markets (Consilium International 2008). Because of smuggling of cooking oil, market prices are not as high as they would be without smuggling, but smuggled products are usually of lower quality.

Turning to the textile industry, Bankole, Ogunkola, and Oyejide (2005) state that import bans did not create production and export growth in most cases. Despite an almost permanent import ban on textile products, exports, output, and employment in the sector have all performed poorly. As a first-generation postcolonial industry, the textile industry started out strongly and constituted a large part of Nigeria's manufacturing sector, accounting for 27 percent of the home textile market and 72 percent of West Africa's textile production in the 1970s and 1980s (Aremu 2005). However, the industry has since suffered a serious decline, from 175 firms at its peak in the mid-1980s to only 10 factories in stable condition in 2004. Employment fell from 350,000 to 40,000 direct workers over the same period, and many of the retrenched workers had difficulty finding new income sources (Aremu 2005). As pointed out by Brenton and Hoppe (2007), there is a general bias against sourcing apparel from African countries, and this has been aggravated by the emergence of India and China as exporting countries and by the rise of global production chains and the removal of quotas from the global trading regime. The global economics of the textile sector has probably had a much greater negative impact on Nigeria's sector performance than the expected positive impact of import bans.

In the construction industry, the current trade policy restrictions for cement, steel, and timber are inflating costs. In particular, cement imports, a major input for construction, are constrained by levies and quantitative restrictions. Due to the fact that import licenses are granted to only a small number of importers—constituting an oligopoly—cement is usually in short supply in the country and at a higher price than it would be if import licenses were unrestricted. Cement importers collude to ensure a high selling price by keeping imports at a low level. In addition, timber imports for carpentry are banned, forcing contractors to use domestic hardwood, which is much more expensive and could be sold internationally at a premium price. Finally, duties on the import of finished steel hover around 50 percent, putting further upward pressure on material costs, while the export of iron scrap[6] is banned, which further distorts the steel market (Consilium International 2008).

Import bans induce onerous and non-transparent border clearance procedures, and these import inefficiencies serve to drive up logistics costs. The cost to haul a load of chemicals[7] by road from Apapa Port to Kano is US$5,000–US$6,000, and the unreliability of the import system makes it necessary for companies to hold inventories for up to six months—with a major impact on logistics costs and therefore on their competitiveness.

The main conclusion of these studies is that the success of domestic production is not contingent on restrictive trade policy, that domestic producers are sensitive not only to trade policy, but also to transport, power, input, and other costs. Therefore, while trade policy can serve as an important tool to boost economic growth, it may not be the most relevant factor. In most cases, macroeconomic policy, infrastructure, and the overall investment climate have a greater impact on the performance of the manufacturing sector. In early 2007, industries had to face, on average, almost 15 hours of power outages per day (the worst being in Cross River State, with 21 hours, and the "best" in Ogun State, with 9 hours). Under these circumstances, it is difficult to imagine that any industry could grow, even with import bans.

Impact on Trade Flows: A High Likelihood of Unofficial Trade

Nigeria imports mainly manufacturing goods, machinery, and equipment, particularly for the capital-intensive oil sector. The import trend was on the rise in the first part of the decade, from US$20.5 billion in 2004 to US$29.4 billion in 2006.

Due to Nigeria's dominant role in the ECOWAS region (64 percent of consumers and 49 percent of regional GDP), and to the limited economic potential of neighboring countries, the real economy in the subregion depends heavily on Nigeria. Therefore, current protective trade policy in Nigeria provides incentives for neighboring countries, particularly Benin, to serve as "warehouse states"[8] for all of Nigeria's banned and highly taxed goods in order to meet Nigerian demand.

One approach to assessing the extent of unofficial trade from Benin to Nigeria is to compare recorded exports and imports from trade partners to Benin. Based on mirror statistics[9] over the last six years, official imports appear to be significantly lower than the value of exports reported by partner countries (mirror imports). On the one hand, Niger's and Nigeria's trade imbalance has tended to decline gradually. On the other hand, since 2000, the flow of goods entering the customs territory of Benin (measured from mirror import data, as reported by exporters) has been significantly higher than what Benin reports for imports, with an average ratio of 219 percent from 2000 to 2005, compared to a ratio of 94 percent for Nigeria and 105 percent for Niger during the same period (table 6.4). This, in turn, suggests that Benin's official statistics do not capture an important part of the imports that leave Benin, either officially or unofficially. This may signify corruption as discussed in more detail below.[10]

While Benin's GDP growth and official imports fell over the 2001–05 period, the value of mirror imports increased by 28 percent in 2005, or by almost three times the value of Benin's reported imports, and amounted to 58 percent of Benin's GDP in 2005 (figure 6.1). In a context of GDP stagnation, such a surge in imports to Benin can only be explained if the bulk of those imports were intended for Nigeria's market; Benin's domestic capacity could never have never absorbed this boom in imports.

To understand the gap between Benin's mirror and official imports, there is a need to analyze Benin's customs regime classification. According to the Benin Customs Code, imports are classified in four categories: imports, transit, re-exports, and other regimes (temporary admission and so on). While domestic consumption is reflected by the official import data, the surplus is mainly destined for Nigeria's market through export,

Table 6.4   Mirror Imports as Share of Total Official Imports of Selected Economies

	2000	2001	2002	2003	2004	2005
Benin	230.9	219.9	206.0	183.0	199.4	275.8
Niger	104.1	120.6	119.6	100.7	111.0	91.1
Nigeria	140.1	134.4	138.2	92.6	77.9	77.1

Source: IMF Direction of Trade Statistics.

Figure 6.1   Benin: Trends in GDP Growth, Imports and Mirror Imports, 2001–05

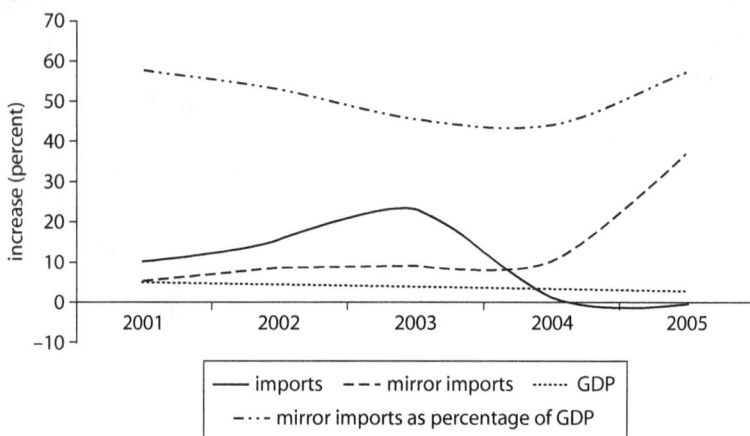

Source: IMF Direction of Trade Statistics.

re-export, transit, or other regimes. (See below on confirmation of the assumption based on unofficial port data.) Based on Benin's customs data, in 2006 the value of goods exiting Benin amounted to more than US$2.4 billion (table 6.5). It is notable that the value of goods in transit was more than two times higher than what was recorded as official imports.[11]

Large discrepancies in Benin's import figures have been reported mainly with Asian economies such as India, Thailand, and the Republic of Korea, which are known as large exporters of manufacturing products, and most prominently with China, which accounts for 27 percent of the total discrepancy. Between 2000 and 2005, mirror imports from China were equivalent to 863 percent of Benin's total reported imports and climbed to 1,602 percent in 2005, which means that less than 10 percent of what China declared as exported to Benin was actually reported by Benin authorities.

By contrast, trade data in the case of Nigeria and selected developed economies (European Union, Japan, United States, United Kingdom) reveal that the values of Nigeria's reported imports are well above the values of mirror imports from China (due to the cost of insurance and freight), which means China's recording of exports flows is fairly accurate (see appendix H).

To identify more precisely the major causes of Benin's underreporting of imports, discrepancies in the COMTRADE database between mirror and official imports were analyzed by product groups. The results are

Table 6.5   Benin Trade Data, 2004–06
(US$)

	2004	2005	2006
World exports to Benin	1,788,980	2,462,410	3,335,060
Imports	893,820	896,696	958,019
Exports	292,178	263,522	217,484
Re-exports	12,587	12,911	25,958
Transit	1,148,248	1,284,587	2,199,884
Other regimes	73,173	77,366	26,998

Source: Nigeria Customs Service.

compelling: the products with the highest discrepancies are those subject to import prohibition or high tariff rates in Nigeria. The largest trade statistics gap appears in two product groups: manufactured goods and miscellaneous manufactured articles (Standard International Trade Classification [SITC] 6 and 8), and accounts for 50 percent of total trade statistics discrepancies.

When trade discrepancies are disaggregated, it appears that a limited number of products are smuggled into Nigeria. At the two-digit level in 2005, textile products (SITC 65) accounted for 77 percent of overall discrepancies within the SITC 6 (manufactured goods) category, and footwear and manufactured products (SITC 85 and 89) accounted for 84 percent of overall discrepancies between mirror and reported imports within SITC 8 (miscellaneous manufactured articles) category. As shown in figure 6.2, Benin's mirror imports of textile products boomed as of 2004, the year Nigeria reintroduced extensive import bans on textiles. Mirror imports from China accounted for the bulk of this gap. In the case of China at the two-digit SITC classification, the share of textile products (SITC 65) and footwear-manufactured products (SITC 85 and 89) accounted for 81 percent of the overall discrepancies in trade statistics.

It is also worth noting that Benin's trade statistics reveal no discrepancy with Nigeria for goods with low tariff rates and non-prohibited imports. For instance, for animals and animal products (Harmonized System Code 01-05), with a simple average tariff of 12.3 percent and a peak of only 20 percent, no trade statistics gap can be found when comparing Benin's mirror and official imports data (figure 6.3).

Furthermore, mirror data show that consumption in Benin for Nigeria's banned and high tariff goods is significantly higher than in Nigeria. Based on mirror statistics, the consumption of manufactured goods and miscellaneous manufactured articles (SITC 6 and 8) is four times higher in

Figure 6.2   Nigeria's and Benin's Mirror and Official Imports of Textile Products, 2000–06

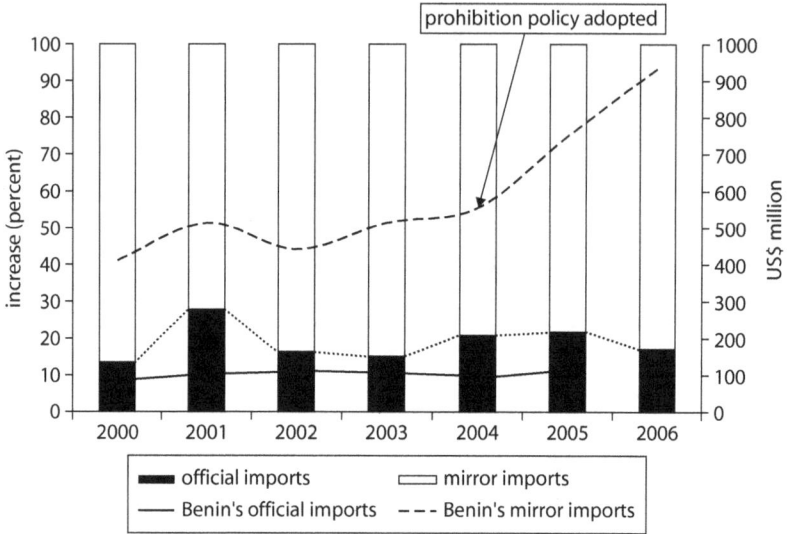

Sources: United Nations Comtrade; Nigerian customs data.

Figure 6.3   Benin's Value of Mirror and Official Imports of Animals and Animal Products, 2004–06

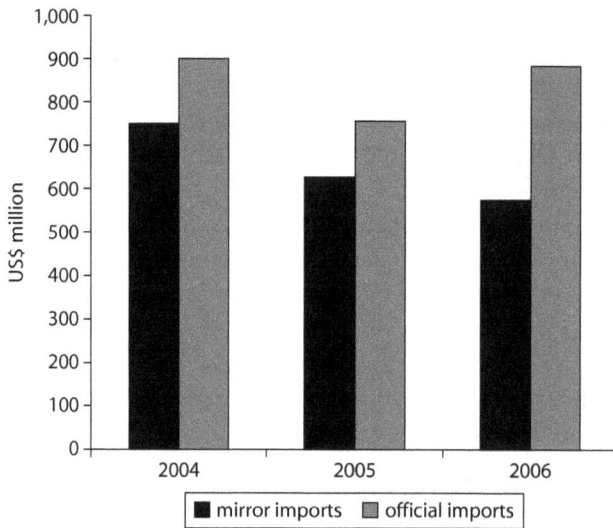

Sources: Authors' calculations, based on World Integrated Trade Solutions and Benin customs data.
Note: The value of official imports is equal to the export price plus the cost of transport from the country of origin, which explains why import values are higher than export values.

Benin than in Nigeria. According to the same statistics, for the period 2001 to 2005, consumption of manufactured goods and miscellaneous manufactured articles in Benin increased by an average of 14 percent, while GDP per capita remained stagnant with an average of one percent increase for the same period. Furthermore, disaggregated mirror data demonstrate that consumption per capita of textile products in Benin in 2005 was 18 times higher than in Nigeria, and the same applies to per capita consumption of rice, on which the tariff is 50 percent in Nigeria and 8.75 percent in Benin. Over the period 2004 to 2006, Benin's mirror imports of rice doubled. Hence, a country of fewer than 10 million people appeared to be importing almost as much rice as a country of more than 130 million. This was all the more incredible considering that experts at the West Africa Rice Development Association say that per capita rice consumption is much lower in Benin than in Nigeria.

Channels of Unofficial Trade to Nigeria[12]

How can mirror statistics be useful to detect trade discrepancies, and what are the main mechanisms through which goods are imported unofficially to Nigeria from Benin? The transmission channels seem to differ widely, depending on the goods. One can conclude that manufactured products such as textiles or footwear are imported in large quantities to Benin and then transit to Nigeria, while consumer goods are probably imported to Benin and then smuggled in small quantities across the porous border.

Based on trade data analysis and investigations, there are four possible channels through which Benin's imported surplus of high-tariff and banned import goods ends up in Nigeria:

- *Channel 1:* smuggled re-exports of imports that pay the ECOWAS CET and Benin's value-added tax (which can be detected by a lack of discrepancy in mirror statistics but high consumption per capita in Benin compared to neighboring countries)
- *Channel 2:* official re-exports to Nigeria from Benin (detected by a high share of official re-exports)
- *Channel 3:* smuggling into Nigeria of imports that are officially in international transit while crossing Benin[13] (detected by a high share of goods declared in transit)
- *Channel 4:* smuggling into Nigeria of imports that were unofficially imported to Benin

Benin's official customs data suggest that the most favorable customs regime for informally importing used cars and textile products into Nigeria is through the special transit regime in place in Benin. Customs data reveal that official re-exports are marginal, which means that channel 2 cannot be taken as a major explanation for unofficial trade. Channel 1 also cannot be taken as a main cause of unofficial trade, since official import flows seem to be comparable to those of neighboring ECOWAS countries, Nigeria excepted, and there is a large discrepancy between mirror and official import statistics. Indeed, if a Benin-based trader were to import goods from China for informal re-export to Nigeria (and were to pay duties in Benin), these imports should show up in the Benin import statistics. Hence, there should be no difference between Chinese export data and Benin import data.

Channels 3 and 4 are considerably more profitable for Nigerian importers than channels 1 and 2, except in cases where the combination of the tariff under the CET and Benin's value-added tax is quite low, which explains why there is no discrepancy for animal products imports. (Traders' costs and profits for the main goods transiting from Cotonou to Nigeria are estimated below.) Channel 4 is the most difficult to estimate. However, it is hard to conceive that millions of tons are smuggled into Cotonou port and then to Nigeria without any oversight by the authorities.

Therefore, channel 3 is probably the most important for unofficial trade of textiles from Benin to Nigeria. Benin's customs data reveal that, in 2006, the value of textile products leaving Benin under a transit regime equaled US$402 million, three times the value of Benin's recorded imports (table 6.6).

In the context of unofficial trade, how are things organized on the ground? For textiles, for instance, the exporting country declares the goods exported to Benin. When the goods arrive at Cotonou port, revised transit papers (invoice, bill of lading, and so forth) are created to show that their final destination is Nigeria. An agent then produces a transit declaration and pays for a bond (and some low official transit fees). Since the goods leave Benin's customs territory, their exit is certified by customs. The goods are then piled at the Nigerian border and illegally smuggled into the Nigerian market. Thus, Benin's import statistics will mainly include transit flows, although in the partner country, the statistics show exports to Benin. This scheme is known as a special transit procedure (Golub 2008).[14]

The story seems to be different, however, for consumer goods such as rice or vegetable oil, where the discrepancy between mirror and official

Table 6.6   Share of Various Customs Regimes for Selected High Tariffs and Banned Goods in Nigeria, 2004–06

	2004 (%)	2005 (%)	2006 (%)
Textile			
Transit	51.04	60.39	79.36
Export	48.59	39.46	20.57
Re-export	0.11	0.06	0.04
Other regime	0.26	0.08	0.03
Rice			
Transit	79.90	66.30	100.00
Other regime	20.10	33.70	0.00
Export	0.00	0.00	0.00
Re-export	0.00	0.00	0.00
Vehicles			
Transit	95.87	96.01	94.93
Other regime	3.59	2.67	2.54
Re-export	0.37	0.64	2.42
Export	0.17	0.67	0.12

Source: Authors' calculations, based on Benin customs data.

imports is much lower but can still be detected through per capita consumption data.

In any case, macrodata analysis shows that unofficial trade from Benin into Nigeria is on a strong upward trend,[15] due largely to Nigeria's policy on import bans.

The Impact of Restrictive Trade Policy on Customs Efficiency

Strong protection encourages underground trade channels. A local industry may officially enjoy a high level of protection, but rampant fraud means that it faces unfair competition on the domestic market from smuggled products, which have been imported without paying customs duties and domestic taxes, enabling them to be sold more cheaply (Geourjon 2004).

Nigeria's trade policies have a negative effect on revenue collection due to their complexity and restrictive nature. These policies provide opportunities and incentives for smuggling, thus leading to a substantial loss in revenues and rampant corruption (all the more, as import licenses are granted to a select few for prohibited import goods). As a proxy for low customs efficiency, revenue collection per staff is also lower in Nigeria than in neighboring countries (table 6.7).

Table 6.7   A Comparison of Customs Revenues Collected per Staff (in US$)

Country	Customs revenue collected per staff	Year
Kenya	954,181	2003
Romania	838,587	2003
Macedonia, FYR	646,282	2004
Russian Federation	644,134	2004
Armenia	603,925	2006
Tajikistan	520,545	2002
Bulgaria	497,917	2002
Thailand	474,051	2004
Bosnia and Herzegovina	466,306	2003
Albania	420,952	2003
Iran, Islamic Rep. of	407,122	2003
Indonesia	392,067	2003
Pakistan	378,169	2006
Cameroon	370,370	2006
Philippines	356,739	2003
Tunisia	342,216	2005
Vietnam	340,460	2004
Kazakhstan	321,695	2004
Yugoslavia, former	288,112	2004
Nigeria	153,846	2006
Georgia	153,530	2003
Moldova	145,257	2003

Sources: Nigerian Customs Service; various data sources for other African countries; World Bank Trade and Transportation Facilitation in South-Eastern Europe Project 2008c.

Nigeria's traders face an array of cumbersome customs procedures, leading to long delays in clearing goods through customs. This high number of physical customs checks[16] and procedures is a result of too many prohibited items and creates opportunities for rent seeking by customs officials.

The current trade regime also undermines the willingness of the Customs Service to undertake procedural reforms, despite the high costs of carrying out operations to detect smuggling activities (without increased revenues), especially at the border with Benin. In the last two years, the detection and seizure of smuggled goods has become more frequent, with more customs officers deployed at border points to physically control every shipment entering Nigeria. These officials unload each truck to see whether traders are trying to import prohibited items into the domestic market, which results in high operational costs to the Customs Service as well as to traders and reduces revenue collected per staff. As an example, at the Idiroko border post between Nigeria and Benin, revenue collected per staff are less than US$10,000 per year[17]—ten times lower than the average figure for customs officers in Nigeria.[18] Customs data illustrate that these operations are heavily focused on curbing smuggling on a limited number of items: in 2007, prohibited textiles and used vehicles (older than 8 years) accounted for 56 percent of the total value of seizures. However, this remains only a fraction of the goods crossing the border from Benin.

The Spillover Effect of Import Prohibitions on Lagos Port

The reform of Lagos port is widely considered one of the best port reforms in Sub-Saharan Africa in the past decade. However, the benefits of this reform are fast dissipating due to the current trade policy. Nigeria's port sector had long been recognized as one of the least efficient in West and Central Africa. It was plagued with an unusual degree of centralization, with any major decision needing the approval of the president or the minister of transport. In 2003, when congestion was very high in Nigeria, the average cost of a call at Lagos port was estimated to be twice the cost of a call at Felixstowe in the United Kingdom. In 2005, a reform process was initiated and a "landlord" model adopted for Lagos port, entailing private operation of the container terminals. In 2006, the initial concessions became operational, and productivity rose within a few months. Chronic delays for berthing space nearly vanished, leading shipping lines to reduce their congestion surcharge from €525 in March 2006 (just before concessioning) to €75 in January 2007. The reduction in congestion charges alone saved the Nigerian economy an estimated US$200 million annually (Harding, Palsson, and Raballand 2007).

Less than three years later, however, the situation had deteriorated to the point that in February 2009, the Nigerian Ports Authority announced a temporary suspension of ship entry, to enable terminals to clear a high level of backlogs. Large vessels now wait an average of 30 days at Lagos port before discharging, at a cost of more than US$500,000 per vessel (*Guardian* 2009). Moreover, cargo port dwell time now averages several weeks; there is insufficient space for empty containers, and infrastructure, including the port access road, is inadequate and decayed.

How could this have happened, particularly in the context of private sector investments and limited traffic growth? Private sector representatives blame the high port charges and the demurrage fees on overtime cargoes, claiming they cannot afford to pay them. But why have costs for importers risen so sharply, and why do importers now abandon their cargo for months, even up to a year? One factor may be Customs Circular 026/2008, issued on June 12, 2008, which forbade the clearance of goods that lack appropriate import clearance documents, including a Risk Assessment Report and Form M.

This circular had the effect of changing the behavior of some importers and customs officials: priority was given to goods that could be easily cleared, while other goods were left to sit at the port. After it was published, the amount of uncleared and abandoned cargo started to grow and congestion increased. The Customs Service explained in February 2009 that it had to physically inspect 100 percent of containers because of the high incidence of concealment and false declarations by importers (*Journal of Commerce* 2009). Port operators confirmed this and insisted that "most of the containers have at least one prohibited item" (*Hong Kong Shipping Gazette* 2009). The Ports Authority also accused Nigerian importers of creating problems by making false cargo declarations.

There are two types of cases of cargo abandonment, both of which rely on the repurchase of the abandoned goods at auction as a way to bypass normal import fees and procedures.

- An importer of prohibited goods abandons the goods in the port and waits for them to be auctioned, at which point he can bypass the import regulation and get the goods at a relatively low price.
- An importer makes a false declaration, including the undervaluation of declared goods. When caught, he abandons the consignment and gets the goods through auction, which is cheaper than full payment of import duties along with penalties for making a false declaration and incidental port charges.[19]

The Customs Service's liberal auction policy encourages low compliance with import procedures. Indeed, in Lagos port, auctioned goods rarely bring more than 500,000 (about US$3500) for a 40-foot container,[20] even for high-value goods such as some textile products.

The question then arises: do operators abandon their cargo mainly because of a false declaration of prohibited imports? One good indicator has been the number of clearances since the suspension of the Circular 026/2008 in February 2009. As a customs official explained at that time, "out of 50 containers that have been examined, only one importer came forward to take delivery of his cargo. In some terminals, no importer whose consignment falls into the category of overtime cargo has shown his face." (All Africa Global Media/Comtex 2009). If it were only a matter of a high tariff, the importers would not have feared seizure and would have taken possession of their cargo. In the case of prohibited imports, however, the best option seems to have been to let the cargo go to auction and repurchase it at a low price.[21]

Impact of Import Bans on Customs Efficiency and Revenue Collection[22]

The Effect of Restrictive Trade Policy

The current trade policy negatively affects stakeholders in the following ways:

- Customs productivity and efficiency are considerably decreased, because almost all containers must be physically inspected for prohibited imports; thus, any risk management strategy cannot be implemented because of the high risk of non-compliance.
- Government revenues are considerably reduced, because (a) smuggling of banned imports, by definition, does not increase duties revenues and (b) some customs officials deliberately approve undervalued, misclassified, or prohibited imports.
- The cost efficiency and competitiveness of several value chains have been reduced because of import bans and high tariffs.
- Lagos port operators lose market share because of the import bans and because important traffic volumes go to other ports in the subregion so importers can avoid paying high tariffs.
- Compliant traders are penalized, because their imported cargo is delayed by the lengthy physical inspection process.

The calculations below, based on selected key items smuggled into Nigeria, show that a revised trade policy, including phasing out of major import bans and instituting tariff duties, would reduce incentives for smuggling and have the following positive effects:

- Increased tariff revenues (provided that tariff duties replace import bans) due to a higher compliance rate
- Increased port revenues due to higher efficiency and reduced diversion to other ports
- Lower transaction costs due to reduced delays at ports and border posts
- Valuation of unofficial trade

Assessing the magnitude of smuggling activities into Nigeria is a difficult and complex task. However, by cross-checking information and using data from public agencies and the private sector, one can arrive at estimates that are useful to demonstrate the impact of the current trade policy.

Officially, 13 percent of Cotonou port traffic originates from or is destined to Nigeria. Unofficially, however, an estimated 75 percent of the containers landing at Cotonou port are headed for Nigeria as is around the same percentage of bulk products. According to current traffic and after subtracting official imports data, 3.5 million tons would then end up in Nigeria through smuggling (since exports through Cotonou from Nigeria are negligible). If one assumes a minimum value of US$1,400 for a ton of cargo, up to US$5 billion of cargo would be smuggled to Nigeria from Cotonou alone, representing one-sixth of Nigeria's total imports.

As noted in the previous section, textiles seem to be the main products smuggled into Nigeria. Assuming that total imports are a computation of official and unofficial imports, the value of smuggled goods to Nigeria can be estimated as

$C = P + (Moff + Munoff) - X$, which can rewritten as:

$$Munoff = C - P - Moff + X \qquad (1)$$

where $Munoff$ = unofficial imports; C = consumption; P = production; $Moff$ = official imports; and X = exports.

C is computed from the formula: C per capita * Population

- C per capita is available from the handbook *Patterns of Consumption* published by the Nigerian Statistical Office (data on textiles [SITC 65] and footwear).
- $Moff$ and X are available from trade statistics published by the Nigerian Statistical Office.
- Production data are published by the Manufacturers Association of Nigeria.

According to these data, the equation becomes

$$2,186 = 2,220 - 40 - 0 + 6 \qquad (2)$$

which means that the value of smuggled textiles to Nigeria is approximately US$2 billion, or more than 50 percent of smuggled goods to the country. In comparison, textile industry experts worldwide estimate that figure to be US$1.6 billion.

The Cost of Restrictive Trade Policy

The various losses from a restrictive trade policy are estimated using a conservative hypothesis for the various cost components. The estimates are mainly limited to the removal of import bans (changed to tariffs peaks) on some key products, with the exception of rice (tables 6.8 to 6.10[23]).

Table 6.8   Comparison of Total Transportation Costs for Textiles at Different Tariff Levels

Tariff level (%)	Total transportation costs (% of goods value)	Total transportation costs (US$ per ton)	Transit fees or import duties (US$ per ton)	Port fees (US$ per ton)	Road informal payment (US$ per ton)	Border informal payment (US$ per ton)
Benin	7.7	192.5	12.5	40	20	120
Nigeria (35)	16.8	420	420	40	—	—
Nigeria (15)	8.8	220	180	40	—	—

Source: Authors' calculations.
Note: Port fees are based on container port charges of US$400 divided by 10 tons; fees are assumed to be similar for all cargo. Informal payments are calculated as 10 percent of US$1,200 per ton. Road informal payment is based on the average payment per roadblock for a truck divided by 40 tons; it is assumed to be insensitive to the type of cargo. Transit fees for Benin are computed on the basis of Benin customs data. Tariff duties for Nigeria are computed as a percentage of goods value; for example, 35 percent of US$1,200 is equal to US$420 tariff duty per ton. — = not available.

Table 6.9   Comparison of Total Transportation Costs for Vegetable Oils at Different Tariff Levels

Tariff level (%)	Total transportation costs (% of goods value)	Total transportation costs (US$ per ton)	Transit fees or import duties (US$ per ton)	Port fees (US$ per ton)	Road informal payment (US$ per ton)	Border informal payment (US$ per ton)
Benin	36.3	163.5	58.5	40	20	45
Nigeria (35)	43.8	197.5	157.5	40	—	—
Nigeria (15)	23.9	107.5	67.5	40	—	—

Source: Authors' calculations.
Note: Port fees are based on container port charges of US$400 divided by 10 tons; fees are assumed to be similar for all cargo. Informal payments are calculated as 10 percent of US$450 per ton (this value is derived from Benin import data). Road informal payment is based on the average payment per roadblock for a truck divided by 40 tons; it is assumed to be insensitive to the type of cargo. Import duties for Benin are computed on the basis of Benin customs data. Tariff duties for Nigeria are computed as a percentage of goods value; for example, 35 percent of US$450 is equal to US$157.5 tariff duty per ton. — = not available.

Table 6.10   Comparison of Total Transportation Costs for Rice at Different Tariff Levels

Tariff level (%)	Total transportation costs (% of goods value)	Total transportation costs (US$ per ton)	Transit fees or import duties (US$ per ton)	Port fees (US$ per ton)	Road informal payment (US$ per ton)	Border informal payment (US$ per ton)
Benin	41.2	136	43	40	20	33
Nigeria (100)	112.1	370	330	40	—	—
Nigeria (50)	62.2	205.5	165	40	—	—
Nigeria (15)	27.1	89.5	49.5	40	—	—

Source: Authors' calculations.
Note: Port fees are based on container port charges of US$400 divided by 10 tons; fees are assumed to be simi-lar for all cargo. Informal payments are calculated as 10 percent of US$330 per ton (this value is derived from Benin import data). Road informal payment is based on the average payment per roadblock for a truck divided by 40 tons; it is assumed to be insensitive to the type of cargo. Import duties are computed on the basis of Benin customs data. Tariff duties for Nigeria are computed as a percentage of goods value; for example, 50 percent of US$330 is equal to US$165 tariff duty per ton. — = not available.

The revenues realized are likely to be a fraction of the losses for the Nigerian economy. Two scenarios could materialize:

- *Scenario 1.* In the case of replacing the main import bans (as on textiles or vegetable oils) or very high tariffs (as on rice) by a 15 percent tariff duty, most traders are likely to redirect imports to Lagos port, since imports through Cotonou will be more expensive than a 15 percent tariff level. In this case, the positive impact for Nigeria in terms of for-mal revenues collected and port charges are higher than in scenario 2 (with higher tariffs level).

- *Scenario 2.* In the case of replacing the main import bans (as on tex-tiles or vegetable oils) or very high tariffs (as on rice) by a 35 percent tariff duty, most traders are likely to redirect imports to Lagos port for goods cleared in Benin (such as rice or vegetable oils). However, due to the fact that textile products and secondhand cars are mostly de-clared to be in transit (and are not subject to the same level of pay-ment in Benin), a 35 percent tariff level would likely not make it attractive for most traders to redirect flows from Cotonou to Lagos.

It is worth noting that the compliance rate, and therefore the expected gains for the budget, depend mainly on two factors: (a) the customs regime in Benin (goods declared in transit are more likely to continue transiting through Cotonou) and (b) the level of informal payments at the border (the higher the payment, the more likely that goods will be redirected to Lagos port). These factors are mainly a function of the type of goods and of the cargo owner.

Detailed results on the shift from import prohibitions to various tariff levels are presented in appendix I. With a very conservative hypothesis, more than US$200 million would be directly gained, mostly for port operators and the Nigerian Treasury.

Concluding Remarks and Next Steps

Data demonstrate that smuggling and unofficial trade to Nigeria are on an upward trend, due mainly to the continued practice of banning imports of numerous products, such as textiles and some agro-processed products.

The impact of this trade policy on the Nigerian economy has a negative direct impact on traders and customs revenues, and a major indirect impact on consumer goods prices and therefore on poverty reduction.

To reduce congestion at Lagos port caused largely by abandoned cargo, import prohibition should be much more limited. The Customs Service auction policy, which encourages traders to import prohibited goods and then abandon them, should also be comprehensively reviewed.

Before attempting any trade liberalization, which may be politically difficult, the government of Nigeria needs to first remove most import prohibitions to significantly reduce incentives for smuggling and trade re-export from Benin. Changing prohibited imports into tariff peaks would bring additional revenues for the Treasury and the Customs Service and would give Customs a stronger incentive to curb unofficial trade. Such a change would also make it easier for the Ministry of Finance to monitor customs efficiency, since it would eliminate distortions in the revenue-per-staff ratio, which is now extremely low at some border stations. Local customs officials would no longer be able to use the import bans to justify their low collection rate. For customs senior management, removing the import bans would give them an incentive to be more efficient, since doing so would expand their revenue base.

A phased comprehensive approach to removing the import bans could be defined along the following lines:

- Quantify the likely impact of removing import prohibitions, distinguish among tariff lines, and demystify their social impact. Removals are likely to have more impact for some tariff lines than for others. The removal of textile products from the list, for example, is likely to have a greater potential impact on employment and value-added than the removal of wheelbarrows.

Notes

1. Import bans are allowed for moral, health, security, and environmental reasons under international conventions.
2. For a discussion of the Tariff Review Board and the political economy of trade policy formulation, see Ajayi and Kwaako-Osafo (2006).
3. Smuggled goods are those that evade customs control and on which lawful duties have been avoided or goods that are not permitted to be imported into Nigeria. Undervalued imports are not included in the category of smuggled goods.
4. It is all the more important that for most prohibited imports, special import licenses (prohibition waivers) are usually granted to a handful of traders and manufacturers, or both, enabling them to make substantial profits.
5. The main import bans lifted were maize, wheat flour, biscuits, and some garment products. There was also a change in the age limit on imported motor vehicles—the prohibition is now on vehicles older than ten years, up from eight years.
6. Iron scrap is the primary input in steelmaking in Nigeria.
7. Imported chemicals are critical to the leather industry, for example. They are subject to high tariff duties, which undermine the competitiveness of domestic leather products, even on the local market.
8. For more details on smuggling between Benin and Nigeria, see Igue and Soule (1992), who investigated the phenomenon based on detailed surveys on both sides of the border.
9. Mirror statistics consist of comparing different measures of a trade flow: for instance, the reported export flows from country A to country B, and the reported import flows from country B from country A. Mirror statistics are a traditional tool for detecting the causes of asymmetries in trade statistics, especially when goods supposedly imported to country A are changed into a transit for country C when arriving in country A.
10. Berger and Nitsch (2008) demonstrated that there is a strong correlation between the extent of trade statistics discrepancies, measured in mirror statistics, and corruption levels.
11. The puzzle can be explained by looking at the value adjustments made by the Benin Customs Service in cases of re-exports and transit goods. In other

words, Benin Customs probably increases the price of goods declared in transit in order to collect more transit fees (for applicable goods), which results in higher revenue collection from goods in transit.

12. This section confirms findings from Golub (2008), who studied these channels in Benin in detail.

13. Goods can also be recorded under temporary admission (and hence not cleared by Benin customs). Some used cars are exported to Nigeria's market through this procedure.

14. It is worth noting that transit to third countries is common: goods are sometimes placed under the transit regime to Niger and then unofficially diverted to Nigeria. Banned import products usually fall under this category.

15. This trend could be reversed in 2009–10 due to the financial crisis and the rapid decrease of international prices, which have recently depressed imports from Nigeria.

16. In Apapa port, 60 percent of goods go through the Red Channel, synonymous with physical inspections.

17. According to interviews with customs officials, two trucks go through the border post every day; assuming a twenty-foot equivalent unit (TEU) value of US$20,000, this means a value of US$80,000 per day. Applying the average tariff rate, US$3.5 million is collected by 600 staff members.

18. In this case, the Customs Service may not be completely efficient in terms of revenue collection, and some agents may undervalue some imported goods.

19. According to the Customs circular, such imports should not be allowed. However, according to professionals, such imports—excluding violation of import prohibition orders on standardization, human and animal health, environment, and intellectual property rights infringement—should be allowed clearance after payment of duties and penalties to avoid congestion in port.

20. Section 31 (subsections 1–9) of the Nigerian Customs regulation deals with "goods uncleared and missing goods" and recommends that the Board of Customs "may sell them" *without specific mention of any price*. Though there are guidelines, they appear to be subject to the discretionary powers of the Comptroller General of Customs, who exerts a delegated power on behalf of the Chairman of the Board (the Minister of Finance). These auction regulations apply only to overtime goods, not to seized goods.

21. It is also worth noting that in order to reduce congestion, the Ports Authority introduced demurrage charges of   100,000 (US$680) per TEU to force owners to move their cargo out of the ports but without much result in the short term (*Tradewinds* 2009).

22. Primary and secondary sources are used to estimate the impact of import bans and high tariff peaks on customs management. Primary data were collected

from the Nigerian Customs Service and from interviews with public and private sector stakeholders. Secondary data were taken from previous research work and from the Statistical Bureau of Nigeria.

23. Values in tables 6.8–6.10 are derived from Benin import statistics (transit or imports), which are undervalued for vegetable oils and rice. The correct values are assumed to be, respectively, US$2500 for textiles, US$450 for vegetable oils, and US$330 for rice.

Methodology for Selecting and Scoring Value Chains

Selecting the Value Chains

The starting point was an analysis of the economy to identify the contribution to growth of the oil and non-oil sectors. This revealed that the non-oil economy had been the main driver of growth (table A.1).

The next step was to assess the contribution to growth of the main non-oil sectors. This revealed that agriculture had been the main contributor to growth, but that services had contributed almost as much, and from a much smaller base (figure A.1).

This led to an analysis of what were the fastest growing industries. This revealed that the service industries were growing fastest, and were leading an economic transformation away from the reliance on primary industries (figure A.2).

Moreover, the analysis revealed that the country's manufacturing sector, though growing rapidly, was not leading transformation. The explanation, as the World Bank's Country Economic Memorandum (World Bank 2007) and Investment Climate Enterprise Survey (World Bank 2008a) had shown, was that infrastructure (especially power) and access to finance were the binding constraints to growth, and that where these were the major components of costs, they were likely to affect the growth of manufacturing more than services. This was confirmed by value chain analysis,

Table A.1   Contribution to Growth of the Oil and Non-Oil Sectors, 2001, 2003–06
(percent)

Indicator	2001	2003	2004	2005	2006
GDP growth (constant prices)	8.40	10.20	10.58	6.50	6.00
Oil growth (constant prices)	5.60	23.80	3.30	0.50	–4.40
Non-oil growth (constant prices)	9.80	5.80	13.20	8.60	9.40
Agriculture growth (constant prices)	3.80	6.60	6.50	7.10	7.20
Manufacturing growth (constant prices)	—	5.66	10.00	9.61	9.71
Services growth (constant prices)	—	0.41	8.83	7.96	8.83
Oil sector (share of GDP)	26.04	26.53	25.72	25.84	24.64
Agriculture sector (share of GDP)	—	41.01	40.98	43.87	47.02

Source: Consilium International 2008.
Note: — = not available. Due to a statistical break in the series, 2002 data are not reliable.

Figure A.1   Contribution to Growth of the Main Non-Oil Sectors, 2001–06

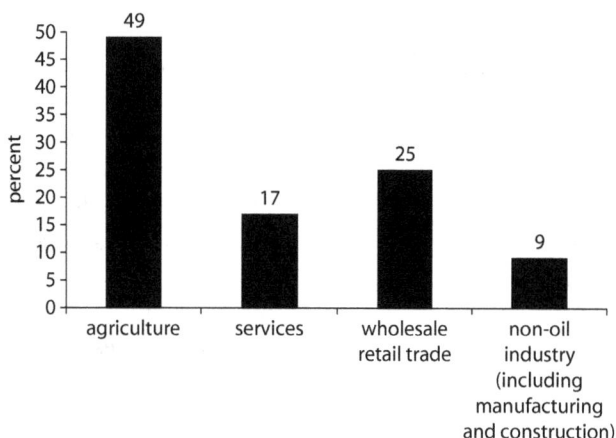

Source: Author's calculations.

which showed many manufacturing industries to be uncompetitive because of high cost of power. The decline of manufacturing industries producing internationally traded goods such as textiles and footwear reinforced these findings.

Finally, analysis of changes in incomes revealed that the growth of the middle class was a decisive factor in the performance of industries, since those that catered to the consumption habits of the middle class

Figure A.2   Sectoral Growth Rates, 2006

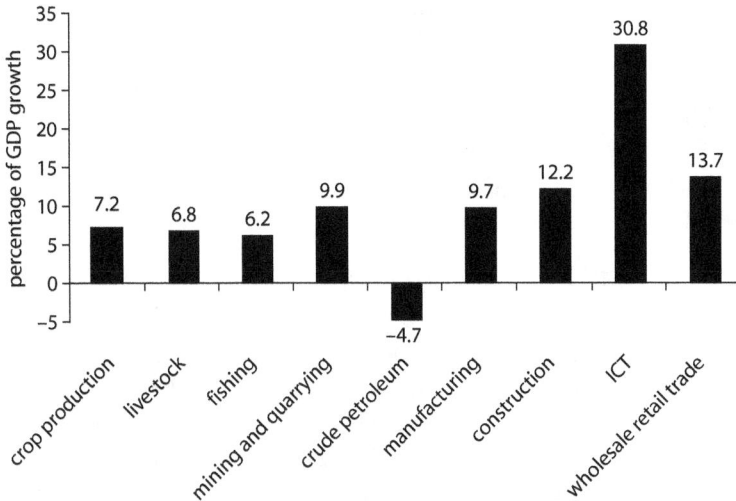

Source: Author's calculations.
Note: ICT = information and communication technology.

were growing faster than others. Wholesale and retail trade, information and communication technology, hotels and restaurants, and housing construction were growing twice as fast as GDP. This analysis gave a list of 14 industries for further study.

Scoring the Value Chains

The next step was to score the value chains across the three *upside potential* criteria—growth, employment, and spillovers—and the *three feasibility criteria*—competitiveness, policy reform, and private sector capability. This approach recognized that what mattered most for successful intervention was not only the potential upside, but also the feasibility of being able to bring about the changes needed to sustain rapid growth of the industry. For production of a simple ordinal ranking, the six criteria were scored as follows:

- *Growth:* Rate of growth in the past and underpinnings of source of growth for the future;
- *Employment:* Level of self and wage employment and rate of increase in the past;
- *Spillovers:* Technological externalities with other industries (i.e., effects on productivity) and links;

- *Competitiveness:* Level and ease of being able to bridge the international gap in competitiveness;
- *Policy:* Extent that policy changes needed to bring about international competitiveness are contested—the more contested, the lower the score;
- *Capability of the private sector:* Extent of private sector's capability to bring about the changes needed for international competitiveness— the greater the capability, the higher the score.

A simple ordinal scale was used, with 1 being the lowest (white) and 4 the highest (black), to plot the 6 criteria. The results of the scoring were then mapped on a plot diagram shown in the main text (figure 1.5).

For creation of this diagram, the sum of each value chain's score from 1 to 4 for each of the three criteria taken from the earlier analysis determined their overall upside potential and hence position on the vertical axis. The sum of the three scores for the feasibility criteria determined their position on the horizontal axis. The combination of upside and feasibility scores places the value chain on the diagram. The color of each circle indicates the state being considered, and the size of the circle represents the estimated current importance of that value chain to that state in terms of proportion of state GDP. The smallest circle represents less than 1 percent, then as the sizes move up, 1 to 2 percent, 2 to 3 percent, and the largest circle, greater than 3 percent.

Regression Analysis of Non-Participation Data

Table B.1 shows the weighted probit regression on the probability of being out of the labor force. The regressors in (A1) are age (in years), education, marital status dummy, and a gender dummy. Age and education are included nonlinearly, and gender is interacted with education, age, and marital status dummy, confirming that education and marital status are more important in increasing the probability of non-participation in the male population.

Regressors in (A2) are as in (A1), with an additional dummy for Muslim faith, including a gender interaction term, demonstrating the gender-specific impact of this faith, that is, increasing labor participation of men while decreasing labor participation of women.

Table B.1 Regression Analysis—Probability of Being Out of the Labor Force

	A1		A2	
	Coefficient	Standard error	Coefficient	Standard error
Age	-.213***	0.0059	-0.2085***	0.0059
Age squared	0.002***	0.00007	0.0023***	0.0001
Years of education	-.030***	0.00752	-0.0172**	0.007
Years of education squared	0.001***	0.0004	0.0011**	0.0004
Male dummy	-0.677***	0.0842	-0.3786***	0.0909
Married dummy	-0.1635***	0.035	-0.2431***	0.0361
Muslim faith dummy	n.a.	n.a.	0.3841***	0.0341
Male–age interaction	0.0004	0.0024	-0.0035	0.0024
Male–education interaction	0.057***	0.0054	0.0484***	0.0055
Male–married interaction	-0.922***	0.0641	-0.8260***	0.0647
Male–Muslim interaction	n.a.	n.a.	-0.4999***	0.0515

Source: Nigeria Living Standard Survey, National Bureau of Statistics 2003.
Note: Both regressions contain a constant, N = 19,350, Pseudo-R² 0.30; *** significant at 0.01 level; ** significant at 0.05 level. n.a. = not applicable.

APPENDIX C

Main Constraints in Selected Agricultural Value Chain

Table C.1 Potential of Selected Value Chains for Short, Medium, and Long-Term Growth

| | Value chain | | |
| | Shrimp | Finished leather | Cassava starch |
Growth cycle	Reversal to uptrend	Reversal to uptrend	Nascent
Financial performance	Profitable	Profitable	Loss
Target markets	International (European Union)	International (Italy, China)	Domestic
Product value	High	Very High	Medium
Exposure to impediments			
Defective and low-yield raw material	High	High	Very High
High-cost financing environment	High	High	High
Rigid and poorly skilled labor market	Medium	High	Medium
Overburdened management	High	Medium	Medium
Disruptive and high-cost public utilities	Low	High	High
Onerous business regulations	High	High	Medium
Onerous cross-border regulations	High	High	Low
Poor inland transport and handling	Low	Medium	Very High

Source: Consilium International 2005.

Marginal Effective Tax Rates

Table D.1 Reform of the Tax Regime—Summary of Key Issues and Recommendations

Issues	Recommendations
Manufacturing (METR: 3–28 percent)	
No VAT recovery on overhead or capital assets hits manufacturers very hard, as does FIRS failure to pay VAT refunds.	Introduce risk-based screening of VAT claims to increase repayment efficiency, reduce 100 percent audit requirement, and create an effective refund system.
Multiplicity of taxes occurs.	Reduce multiplicity of taxes through legislative and administration reform, which should include precise guidelines for definition of taxes, fees, levies, and other charges; rules on their application at state and local levels (including ministries, agencies, tax authorities); and regulations specifying how these charges shall be applied. Changes should strive to be revenue neutral.
	Introduce registration threshold for VAT.
	Remove restrictions on VAT input tax deduction with respect to capital goods and business overhead.
	Replace pharmaceuticals VAT exemption with either the standard rate or a zero rating.
Mining (METR: −25–27 percent)	
Overly generous capital allowances, combined with tax holidays and unlimited loss carry forward, create negative METR.	Eliminate tax holidays.
	Reduce capital allowances on ongoing capital expenditures from 100 percent to normal depreciation rates.
Financial services (METR: 18 percent)	
Exemption from capital gains tax on Nigerian-listed securities is overly generous.	Consider eliminating the tax exemption on shares and other listed instruments, and subjecting them to normal 10 percent capital gains tax.
High property transfer taxes stifle growth of mortgage lending.	Consider exempting income from insurance policies from tax.
Taxation of income within unit trusts and insurance policies reduces incentives to invest.	Consider exempting income from unit trusts from tax.
	Treat unit trusts as pass-throughs rather than as corporations subject to tax.
	Consider reforming national guidelines on property taxes and property transfer taxes.
Agriculture (METR: −0.5–1 percent)	
Tax is not a major constraint to investment in the agriculture sector.	Change the VAT status of agricultural inputs from "exempt" to "zero rated" to allow reclamation of VAT on imported inputs.
Agricultural inputs and outputs are VAT exempt, but VAT is levied on imported inputs.	

238

Double and multiple taxes (onerous and illegal) produce inspection fees, as well as roadblocks of questionable legality.	Ensure that state and local government taxes and fees are properly enforced, that charges such as agricultural inspection fees are imposed only by state governments, and that fees are related to the cost of carrying out legitimate inspections.
Tourism (METR: 2–5 percent)	
Proof that withholding tax has been remitted is often delayed or not received, leaving firms unable to offset withholding tax paid against corporate tax payable.	Move away from sector-based incentives, which are usually poorly administered, as they distort the playing field. A tourism tax could possibly be introduced at the federal and/or state level.
Small business (METR: 32–48 percent)	
No special tax regime for small businesses.	Introduce small business tax regime.
Small businesses pay VAT but are unable to reclaim it.	Revise VAT deduction rules to allow reclamation of VAT on overhead.
Lack of knowledge of tax rights and responsibilities is prevalent.	Create a "Charter of Rights" for taxpayers, and publicize it through a communications and information campaign.
	Make tax appeals system more effective for small businesses.
	Establish an independent body to investigate complaints.
General tax issues	
Multiplicity of taxes	Revise Federal Act 21, which allows states to legislate new taxes. A draft law, which aims to limit these powers at the state level, has been approved by the Council of Ministers, but has not yet been presented before Parliament.
Double taxation	Coordinate tax administration reform in four pilot states.
Illegal practices	Launch information and education campaign.
Lack of Information	Provide training for tax officials.
Vague federal tax law on allocation of powers and responsibilities for tax administration	Revise VAT deductibility rules in advance of any increase in VAT rates.
Inefficient tax administration	
Limits on deductibility of VAT	

Source: International Finance Corporation/Foreign Investment Advisory Service 2008.
Note: FIRS = Federal Inland Revenue Service; METR = marginal effective tax rate; VAT = value-added tax.

Bank of Industry—Assessment of Service and Performance, 2001–07

Table E.1 Assessment Criteria and Summary of Findings

Assessment criteria	Summary of findings
Background	Bank established in 2001 following reconstruction of the Nigerian Industrial Development Bank Ltd. (NIDB), with headquarters in Lagos and 6 zonal offices (Abuja, Aba, Akure, Bauchi, Asaba, Kaduna).
Sector exposure	Agro-allied, petrochemicals, manufacturing
Firm sizes, examples of clients and products	Bank assists small, medium-size, large, and cottage industries; examples include: • Maslaha Nig, Ltd., Gasau, Zamfara State—production of woven sacks from petroleum-based resins • Aso International Ltd., Abuja FCT—production of bottled water • Afrotec Industries Ltd., Isolo, Lagos State—polymer-based products from petroleum bi-products • Jumac Int. Co. Ltd., Ikeja, Lagos—production of suitcases using flat sheets from petrochemicals • Seamaster Industries Ltd., Orlu, Imo State—agro-based products, including palm kernel oil • Apaco Foam & Chemical Industries Ltd., Agbor, Delta State—production of polyurethane flexible foams

(continued)

Table E.1   Assessment Criteria and Summary of Findings *(continued)*

Assessment criteria	*Summary of findings*
Loan/investment criteria	• Creditworthiness of firm
	• Probability of loan repayment
	• Viability of project
	• Ability to contribute at least 25 percent of project cost, excluding land
	• High percentage of domestic raw materials
	• High employment potential
	• Submission of feasibility study, site plan, land title, tenancy agreements
	• Provision of collateral or director's personal guarantee, quotations for machinery and equipment
	Audited accounts for at least three years
Growth performance	Cumulative number of loans and investments
	• December 2005: 88; June 2006: 145; December 2006: 194; June 2007: 267
	Cumulative value of loans and investments (N billion)
	• December 2005: 9.8; June 2006: 15.1; December 2006: 21.6; June 2007: 29
	Number of approvals by firm size
	• 2001–2005: SME 65%; large 35%
	• January–June 2006: SME 70%; large 30%
	• July–December 2006: SME 75%; large 25%
	• January–June 2007: SME 79%; large 21%
	Increases from January–June 2007
	• 96.8% (about N7.4 billion) in loans and investments
	• 34% (about N29 billion) in cumulative loans and investments
	• 33% (about N90 billion) in cumulative capital formation
	No direct data or projections on employment
Return on investment	From infrastructure expansion, 2001–07 (year: N thousand)
	2001: 31.08 2002: 7.67 2003: 8.63
	2004: 7.02 2005: 0.52 2006: 5.36
	2007: 7.34

Note: N = naira; SME = small and medium-size enterprise.

Nigeria's Import Prohibition List as of October 2008

Live or dead birds, including frozen poultry. H.S. codes 0105.1100–0105.9900; 0106.3100–0106.3900; 0207.1100–0207.3600; and 0210.9900.

Pork and pork products, beef and beef products, mutton, lamb, goat meat. H.S. codes 0201.1000–0204.5000; 0206.1000–0206.9000; 0210.1000–0210.2000; 0511.1000; 0511.9900; 1601.0000; 1602.1000–1602.2000;1602.4100–1602.9000.

Birds eggs. H.S. code 0407.0000.

Flowers (plastic and fresh). H.S. codes 0603.1000–0603.9000; 6702.1000–6702.9000.

Cassava/cassava products. H.S. codes 0714.1000; 1106.2000; 1108.1400; 1903.0000.

Fresh and dried fruits. H.S. codes 0801.1100–0814.0000.

Maize, sorghum, millet. H.S. codes 1005.1000–1005.9000; 1007.0000; 1008.1000–9000.

Wheat flour, maize flour, cereal groats, meal, pallets. H.S. codes 1101.0000; 1102.1000–1103.2000.

Vegetable oils and fats. H.S. codes 1507.1000–1516.2000 (excluding linseed and castor oils, hydrogenated vegetable fats used as industrial raw materials, olive oil in bottles); 1515.1100–1515.1900; 1515.3000; 1515.9000; 1516.2000; 1509.1000–9000.

Sugar confectionaries (other than chocolate). H.S. codes 1704.1000–1704.9000.

Cocoa butter, powder, cakes. H.S. codes 1802.–1803.2000; 1805.0000; 1806.1000–1806.2000; 1804.0000.

Spaghetti/noodles (excluding lasagna, gnocchi, ravioli, cannelloni). H.S. codes 1902.1100–1902.3000.

Biscuits. H.S. codes 1905.3100–1905.3200.

Fruit juice in retail packs. H.S. codes 2009.1100–2009.9000.

Waters (including mineral waters and aerated waters not containing added sugar or sweetening matter or flavored; ice snow). H.S. codes 2201.1000–2201.9000.

Waters (including mineral waters and aerated waters containing added sugar or sweetening matter or flavored, and other non-alcoholic beverages). H.S. codes 2202.1000–2202.9000 (excluding power or health drinks, liquid dietary supplements).

Beer (bottled, canned, otherwise packed). H.S. codes 2203.0000; 2206.0000.

Bentonites and barytes. H.S. codes 2508.1000–2508.0000; 2511.1000.

Bagged cement (excluding white cement). H.S. code 2523.2900.22.

Medicaments falling under H.S. headings 3003 and 3004. Paracetamol tablets and syrups; cotrimoxazole tablets and syrups; metronidazole tablets and syrups; chloroquine tablets and syrups; haematinic formulations; ferrous sulphate and ferrous gluconate tablets; folic acid tablets; vitamin B complex tablets (except modified released formulations); multivitamin tablets, capsules, and syrups (except special formulations); aspirin tablets (except modified released and soluble formulations); magnesium trisilicate tablets and suspensions; piperazine tablets and syrups; levamisole tablets and syrups; clotrimazole cream; ointments (penicillin/gentamycin); pyrantel pamoate tablets and syrups; intravenous fluids (dextrose, normal saline, etc.)

Waste pharmaceuticals. H.S. code 3006.8000.

Toothpaste of all kinds. H.S. code 3306.1000.

Finished soaps (including soap noodles and flakes) and detergents (excluding all raw materials which shall also attract 10 percent duty rate). H.S. codes 3401.1100–3402.9000.

Mosquito repellent coils, disinfectants, germicides. H.S. codes
3808.1000.11; 3808.4000–3808.9000.

Sanitary plastic wares, domestic plastic articles and wares (excluding baby
feeding bottles). H.S. codes 3922.1000–3922.9000.

Polypropylene woven/laminated sacks and bags. H.S. codes 3923.2100;
3923.2900.

Toothpicks. H.S. codes 3926.9000; 4421.9000.

Rethreaded and used pneumatic tires. H.S. codes 4012.1100–4012.9000.

*Corrugated paper and paper boards; all forms of paper cartons, boxes, and
cases.* H.S. codes 4808.1000a; 4819.1000–4819.2000.

Envelopes, diaries, greeting cards, calendars. H.S. codes 4817.1000;
4820.1000; 4909.0000; 4910.0000.

Toilet paper, cleansing and facial tissues, towels, similar sanitary articles.
H.S. codes 4818.1000–4818.9000; 5601.1000–5601.3000 (excluding
baby diapers H.S. codes 4818.4000 and 5601.1000, which importation
shall be allowed for a period of one year beginning 28 November 2006,
at a duty rate of 20 percent).

*Textile fabrics, African prints, lace fabrics, georges, other embroidered fabrics,
and articles thereof.* H.S. codes 5208.5100–5208.5900;
5209.5100–5209.5900; 5210.5100; 5210.5900; 5211.5100–5211.5900;
5212.5100; 5212.2500; 5407.4400; 5407.5400; 5407.7400; 5407.8400;
5407.9400; 5408.3400; 5408.2400; 5513.4100–5513.4900;
5514.4100–5514.4900; 5516.1400; 5516.2400; 5516.3400; 5516.4400;
5514.9400; 5801.1000–5811.0000.

Yam fabric. H.S. codes; 5004.0000–5006.0000; 5106.1000–5110.0000;
5204.1100–5207.9000; 5306.1000–5308.9000; 5401.1000–5406.2000;
5402.3300; 5402.6200; 5508.1000–5511.3000.

Carpets. H.S. codes 5701.1000–5705.0000.

Made-up garments and other textile articles, including towels. H.S. codes
6101.1000–6310.9000.

Note: No importation of textile fabrics and articles thereof shall be
allowed through land borders. Polyester filament yarn, although still
under prohibition, attracts 20 percent duty, as against 10 percent
contained in the new tariff.

Exercise books. H.S. code 4820.2000.

All types of footwear and bags, including suitcases of leather and plastics
(excluding safety shoes used in oil industry, hospitals, firefighting,

factories; sport shoes, all completely knocked down parts of footwear, bags, and suitcases). H.S. codes 6401.1000–6405.9000; 4202.1100–4202.9900; 6305.3300; 6305.3900.

Hollow glass bottles with capacity greater than 150 mls (0.15 liters), of a kind used for packaging of beverages by breweries and other drink companies. H.S. code 7010.9000.92.

Cutlasses, axes, pick axes, spades, shovels, and similar hand tools (excluding blanks of these tools, which fall under the same H.S. codes but shall attract a 10 percent duty rate effective 28 November, 2006). H.S. codes 8201.1000–8201.9000.

Used compressors, air conditioners, refrigerators/freezers. H.S. codes 8414.3000; 8415.1000–8415.9000; 8418.1000–8418.6900.

Used motor vehicles older than 8 years. H.S. codes 8703.1000–8703.9000.

Fully built and knocked down bicycles, frames, forks, and mudguards. H.S. codes 8712.0000; 8714.9100; 8714.9200; 8714.9900 (excluding rims, H.S. code 8714.9200.94, which shall attract a 50 percent duty rate effective 28 November, 2006).

Wheel barrows. H.S. code 8716.8000.

Furniture (excluding stadium chairs and all fittings and accessories used in furniture making; e.g., veneer chair skeleton/shell, arm guide, headrest support, back frame height adjustment device, injection-molded memory, seat frame, control mechanism unit), for a period of 18 months at 5 percent duty rate. H.S. codes 9401.1000–9401.9000; 9403.1000–9404.9000.

Electric generating sound-proof casings, excluding other prefabricated buildings. H.S. code 9406.0000.

Gaming machines (excluding those imported directly by five-star hotels of 100 or more rooms). H.S. code 9504.3000.

Ball point pens. H.S. code 9608.1000.

Telephone recharge cards. H.S. code 4911.9900.91.

List of Lines/Products Removed from Import Prohibition List in October 2008

Pork and pork products, beef and beef products, mutton, lamb, goat meat. H.S. codes 0511.1000; 0511.9900; 1601.0000; 1602.1000–1602.2000; 1602.4100–1602.9000.

Flowers (plastic and fresh). H.S. codes 0603.1000–0603.9000; 6702.1000–6702.9000.

Cassava products. H.S. codes 0714.1000; 1106.2000; 1108.1400; 1903.0000.

Fresh and dried fruits. H.S. codes 0801.1100–0814.0000.

Maize, sorghum, millet. H.S. codes 1005.1000–1005.9000; 1007.0000; 1008.1000–10018.9000.

Wheat flour, maize flour, cereal, groats, meal, pallets. H.S. codes 1101.0000; 1102.1000–1103.2000.

Sugar confectionaries (other than chocolate). H.S. code 1704.1000–1704.9000.

Cocoa butter, powder, cakes. H.S. codes 1802.–1803.2000; 1805.0000; 1806.1000–1806.2000; 1804.0000.

Biscuits. H.S. codes 1905.3100–1905.3200.

Beer (bottled, canned, otherwise packed). H.S. code 2203.0000; 2206.0000.

Bentonites and barytes. H.S. codes 2508.1000–2508.0000; 2511.1000.

Toothpaste of all kinds. H.S. code 3306.1000.

Disinfectants and germicides. H.S. codes 3808.4000–3808.9000.

Polypropylene woven/laminated sacks and bags. H.S. code 3923.2100; 3923.2900.

Trucks tires for retreading, size 11 × 20 m and above. H.S. code 4012.2010.00.

Envelopes, diaries, greeting cards, calendars. H.S. codes 4817.1000; 4820.1000; 4909.0000; 4910.0000.

Lace fabrics, georges, and other embroidered fabrics falling after H.S. code 5805.0000.

Made-up garments and other textile articles, including towels:

- *Made-up lining articles.* H.S. codes 6117.8000–6117.9000; 6217.1000–6217.9000.
- *Insecticide-treated mosquito nets* (ITNs) and long-lasting (LLITNs). H.S. codes 6304.9100.92; 6304.9200.94; 6304.9300.96; 6304.9900.98.
- *Industrial gloves.* H.S. code 6116.1000.11–6116.9900.99; 6116.1000.11; 6116.9200.92; 6116.9900.98.
- *Molding cup,* lycra. H.S. code 6212.9000.
- *Mutilated rags.* H.S. Code 6310.1000.11, 6310.9000.91
- *Jute bags.* H.S. code 6305.1000.

Yarn falling under H.S. codes 5004.0000–5006.0000; 5106.1000–5110.0000; 5204.1100–5207.9000; 5306.1000–5308.9000; 5401.1000–5406.2000; 5402.3300; 5402.6200; 5508.1000–5511.3000.

Exercise books. H.S. code 4820.2000.

Cutlasses, axes, pick axes, spades, shovels, and similar hand tools. H.S. codes 8201.1000–8201.9000.

Used motor vehicles. above H.S. codes 8703.1000–8703.9000 (prohibition is extended from 8 to 10 years from the date of manufacture).

Fully built and CKD bicycle frames, forks, and mudguards. H.S. codes 8712.0000; 8714.9100; 8714.9200; 8714.9900.

Wheel barrows. H.S. code 8716.8000.

Gaming machines. H.S. code 9504.3000.

APPENDIX H

Benin's Mirror Imports from China

Figure H.1 Benin's Mirror Imports from China in Official Recorded Imports

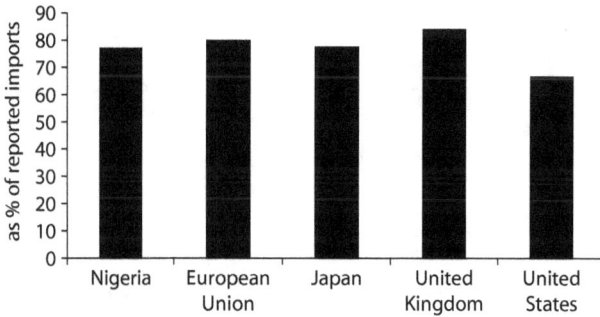

Source: Derived from Direction of Trade Statistics database.

APPENDIX I

Possible Impact of Tariff Policy Changes on Textiles, Vegetable Oils, and Rice

Table I.1   Possible Impact of Tariff Policy Changes on Textile Imports

Tariff level (%)	Benefits transferred to Nigeria (US$ million)	Total benefits (US$ per ton)	Import duties (US$ per ton)	Port fees (US$ per ton)
35	37.8	420	420	40
15	66.0	220	180	40

Source: Authors' calculations.
Note: Calculations assume that with a 35 percent tariff, 15 percent of flows will be redirected to Lagos port and Cotonou will continue to be more attractive for most traders. However, with a 15 percent tariff, we assume that 50 percent of flows will be redirected to Lagos.

Table I.2   Possible Impact of Tariff Policy Changes on Vegetable Oil Imports

Tariff level (%)	Benefits transferred to Nigeria (US$ million)	Total benefits (US$ per ton)	Import duties (US$ per ton)	Port fees (US$ per ton)
35	49.4	197.5	157.5	40
15	53.8	107.5	67.5	40

Source: Authors' calculations.
Note: Calculations assume that with a 35 percent tariff, 15 percent of flows will be redirected to Lagos port and Cotonou will continue to be more attractive for most traders. However, with a 15 percent tariff, we assume that 50 percent of flows will be redirected to Lagos.

Table I.3   Possible Impact of Tariff Policy Changes on Rice Imports

Tariff level (%)	Benefits transferred to Nigeria (US$ million)	Total benefits (US$ per ton)	Import duties (US$ per ton)	Port fees (US$ per ton)
50	33.9	205.5	115.5	40
15	44.75	89.5	49.5	40

Source: Authors' calculations.

Note: Calculations assume that with a 50 percent tariff, only 33 percent of flows will be redirected to Lagos port, because for many traders, Cotonou will continue to be more attractive. However, with a 15 percent tariff, we assume that all traders will redirect flows to Lagos.

Bibliography

Adams, A. V. 2008. "A Framework for the Study of Skills Development in the Informal Sector of Sub-Saharan Africa." World Bank, Washington, DC.

African Development Fund. 2005. "Appraisal Report." Nigeria Skills Training and Vocational Education Project.

Aghenta, J. 2008. "Graduate Employability and Performance on the Job." Occasional Paper, Nigerian Ministry of Education, Abuja.

Ajayi, K., and P. Kwaako-Osafo. 2006. "Research and Trade Policy Formulation: The Case of Nigeria's Adoption of the ECOWAS Common External Tariff." Working paper, Latin American Trade Network.

Akinlo, E. 1996. "Improving the Performance of the Nigerian Manufacturing Subsector after Adjustment: Selected Issues and Proposals." *Nigerian Journal of Economic and Social Sciences* 38 (2): 98–110.

All Africa Global Media/Comtex. 2009. February 29.

Aremu, I. 2005. *End of (Textile) Industry? A Critical Study of the Collapse of Textile Industry in Nigeria and the Implications for Employment and Poverty Eradication.* Lagos: Friedrich Ebert Stiftung.

Arnold, J. 2006. "Best Practices in Management of International Trade Corridors." Transport Paper 13, World Bank, Washington, DC.

Babalola, A. 2008. "Stocktaking of Tax, Trade, and EPZ Incentives for Industrial Development in Nigeria." Background paper, World Bank, Washington, DC.

Bankole, A., O. Ogunkola, and A. Oyejide. 2005. "Import Prohibition as a Trade Policy Instrument: The Nigerian Experience." In *Managing the Challenges of WTO Participation*, ed. P. Gallagher, P. Low, and A. Stoler. Geneva: World Trade Organization.

Baptist, S., and F. Teal. 2008. "Why Do South Korean Firms Produce So Much More Output Per Worker than Ghanaian Ones?" Working paper, Centre for the Study of African Economies, University of Oxford, U.K.

Berger, H., and V. Nitsch. 2008. "Gotcha! A Profile of Smuggling in International Trade." Working Paper 2475, CESifo, Munich.

Bigsten, A., P. Collier, S. Dercon, M. Fafchamps, B. Gauthier, J. Willem Gunning, A. Oduro, R. Oostendorp, C. Pattillo, M. Söderbom, F. Teal, and A. Zeufack. 2004. "Do African Manufacturing Firms Learn from Exporting?" *Journal of Development Studies* 40 (3): 115–41.

Bigsten, A., P. Collier, S. Dercon, B. Gauthier, J. Gunning, J. Habarurema, A. Isaksson, A. Oduro, R. Oostendorp, C. Patillo, M. Söderbom, F. Teal, and A. Zeufack. 1999. "Exports of African Manufactures: Macro Policy and Firm Behavior." *Journal of International Trade and Economic Development* 8 (1): 53–71.

Bigsten, A., M. Gebreeyesus, and M. Söderbom. 2008. "Agglomeration Effects in Ethiopian Manufacturing." Background paper, United Nations Industrial Development Organization, Vienna.

Brenton, P., and M. Hoppe. 2007. "Clothing and Export Diversification: Still a Route to Growth for Low-Income Countries?" Policy Research Working Paper 4343, World Bank, Washington, DC.

Bryson, J. R. 2007. "The Second Global Shift: The Offshoring or Global Sourcing of Corporate Services and the Rise of Distanciated Emotional Labour." *Geografiska Annaler: Series B, Human Geography* 89 (Suppl. 1): 31–43.

Canning, D., and P. Pedroni. 2004. "The Effect of Infrastructure on Long-Run Economic Growth." Unpublished working paper, Harvard University, Cambridge, MA.

Central Bank of Nigeria. 2007. "Financial System Strategy 2020." Abuja.

Chuta, E. 2007. "Final Report on Labor Market Data Audit/Statistical Analysis." World Bank, Abuja.

Collier, P. 2000. "Africa's Comparative Advantage." In *Industrial Development and Policy in Africa: Issues of Deindustrialization and Development Strategy*, ed. M. T. H. Jalilian and J. Weiss. Cheltenham: Edward Elgar.

———. 2007. *The Bottom Billion: Why the Poorest Countries Are Failing and What Can Be Done About It*. New York: Oxford University Press.

Collier, P., and J. W. Gunning. 1999. "Explaining African Economic Performance." *Journal of Economic Literature* 37 (1): 64–111.

Collier, P., C. Pattillo, and C. Soludo, eds. 2008. *Economic Policy Options for a Prosperous Nigeria.* New York: Palgrave Macmillan.

Combes, P. P. 2000. "Economics Structure and Local Growth: France, 1984–1993." *Journal of Urban Economics* 47 (3): 329–55.

Consilium International. 2005. "Nigeria: Value and Supply Chain Study—A Report for the World Bank." Washington, DC.

Comtrade [United Nations Commodity Trade Statistics Database]. http://comtrade.un.org/db/. United Nations, New York, NY.

———. 2008. "Product Value Chain Analysis in Nigeria—Real Estate and Construction, Retail and Wholesale Markets and Meat and Leather." Washington, DC.

Dabalen, A., B. Oni, and D. Adekola. 2000. "Labor Market Prospects of University Graduates in Nigeria." World Bank, Abuja.

Desmet, K. and M. Fafchamps. 2006. "Employment Concentration across U.S. Counties." *Regional Science and Urban Economics* 36 (4): 482–509.

Devarajan, S. 2008. "To promote exports, look behind the border." Africa Can. . . End Poverty Blog. September 12.

Dicken, P. 1992. *Global Shift: The Internationalization of Economic Activity.* 2d ed. London: Paul Chapman.

Direction of Trade Statistics (database). http://www2.imfstatistics.org/DOT/. International Monetary Fund, Washington, DC.

Doing Business Indicators (database). http://www.doingbusiness.org/. World Bank, Washington, DC.

Eifert, B., A. Gelb, and V. Ramachandran. 2005. "Business Environment and Comparative Advantage in Africa: Evidence from the Investment Climate Data." Working Paper 56, Center for Global Development, Washington, DC.

Emerging Market Economics. 2008. "Identifying Growth Pole Value Chains for Cross River, Kaduna, Kano and Lagos States." Report prepared for World Bank and U.K. Department for International Development, London.

Estache, A. 2008. "Infrastructure and Development: A Survey of Recent and Upcoming Issues." In *Rethinking Infrastructure for Development. Annual World Bank Conference on Development Economics 2007,* ed. F. Bourguignon and B. Pleskovic. Washington, DC: World Bank.

Fafchamps, M. 2004. "Manufacturing Growth and Agglomeration Effects." Working Paper 233, Centre for the Study of African Economies, University of Oxford, U.K.

Federal Ministry of Commerce and Industry. 2003. "Industrial Policy of Nigeria—Policies, Incentives, Guidelines and Institutional Framework." Abuja.

———. 2007. "Nigeria's Industrial Development Strategy 2007–2011: A Cluster Concept." Abuja.

Federal Ministry of Education. 2000. "National Masterplan for TVE in Nigeria in the 21st Century." Abuja.

———. 2008. "Reforms/Policies for Science, Technology and Vocational Education in Nigeria." Occasional Paper, Abuja.

Federal Ministry of Finance. 2003. "Comprehensive Review of Nigeria's Customs and Excise Tariffs: Framework Paper and Summary of Reports." Abuja.

Federal Ministry of Labor and Productivity. 1989. "National Employment Policy." Abuja.

———. 2004a. "Trade Test Syllabuses." Abuja.

———. 2004b. "Bulletin of Labor Statistics." Department of Planning, Research, and Statistics, Abuja.

———. 2008a. "Advanced Trade Test Syllabuses." Abuja.

———. 2008b. "National Electronic Labor Exchange." Abuja.

Federal Public Service Program. 2008. "Draft Final Report on Demand Assessment of Vocational and Technical Skills Required in the Federal Capital Territory." Abuja.

Federal Republic of Nigeria. 1977. "Federal Republic of Nigeria National Policy on Education." Federal Ministry of Information, Print. Division, Lagos.

Geourjon, A-M. 2004. "Trade Policy and Customs Administration." In *Changing Customs: Challenges and Strategies for the Reform of Customs Administration*, ed. M. Keen. Washington, DC: International Monetary Fund.

Giuliani, E., R. Rabellotti, and M. P. Van Dijk. 2005. *Clusters Facing Competition: The Importance of External Linkages*. Hampshire, U.K: Aldershot Ashgate.

Golub, S. 2008. "Transit Trade and Smuggling in Benin." Background paper for Benin Country Economic Memorandum, World Bank, Washington, DC.

Goorman, A. 2003. "Customs Modernization: The Case of Peru." In *Customs Modernization Initiatives: Case Studies*, ed. L. de Wulf and J. B. Sokol. Washington, DC: World Bank.

Grossman, G. M., and E. Helpman. 1991. *Innovation and Growth in the Global Economy*. Cambridge, MA: MIT Press.

Guardian. 2009. March 2.

Harding, A., G. Palsson, and G. Raballand. 2007. "Port and Maritime Transport Challenges in West and Central Africa." Working Paper 84, Sub-Saharan Africa Transport Policy Program, World Bank, Washington, DC.

Hausmann, R., and D. Rodrik. 2006. "Doomed to Choose: Industrial Policy as Predicament." Harvard University, Cambridge, MA.

Haywood, L. 2007. "The Performance of the Labor Market in Nigeria: A Report on the 2003–2004 Nigeria Living Standards Survey." Centre for the Study of African Economies, University of Oxford, U.K.

———. 2008. "The Performance of the Labor Market in Nigeria." World Bank, Abuja.

Haywood, L., and F. Teal. 2008. "Employment, Unemployment, Joblessness and Incomes in Nigeria: 1999–2006." Centre for the Study of African Economies, University of Oxford, U.K.

Henderson, V. 1997. "Externalities and Industrial Development." *Journal of Urban Economics* 42 (3): 449–70.

———. 2003. "Marshall's Scale Economies." *Journal of Urban Economics* 53 (1): 1–28.

Hermelin, B., and G. Rusten. 2007. "The Organizational and Territorial Changes of Services in a Globalised World." *Geografiska Annaler: Series B, Human Geography* 89 (Suppl. 1): 5–11.

Hong Kong Shipping Gazette. 2009. February 3.

Hors, I. 2001. "Fighting Corruption in Customs Administration: What Can We Learn from Recent Experiences?" Development Center Working Paper 175, Organisation for Economic Co-operation and Development, Paris.

Iarossi, Giuseppe, Peter Mousley, and Ismail Radwan. 2009. *An Assessment of the Investment Climate in Nigeria.* Washington, DC: World Bank.

Ifeyinwa, O. 2008. "Nigeria: Our Import Duties Are Punitive, Reduce Them, NPA, Customs Tell FG." http://allafrica.com/stories/200805120341.html.

Igue, J. O., and B. G. Soule. 1992. *L'Etat-entrepôt au Bénin.* Paris: Karthala.

ILO (International Labour Organization). 2007a. "Database for Export Processing Zones." Geneva.

———. 2007b. Key Indicators of the Labor Market (KILM) database. Geneva.

IMF (International Monetary Fund). 2005. "Nigeria: Selected Issues and Statistical Appendix." Country Report 05/303, Washington, DC.

———. 2007. "Nigeria: Fourth Review under the Policy Support Instrument— Staff Report." Country Report 07/353, Washington, DC.

———. 2008. *World Economic Outlook.* Washington, DC: IMF.

Industrial Training Fund. 2008. "Developing the Nation's Human Resources: Manpower Training and Development Programs." Abuja.

Industrial Training Fund and Nigeria Employers' Consultative Association. 2007. "A Survey of Contemporary Manpower Requirements in the Nigerian Economy." Abuja.

International Finance Corporation, Foreign Investment Advisory Service. 2008. "Sector Study of Effective Tax Burden." Investment Climate Program, U.K. Department for International Development–World Bank Group, Washington, DC.

Iyigun, M., and D. Rodrik. 2004. "On the Efficacy of Reforms: Policy Tinkering, Institutional Change and Entrepreneurship." Policy Discussion Paper 4399, Centre for Economic Policy Research, London.

Johanson, R., and A. V. Adams. 2004. "Skills Development in Sub-Saharan Africa." World Bank, Washington, DC.

Journal of Commerce. 2009. January 23.

Kaminski, B., and G. Raballand. 2008. "Bazaar Trade in Central Asia: A Major Positive Welfare Impact." World Bank, Washington, DC.

Kingdon, G., J. Sandefur, and F. Teal. 2006. "Labour Market Flexibility, Wages and Incomes in Sub-Saharan Africa in the 1990s." *African Development Review* 18 (3): 392–427.

Lin, J. 2008. "Poverty, Inclusive Growth and Development Strategy." Presentation at the University of Ibadan, Nigeria.

Malik, A., and F. Teal. 2008. "Policy Lessons from Nigerian Firm Survey." In *Economic Policy Options for a Prosperous Nigeria*, ed. P. Collier, C. Pattillo, and C. C. Soludo. London: Palgrave Macmillan.

Malik, A., F. Teal, and S. Baptist. 2006. "The Performance of Nigerian Manufacturing Firms: Report on the Nigerian Manufacturing Enterprise Survey 2004." Research report, Centre for the Study of African Economies, United Nations Industrial Development Organization, and Nigerian Federal Ministry of Industry, Abuja.

National Board of Technical Education. 2008. Unpublished data and interviews. Abuja.

National Bureau of Statistics. 1999. General Household Survey. Abuja.

———. 2003. Nigeria Living Standard Survey. Abuja.

———. 2004. General Household Survey. Abuja

———. 2005. "Social Statistics in Nigeria." Abuja.

———. 2006a. General Household Survey. Abuja

———. 2006b. "Nigerian Statistical Fact Sheets on Economic and Social Development." Abuja.

National Directorate of Employment. 2004a. "Background Paper on Employment and Poverty Alleviation in Nigeria." Abuja.

———. 2004b. "Some of NDE's Sponsored Projects in the States and FCT." Abuja.

———. 2006. "Mandate, Strategies, Activities and Socio-economic Impact." Abuja.

National Directorate of Employment, Vocational Skills Department. 2006a. "National Open Apprenticeship Scheme—Analysis by State and Trade." Abuja.

———. 2006b. "Number of Unemployment Youths Assisted in Setting Up Workshops under Resettlement Scheme." Abuja.

Ndibe, C. 2007. "Understanding the Free Zones Scheme—The Nigeria Perspective." Africa Free Zone Association, Cape Town, South Africa.

Nicita, A., and M. Olarreaga. 2007. "Trade, Production, and Protection Database, 1976–2004." *World Bank Economic Review* 21 (1): 165–71.

NISER (Nigerian Institute of Social and Economic Research). 2007. "Report of Baseline Study on Employment Generation in the Informal Sector of Nigerian Economy." African Capacity Building Foundation/International Labour Organization Project on Strengthening the Labour Market Information and Poverty Monitoring System in Africa, Ibadan, Nigeria.

Njikam, O., J. N. Binam, and S. Tachi. 2006. "Understanding Total Factor Productivity Growth in Sub-Saharan Africa Countries." Working paper, *Les Cahiers du SISERA*, Dakar.

Ogunkola, O. 2005. "Advancing Nigeria's Agricultural Development through Doha Development Round (DDR)." In *Nigeria's Imperatives in the New World Trade Order*, ed. O. Ogunkola and A. Bankole. Ibadan, Nigeria: New World Press.

Organisation for Economic Co-operation and Development /African Development Bank. 2008. *African Economic Outlook 2007/08*. Paris: Organisation for Economic Co-operation and Development /African Development Bank.

Oyelaran-Oyeyinka, B., and K. Lal. 2006. "Institutional Support for Collective Learning: Cluster Development in Kenya and Ghana." *African Development Review* 18 (2): 258–78.

Oyelaran-Oyeyinka, B., and D. McCormick. 2007. *Industrial Clusters and Innovation Systems in Africa*. New York and Geneva: United Nations University Press.

Phoenix Logistics Inc. 2004. "Nigerian Urban Youth Employment Project—Labor Market Research Study." Tempe, AZ.

Resman Associates Ltd. 2007. "Informal Case Studies: Consolidated Final Report." Prepared for United Nations Development Programme, Abuja.

Rodrik, D. 2007. *One Economics, Many Recipes: Globalization, Institutions and Economic Growth*. Princeton, NJ: Princeton University Press.

———. 2004. "Industrial Policy for the Twenty-First Century." Research report prepared for United Nations Industrial Development Organization.

Sandefur, J., P. Serneels, and F. Teal. 2006. "African Poverty through the Lens of Labor Economics: Earnings and Mobility in Three Countries." Working Paper GPRG-WPS-060, Department of Economics, University of Oxford, U.K.

———. 2007. "Poverty and Earnings Mobility in Three African Countries." In *Employment and Shared Growth*, ed. P. Paci and P. Serneels. Washington, DC: World Bank.

Schmitz, H., and K. Nadvi. 1999. "Clustering and Industrialisation: Introduction." *World Development* 27 (9): 1503–14.

Sirtaine, S., M. E. Pinglo, J. L. Guasch, and V. Foster. 2005. "How Profitable Are Private Infrastructure Concessions in Latin America? Empirical Evidence and Regulatory Implications." *Quarterly Review of Economics and Finance* 45 (2–3): 380–402.

Söderbom, M., and F. Teal. 2000. "Skills, Investment and Exports from Manufacturing Firms in Africa." *Journal of Development Studies* 37 (2): 13–43.

———. 2003. "Are Manufacturing Exports the Key to Economic Success in Africa?" *Journal of African Economies* 12 (1): 1–29.

Tallapragada, P. V. S. N., and B. S. Adebusuyi. 2008. "Nigeria's Power Sector: Opportunities and Challenges." In *Economic Policy Options for a Prosperous Nigeria*, ed. P. Collier, C. Pattillo, and C. C. Soludo. London: Palgrave Macmillan.

Teal, F. 1999. "Why Can Mauritius Export Manufactures and Ghana Not?" *World Economy* 22 (7): 981–93.

Thompson, F. 2006. "The Impact of Location on Firm Performance in Moroccan Manufacturing." DPhil Thesis, Department of Economics, University of Oxford, U.K.

Tradewinds. 2009. February 26.

Ukaegbu, I. 2008. "Education and Employment." Occasional Paper, Nigerian Ministry of Education, Abuja.

UNCTAD (United Nations Conference on Trade and Development). 2004. *World Investment Report 2004.* New York and Geneva: United Nations University Press.

———. No date. "The Role of Research in Trade Policy Formulation." http://vi .unctad.org/tda/papers/Research%20Questions_Sam/ajayi_kwaako%20 %282006%29%20Role%20of%20research%20in%20trade%20policy%20 formulation_Nigeria.pdf.

UNESCO (United Nations Educational, Scientific and Cultural Organization). 2008. "Final Report of the Sub-Regional Seminar for West Africa on Implementing the UNESCO/ILO Recommendations Concerning Technical and Vocational Education and Training." Paris.

UNIDO (United Nations Industrial Development Organization). 2004. Industrial Statistics database. Vienna.

———. 2009. *Industrial Development Report.* Vienna: UNIDO.

Venables, A. 2005. "Spatial Disparities in Developing Countries: Cities, Regions, and International Trade." *Journal of Economic Geography* 5 (1): 3–21.

World Bank. 2006a. *Governance, Investment Climate, and Harmonious Society: Competitiveness Enhancements for 120 Cities in China.* Report No. 37759-CN. Washington, DC: World Bank.

———. 2006b. "Review of Science and Technology Education at Post-Basic Level." Africa Human Development Department, Nigeria Country Office, Abuja.

———. 2007a. *Nigeria Competitiveness and Growth—Country Economic Memorandum.* Report No. 36483-NG. Washington, DC: World Bank.

———. 2007b. World Development Indicators database. Washington, DC.

———. 2008a. Investment Climate Enterprise Survey. Washington, DC.

———. 2008b. "Nigeria Economic Report." Washington, DC.

———. 2008c. Trade and Transport Facilitation in South East Europe Project. World Bank, Washington, DC.

World Development Indicators (database). http://data.worldbank.org/data-catalog/world-development-indicators. World Bank, Washington, DC.

World Integrated Trade Solution (database). http://wits.worldbank.org/witsweb/. World Bank, Washington, DC.

WTO (World Trade Organization). 2005. "Trade Policy Review, Federal Republic of Nigeria: Report by the Secretariat." Geneva.

Yeaple, S. R., and S. S. Golub. 2007. "International Productivity Differences, Infrastructure, and Comparative Advantage." *Review of International Economics* 15 (2): 223–42.

Yeats, A. J. 1990. "On the Accuracy of Economic Observations: Do Sub-Saharan Trade Statistics Mean Anything?" *World Bank Economic Review* 4 (2): 135–56.

Zhihua Zeng, D. 2008. "Knowledge, Technology and Cluster-Based Growth in Africa." World Bank, Washington, DC.

Index

Page numbers followed by *b*, *f*, or *t* refer to boxed text, figures or tables, respectively. Page numbers followed by *n*. refer to numbered notes.

www.ingramcontent.com/pod-product-compliance
Lightning Source LLC
Chambersburg PA
CBHW050702280326
41926CB00088B/2428